Queer(y)ing Bodily Norms in Francophone Culture

Modern **F**rench **I**dentities

Edited by Jean Khalfa

Volume 140

PETER LANG
Oxford • Bern • Berlin • Bruxelles • New York • Wien

Polly Galis, Maria Tomlinson and Antonia Wimbush (eds)

Queer(y)ing Bodily Norms in Francophone Culture

PETER LANG
Oxford • Bern • Berlin • Bruxelles • New York • Wien

Bibliographic information published by Die Deutsche Nationalbibliothek
Die Deutsche Nationalbibliothek lists this publication in the Deutsche Nationalbibliografie; detailed bibliographic data is available on the Internet at http://dnb.d-nb.de.

A catalogue record for this book is available from the British Library.

Library of Congress Cataloging-in-Publication Data

Names: Galis, Polly, 1991- editor. | Tomlinson, Maria, 1990- editor. | Wimbush, Antonia, 1989- editor.
Title: Queer(y)ing bodily norms in francophone culture / [edited by] Polly Galis, Maria Tomlinson, Antonia Wimbush.
Description: Oxford ; New York : Peter Lang, [2021] | Series: Modern French identities, 1422-9005 ; 140 | Includes bibliographical references and index.
Identifiers: LCCN 2020036297 (print) | LCCN 2020036298 (ebook) | ISBN 9781789975147 (paperback) | ISBN 9781789975154 (ebook) | ISBN 9781789975161 (epub) | ISBN 9781789975178 (mobi)
Subjects: LCSH: French fiction--20th century--History and criticism. | French fiction--21st century--History and criticism. | Gender identity in literature. | Subject (Philosophy) in literature. | Human body in literature. | Queer theory.
Classification: LCC PQ673 .Q44 2021 (print) | LCC PQ673 (ebook) | DDC 843/.9093521--dc23
LC record available at https://lccn.loc.gov/2020036297
LC ebook record available at https://lccn.loc.gov/2020036298

Cover image: Sophie Ann Lillywhite, *Fruits of my Labor*. Reproduced with permission from the artist.
Cover design by Peter Lang Ltd.

ISSN 1422-9005
ISBN 978-1-78997-514-7 (print) • ISBN 978-1-78997-515-4 (ePDF)
ISBN 978-1-78997-516-1 (ePub) • ISBN 978-1-78997-517-8 (mobi)

Published by Peter Lang Ltd, International Academic Publishers,
52 St Giles, Oxford, OX1 3LU, United Kingdom
oxford@peterlang.com, www.peterlang.com

This publication has been peer reviewed.

Contents

Acknowledgements ix

POLLY GALIS, MARIA TOMLINSON AND ANTONIA WIMBUSH
Introduction 1

PART I Queering the Body 27

BRIAN TROTH
1 Hookups: Social Networking and Digital Bodies in Twenty-First-Century France 29

ADINA STROIA
2 Lesbian Selves: The Figure of the (Body) Double in Marie Nimier's Works 47

RAY BALSTAD
3 Children Out of Line: Gender (Dis)Orientations and Paths of Queer Resistance in the Heterotopia 67

PART II Rethinking Gendered Bodily Norms 87

KATHLEEN RIZY
4 Motherhood Reconceived: The Posthuman Future Is Female in 'Mon mari le clone' by Marie Darrieussecq 89

VANESSA LEE

5 The Female Body in the Plays of French Caribbean Women Writers 107

SETH COMPAORÉ

6 Male Bodily Poetics in André Téchiné *Quand on a 17 ans* (2016): Physical Violence and Teenage Passion 127

PART III Hybrid and Dysfunctional Bodies 147

CRISTINA ONESTA

7 Dysfunctional Bodies, Dysfunctional Gazes: Artistic Creation and Death in *Manger l'autre* by Ananda Devi and *Le Génie d'Abou* by Isabelle Boni-Claverie 149

SARA BÉDARD-GOULET

8 *14* or the Missing Arm: Ontological Instability of the French Contemporary Novel in Jean Echenoz's Work 167

KATE FOSTER

9 The Cyborg's Undecidable Body: A Game of 'Who am I?' in Gaston Leroux's *La Poupée sanglante* 187

PART IV Bodies in Flux 207

LOREN K. WOLFE

10 Mediating Eve: Female Protagonists and the Contingent Body in Hervé Guibert's Late Narratives 209

JENNIFER BOUM MAKE

11 Exploring Encounters in *Passages* by Emile Ollivier: The Role of Testimonial Responsibility to Othered Bodies 227

KATHRYN CHAFFEE

12 Dance as Encounter in the Films of Claire Denis 247

POLLY GALIS, MARIA TOMLINSON AND ANTONIA WIMBUSH

Conclusion 263

Notes on Contributors 267

Index 273

Acknowledgements

First and foremost, we would like to thank all of our contributors for their hard work in writing the incredible chapters of which this book comprises. Your work has produced an exciting and varied volume which we are so delighted to be able to share with the world. We are also particularly grateful to Sophie Lillywhite, who created the stunning image on our front cover. We would especially like to extend our thanks to Laurel Plapp at Peter Lang, who has supported and advised us throughout the whole process, and we thank the reviewers, too, for their helpful comments and feedback.

This edited volume arose from a conference that we organized in Birmingham in January 2018 entitled 'Imagining the Body in France and the Francophone World', along with a special issue of *L'Esprit Créateur* entitled 'Challenging Normative Spaces and Gazes: The Body in 20th- and 21st-Century Francophone Culture' (2020). The vast majority of our contributors are early career researchers and this book therefore celebrates the innovative research that our cohort is undertaking.

We would also like to extend our thanks to a variety of organizations which either subsidized our conference or have funded our own individual research projects which we were undertaking at the time of editing this book. These include The Leverhulme Trust, the Institute of Modern Languages Research, the Society for French Studies, the Arts and Humanities Research Council, the University of Birmingham and the University of Leeds.

Of course, we would also like to thank our partners, family, friends and colleagues who have supported us during this process. You know who you are!

Finally, we would like to acknowledge our longstanding friendship as early career researchers. All three editors of this volume met around 2015 when we were at different stages of our PhDs. Since we started to organize the 'Imagining the Body' conference, we have stayed in close contact and our friendship has grown. Over the past few years, we have supported each other through the highs and lows of our careers. With the uncertainty and instability of academic careers, now compounded by the COVID-19 pandemic, we know that our friendship will be even more valuable than ever as we continue on our quest to one day find that elusive permanent academic position. We are also heartened by the fact that academic 'bubbles' appear to be growing increasingly supportive and inclusive, and long may it continue!

'Le monde est si vaste et nous si petits, mais unis par l'amitié, nous sommes des géants'.

– *Lisa Rochambeau*

POLLY GALIS, MARIA TOMLINSON AND ANTONIA WIMBUSH

Introduction

A Queer(y)ing Approach to the Body: Questioning Normativity beyond LGBTQ+ Spaces

As this edited volume testifies, the meaning of the term 'queer' has evolved significantly during the twentieth and twenty-first centuries. The word 'queer' appeared in the English language in the sixteenth century to mean something that is different from the norm, and its etymology is rooted in the German word 'quer' which signifies something that is askew.[1] In the early twentieth century 'queer' was pejoratively applied to homosexual men, until the 1990s when this term was reappropriated by the LGBTQ+ community in order to denounce homophobia and express pride.[2] The term 'queer' has therefore had a history of challenging normative beliefs, identities and ideologies. In recent years, scholars have opened up the term 'queer' to question normative ideas that are not strictly related to LGBTQ+ identity. Building on queer scholarship, researchers in other fields have considered the potential of queer approaches, theories and ideas to aid our questioning of a variety of normative discourses. These fields range from disability studies, to research about menstrual experience, and to identity studies more broadly.

A variety of academic works have already commented on how scholarly work is broadening the term 'queer'. Jean Bessette demonstrates that, within queer studies itself, the term 'queer' has been expanded to describe

1 Eric Partridge, *The World of Words: An Introduction to Language in General and to English and American in Particular* (London: Routledge, 2015).

2 Anne Curzon, *Fixing English: Prescriptivism and Language History* (Cambridge: Cambridge University Press, 2014).

a general 'orientation against normativity' which can incorporate socio-economic status and ethnicity.[3] Bessette argues that 'someone, or something, is queer when s/he or it challenges the social processes that consolidate and normalize gendered, sexual, raced, and classed identities'.[4] In *Tendencies* (1993), Eve Sedgwick also illustrates how a queer approach can shed light on other markers of identity. She explains, 'a lot of the most exciting recent work around "queer" spins the term outward along dimensions that can't be subsumed under gender and sexuality at all: the ways that race, ethnicity, postcolonial nationality criss-cross with these and other identity-constituting, identity fracturing discourses, for example.'[5] Sedgwick, here, links the term 'queer' with other fractured and marginalized identities. She therefore highlights the value of viewing marginalized identities through a queer lens. She finds a parallel between the marginalized queer community and marginalized, or low brow, cultural production. She explains that during her childhood she enjoyed engaging with a variety of cultural texts that included both popular and highbrow materials, and that became necessary to her survival. She demonstrates an admiration for those of her generation and the new generation of queer youth who have found their identity in less formal works: 'It's impressed me deeply the way others of my generation and since seem to have invented for themselves, in the spontaneity of great need, the tools for a formalist apprehension of other less prestigious, more ubiquitous kinds of text: genre movies, advertising, comic strips.'[6] Hence, we can infer from Sedgwick's assertion that queer theories and ideas may help to unlock the meaning behind literature that is neither canonical, highbrow, traditional, nor highly regarded. This volume likewise draws on sources that vary considerably in terms of genre and social 'ranking'.

Numerous academic studies have based their methodological approaches on the intersecting aspects of queer and postcolonial studies.[7]

3 Jean Bessette, 'An Archive of Anecdotes: Raising Lesbian Consciousness after the Daughters of Bilitis', *Rhetoric Society Quarterly* 43/1 (2013), 22–45, 28.

4 Jean Bessette, 'An Archive of Anecdotes: Raising Lesbian Consciousness after the Daughters of Bilitis', 28.

5 Eve Kosofsky Sedgwick, *Tendencies* (Durham, NC: Duke University Press, 1993), 8.

6 Sedgwick, *Tendencies*, 3.

7 See, for example, John Hawley and Dennis Altman, *Postcolonial, Queer: Theoretical Intersections* (New York: SUNY Press, 2001).

Both disciplines examine power dynamics, identity politics, institutions and knowledge creation. Studies which take a queer or postcolonial approach often question normative categories or binaries. Alberto Fernández Carbajal exemplifies this rejection of normativity in an article that offers a joint postcolonial and queer reading of Zadie Smith's novel *NW* (2012). Carbajal argues that a resistance to normativity 'is articulated at the crossroads between postcolonial and queer discourses, a joint battleground that dissolves a singular envisioning of national identity by favouring the mixing of cultural perspectives and sexualities'.[8] Thus, a queer and postcolonial reading can offer a multiplicity of viewpoints that deconstruct essentialism and monolithism.

Within feminist scholarly work, studies have drawn on a combination of queer and feminist approaches in order to examine a societal marginalization of women or women's bodies. In an article on the intersections between radical feminism and queer theory, Debbie Cameron and Joan Scanlon argue that the notion of 'queer' brings together 'whatever is at odds with the normal, the legitimate, the dominant'.[9] The authors build on this by arguing that 'queer' signifies a marginal status which is imposed from without and is often applied to a person who has 'no buffer against social prejudice'.[10] They give female sex workers as an example of this queerness. Even though they may be cisgender and heterosexual, they are marginalized for their sexual activity. We can find another pertinent example of a feminist queering of bodily norms in Iris Marion Young's *On Female Body Experience: 'Throwing Like a Girl' and Other Essays* (2005). In her essay about menstrual experience and normative societal ideals about the body, Young argues that the menstruating body has a marginal status in society. She illustrates that societal discourses about menstruation position it as something dirty and shameful that must always remain hidden. She thus

8 Alberto Fernández Carbajal, 'On Being Queer and Postcolonial: Reading Zadie Smith's *NW* through Virginia Woolf's *Mrs Dalloway*', *Journal of Commonwealth Literature* 51/1 (2016), 76–91, 77–8.

9 Debbie Cameron and Joan Scanlon, 'Talking about Gender', *Trouble and Strife* (2010), <https://www.troubleandstrife.org/new-articles/talking-about-gender/>, accessed 24 June 2020.

10 Cameron and Scanlon, 'Talking about Gender'.

posits that society queers the menstruating body by placing it in a marginalized position:

> The normal body, the default body, the body that everybody is assumed to be, is a body not bleeding from the vagina. Thus to *be* normal and to be taken as normal, the menstruating woman must not speak about her bleeding and must conceal evidence of it [...] It seems apt, then, in this normatively masculine, supposedly gender-egalitarian society, to say that the menstruating woman is queer. As with other queers, the price of a woman's acceptance as normal is that she stay in the closet as a menstruator.[11]

Although Young offers a fitting analogy for the experience of cisgender female menstruators, she does not consider the existence of non-binary, transgender or intersex menstruators who may define themselves as 'queer'. We could argue then, perhaps, that their bodies are doubly queered both through being menstruators and for being a part of the LGBTQ+ community.

Another field which has drawn on queer theories and approaches is disability studies. As Tim Dean explains, there is a common desire to reappropriate stigmatizing labels that exist in both disabled and/or LGBTQ+ spaces. Dean also draws on ideas of normativity to bring together queer and disabled identity:

> In recent decades, sexual minorities have reclaimed 'queer' as a badge of pride and a mark of resistance to regimes of the normal, mirroring the embrace of terms like 'crip' and the capaciousness of the term 'disability' itself. These are all political, highly contested terms that refuse essentializing meanings.[12]

Here, Dean illustrates that both the terms 'queer' and 'disabled' resist essentialism and categorization. A further parallel drawn by Dean is between heteronormativity and ableism. He argues that queer studies and disability studies criticize 'the effects of normalization on embodiment, desire, and access'.[13] Thus, as Dean's article demonstrates, the body is at the

11 Iris Marion Young, *On Female Body Experience: 'Throwing Like a Girl' and Other Essays* (New York: Oxford University Press, 2005), 107.

12 Tim Dean, 'Queer', in Rachel Adams, Benjamin Reiss, David Serlin, eds, *Keywords for Disability Studies* (New York: NYU Press, 2015), 143–5, 143.

13 Dean, 'Queer', 143.

centre of both queer studies and disability studies. Both disciplines reveal, question and denounce the monolithic application of normative perspectives to all bodies. Instead, these disciplines encourage intersectionality, nuance and contextualization.

Queer(y)ing Bodily Norms in Francophone Culture builds on these studies that 'queer' societal norms and values through our 'queer(y)ing' methodology. Since the volume combines chapters which focus on LGBTQ+ identity and those which question normativity outside an LGBTQ+ space, we coined the term 'queer(y)ing' to illustrate the value of applying approaches informed by a queer perspective in a variety of different sociocultural and generic contexts. At its heart, the term 'queer(y)ing' articulates an approach to society that examines, questions and challenges normativity in all of its manifestations. Since the word 'queer' today epitomizes the pride of the LGBTQ+ community and expresses their marginalization, we created a term that celebrates this influence but does not appropriate it. The term amalgamates the ideas of queering and questioning to encompass a variety of approaches that question normativity in all of its guises. For instance, a queer(y)ing approach can be used to criticize a range of discourses such as ableism, neocolonialism, ciscentrism and trans-exclusionary feminism, but is nevertheless inspired by the contestatory movement of queer studies.

The Origins of Queer Theory in French and Francophone Thought

In France specifically, queer thinking has been strongly associated with political activism,[14] and organizations such as the Front homosexuel d'action révolutionnaire (founded in 1971) and Les Gouines rouges (also founded in 1971) have been at the forefront of revolutionary queer activism in France during the twentieth century. Although, as Michael Sibalis argues,

14 Elliot Evans, *The Body in French Queer Thought from Wittig to Preciado: Queer Permeability* (Abingdon; New York: Routledge, 2020), 4.

it is too simplistic to attribute the emergence of gay rights movements in France to the events of May '68,[15] it is true that May '68 gave an impetus to activists striving for social, political and sexual equality. However, the francophone academy has been somewhat reluctant to engage with queer theory. The best-known anglophone works of queer theory have only appeared in French translation relatively recently: Judith Butler's *Gender Trouble*, initially published in 1990, was translated into French in 2005,[16] while Sedgwick's *Epistemology of the Closet* (1990) was published in French in 2008.[17] French queer theorists themselves also seem to lag behind their anglophone contemporaries to a certain extent, perhaps because the French Republican model results in a 'supposed blindness to all particularities, including of course sexual orientation'.[18] As Oliver Davis and Hector Kollias observe:

> Queer theory is now an established term in the Anglo-American academic lexicon, so much so that it has already started to engender the kind of internal criticism which intimates that it may no longer be as avant-garde, as radical, or indeed as queer, as was thought in the heady days of the 1900s. The impetus behind this special issue is the realization that the same cannot be said about queer theory in Europe in general and in France in particular, where it still connotates that which is radical and avant-garde in thinking about sexuality and sociality. [...]. Queer theory has arrived in France – late.[19]

Yet as they then go on to explain, and as the title of their special issue – *Queer Theory's Return to France* – makes clear, it is erroneous to think that

15 Michael Sibalis, 'The Gay Liberation Movement in France', in Gert Hekma and Alain Giami, eds, *Sexual Revolutions* (Basingstoke: Palgrave Macmillan, 2014), 188–202, 188.

16 Judith Butler, *Gender Trouble: Feminism and the Subversion of Identity* (New York and London: Routledge, 1990); *Trouble dans le genre: le féminisme et la subversion de l'identité*, trans. Cynthia Kraus (Paris: La Découverte, 2005).

17 Eve Kosofsky Sedgewick, *Epistemology of the Closet* (Berkeley and Los Angeles, CA: University of California Press, 1990); *Epistémologie du placard*, trans. Maxime Cervulle (Paris: Amsterdam, 2018).

18 Camille Robcis, 'How the Symbolic Became French: Kinship and Republicanism in the PACS Debates', *Discourse: Journal for Theoretical Studies in Media and Culture* 26/3 (2004), 110–35, 113.

19 Oliver Davis and Hector Kollias, 'Introduction', *Queer Theory's Return to France*, *Paragraph* 35/2 (2012), 139–43, 139.

France has no history of queer theoretical discourse: 'This arrival is not that of a total newcomer, but a return, the return of a native.'[20] Rather, much contemporary francophone and anglophone queer theory has been strongly influenced by the seminal French thinkers of the twentieth century. Claire Boyle notes in her contribution to Davis and Kollias's special issue of *Paragraph* that 'American queer theory is deeply rooted in European, and specifically French, thought'; Butler draws on Michel Foucault and Luce Irigaray, Sedgwick engages with Marcel Proust, and Diana Fuss develops her ideas on sexuality through a discussion of the work of Jacques Lacan and Frantz Fanon.[21] Boyle goes on to propose that French queer subjects and thinkers will act as a 'critical interlocutor' to post-queer theory that has emerged from the USA – a field still in its infancy but marked by the importance of the virtual world and the blurring of human and machine *à la* Donna Haraway's cyborg – just as it inspired queer theory there in the first place.[22] Bruno Perreau agrees that Anglo-American queer theory has been greatly inspired by French thought, largely thanks to Foucault who acts as a 'bridge' between both transatlantic schools of thought.[23] Moreover, in *Queering Transcultural Encounters* (2019), Luis Navarro-Ayala outlines how Frenchness itself is equated with sexual deviance in Latin America and North Africa, meaning that to adopt certain French traits allows for queer sexual exploration, even in places where this is strictly policed.[24] Following in the footsteps of these influential gender studies scholars, our own contribution to queer studies in France seeks to query what queer means, and how it has been theorized, at different stages of French and francophone history.

20 Davis and Kollias, 'Introduction', 139.

21 Claire Boyle, 'Post-Queer (Un)Made in France?', *Queer Theory's Return to France, Paragraph* 35/2 (2012), 265–80, 266.

22 Boyle, 'Post-Queer (Un)Made in France?', 269.

23 Bruno Perreau, 'The Queer Mind Through the Transatlantic Looking Glass', *Contemporary France and Francophone Studies* 18/1 (2014), 75–85.

24 Luis Navarro-Ayala, *Queering Transcultural Encounters: Bodies, Image, and Frenchness in Latin America and North Africa* (Cham, Switzerland: Palgrave Macmillan, 2019).

Much of contemporary queer theory is rooted in distinctions between sex and gender, a key aspect of Simone de Beauvoir's feminist thought. Beauvoir's *Le Deuxième sexe* (1949) needs little introduction, so seminal has it been in Western feminist discourse. The oft-quoted phrase 'one is not born, but rather becomes, a woman' has been crucial to understanding this division between sex and gender.[25] Beauvoir considers sex to be the anatomically stable condition determined by birth, whereas gender is the cultural and societal meaning given to the body. As Butler explains in an article dedicated to sex and gender in Beauvoir's work, 'with the distinction intact, it is no longer possible to attribute the values or social functions of women to biological necessity, and neither can we refer meaningfully to natural or unnatural gendered behaviour: all gender is, by definition, unnatural'.[26] Butler develops Beauvoir's thinking further in her own analysis of sexuality. She questions whether, if it is possible to conceive of gendered and sexed identity as a relative concept, we should abandon gendered and sexed binaries altogether.[27] The American poet, essayist and feminist Adrienne Rich also argues that such binaries are counter-productive, and she advocates that sexuality be seen as shifting points on a 'lesbian continuum' rather as binary positions.[28] For Rich, this continuum should include 'a range – through each woman's life and throughout history – of woman-identified experience'[29] because only then can we fully understand how diverse women experience lesbianism differently, as both 'the breaking of a taboo and the rejection of a compulsory way of life'.[30] Queer theorists have thus drawn on and expanded Beauvoir's feminist thinking in order to call for an eradication of sexual as well as gendered normativity.

25 Simone de Beauvoir, *Le Deuxième sexe tome II: l'expérience vécue* (Paris: Gallimard, 1949), 13.

26 Judith Butler, 'Sex and Gender in Simone de Beauvoir's Second Sex', *Yale French Studies* 72 (1986), 35–49, 35.

27 Butler, *Gender Trouble*, 196–7.

28 Adrienne Rich, 'Compulsory Heterosexuality and Lesbian Existence', *Signs: Journal of Women in Culture and Society* 5/4 (1980), 631–60, 648.

29 Rich, 'Compulsory Heterosexuality and Lesbian Existence', 648.

30 Rich, 'Compulsory Heterosexuality and Lesbian Existence', 649.

Of course, many francophone second-wave feminists, including Beauvoir but also Annie Leclerc, Julia Kristeva, Marie Cardinal and Christine Delphy, have been criticized by subsequent feminist movements for their monolithic approach to women's issues. However, it must also be remembered that second-wave feminist activists, under the auspices of the Mouvement de libération des femmes, did win some major legislative and legal victories in France, such as the legalization of contraception in 1967 and the legalization of abortion in 1975.[31] The economic and political progress made during this period, then, should not go unnoted. Yet, the above feminist theorists have been taken to task particularly for their failure to include non-normative gendered and sexual identities in their struggle for equality. Indeed, since gender and sexuality also intersect with other aspects of identity such as ethnicity, religious beliefs and class, the second-wave feminists have also been criticized for basing their broad theories about women on their own experiences as white privileged women. For instance, black and lesbian feminist Audre Lorde writes: 'White women focus upon their oppression and ignore differences of race, sexual preference, class and age. There is a pretense to a homogeneity of experience covered by the word *sisterhood* that does not in fact exist.'[32] Indeed, Lorde's words resonate very strongly with contemporary movements today such as #BlackLivesMatters and #BlackintheIvory (an online movement to amplify black voices in academia founded by Shardé Davis and Joy Melody Woods, scholars in the field of communication studies). The online responses to these hashtags, which were trending on social media in June 2020, highlight the importance of amplifying black voices rather than speaking on behalf of black people.

Irigaray is another feminist theorist who has been criticized for failing to acknowledge intersectional considerations, even if her work on sexual difference has been a cornerstone of contemporary queer theory. Adopting a similar approach to psychoanalytic theory as Beauvoir, Irigaray nevertheless foregrounds issues of female sexuality as well as issues of gender. Irigaray is particularly critical of Freudian and Lacanian theory which

31 See Claire Duchen, *Feminism in France: From May '68 to Mitterrand* (London: Routledge and Kegan Paul, 1986).

32 Audre Lorde, *Your Silence Will Not Protect You* (London: Silver Press, 2017), 96.

positions women in opposition to men, defining women as 'not-man'.[33] Just as Beauvoir argues that women are culturally determined to adopt an object-status within society because they are considered to be 'not-man',[34] Irigaray asserts that female sexuality is also defined in relation to male sexuality, a fact which is key to understanding gendered and sexual inequality in society.[35] For Irigaray, Freudian and Lacanian theory is an inappropriate lens through which to understand female development because it is immediately conditioned by a phallocentric viewpoint which posits that female sexuality is a negative entity, a 'not-male sexuality'.[36] Irigaray also argues that the female sexual organ suffers a similar fate: it is considered an inferior version of the male genitalia. For Irigaray, Freud's emphasis on the vagina as the key source of sexual pleasure demonstrates a limited understanding of female sexuality because she asserts that women in fact have multiple sources of sexual pleasure.[37] Irigaray's most important contribution to discussions of female sexuality is the conclusion that female sexuality has never been truly defined because it has also been understood relatively, in opposition to male sexuality – hence the description of 'woman' as the 'sex which is not one' in the title of her most famous work.

The self-identified 'radical lesbian' Monique Wittig is also acutely aware that for many theorists, the category of 'woman' only exists in relation to its opposed category of 'man'. In her landmark essay 'The Straight Mind' (1980), she argues that these categories are 'political concepts of opposition' rather than ontological categories of being which should be abolished altogether rather than celebrated.[38] Wittig is also critical of French feminists who construct their own arguments around the binary concepts of 'man' and 'woman'. For Wittig, such feminist discourse excludes non-heterosexual women, and therefore is not a discourse which represents all women because it neglects to consider sexual difference: 'The consequence of this

33 Luce Irigaray, *Ce sexe qui n'en est pas un* (Paris: Minuit, 1977), 23.

34 Simone de Beauvoir, *Le Deuxième Sexe tome 1: les faits et les mythes* (Paris: Gallimard, 1986), 15.

35 Luce Irigaray, *Éthique de la différence sexuelle* (Paris: Minuit, 1984), 13–14.

36 Irigaray, *Ce sexe qui n'en est pas un*, 57–8.

37 Irigaray, *Ce sexe qui n'en est pas un*, 24.

38 Monique Witting, 'The Straight Mind', *Feminist Issues* 1 (1980), 103–11, 108.

tendency toward universality is that the straight mind cannot conceive of a culture, a society where heterosexuality would not order not only all human relationships but also its very production of concepts and all the processes which escape consciousness, as well.'[39] Here, Wittig is criticizing feminists who treat the category 'women' as a single, unique entity, and do not consider how such a heteronormative and monolithic approach to women's identity silences lesbian women and women who do not fit into the gendered and sexual norm. For Wittig, the oppression of lesbians occurs on two counts – they are marginalized for their gender and for their sexuality – meaning that their oppression is even more acute than that of their female heterosexual counterparts. Quebecois writers Isabelle Boisclair and Lori Saint-Martin, meanwhile, consider the oppression of trans identities, a category which calls into the question the very meaning of woman itself, due to a reconfiguration of diversity and multiplicity.[40] The term 'womxn' is now usefully employed to steer terminology away from the sexist implications of the suffixes -man and -men, and to be inclusive of queer, trans and non-binary women.

It is clear, then, that twentieth-century French feminist thought has been at the heart of debates about queer identity and queer culture, even if queer studies as a theoretical discourse has been slow to launch in France. As Cameron and Scanlon point out, 'we often forget that thinkers within the gay liberation movement in the early days had much in common with feminism: deconstructing masculinity, questioning the nuclear family, challenging misogyny, and seeking a sexuality of equality.'[41] Yet contemporary queer activists and thinkers have sought to push these debates further to examine how gendered inequalities are perpetuated in a heterosexual society. It is important to again acknowledge here that many of the key feminist and queer thinkers explored above demonstrate a white, Eurocentric attitude. Their application, therefore, within a broader francophone context requires a nuanced and mediated response, taking into account intersectional issues

39 Wittig, 'The Straight Mind', 107.

40 Isabelle Boisclair and Lori Saint-Martin, 'Les Conceptions de l'identité sexuelle, le postmodernisme et les textes littéraires', *Recherches féministes* 19/2 (2006), 5–27, 10.

41 Cameron and Scanlon, 'Talking about Gender'.

of race, ethnicity, class and ableism, which, of course, is a key concern of third-wave feminists.

Queer Bodies *à la française*: Resistance, Interrogation and Celebration

More inclusive visions of the body of this kind are very much the order of the day given recent global events. The global health crisis of 2020/2021, more than any other historic event, placed the human body at the centre of social and political conversation. This crisis highlighted the enduring importance of biological matter on our livelihoods and sense of self, and called into question the ways in which we interact with fellow bodies in the world around us. It also provided a vivid figuration of Gilles Deleuze and Félix Guattari's 'Body without Organs' (BoW).[42] Our lives have been controlled by an untenable entity – COVID-19 – that establishes connections between people in a disorderly fashion, producing rhizomatic maps of infection across the globe.[43] This had paradoxical outcomes: on the one hand, this made many people look closer to home. People solidified relationships with their family members and childhood friends, reinforcing nuclear units and neatly related 'bubbles', and proud acts of patriotism played a large part in the fight mounted against the global virus. We can think back, for instance, to Macron's closing statement to his 'compatriotes' when he first formally announced lockdown from the Elysée Palace: 'Nous tiendrons tous ensemble. Vive la République. Vive la France.'[44] Our bodily horizons also became extremely limited as we found

42 See Gilles Deleuze and Félix Guattari, *A Thousand Plateaus: Capitalism and Schizophernia*, trans. and intro. Brian Massumi (London: Bloomsbury, 2013), 173–93.

43 Deleuze and Guattari privilege rhizomatic over arborescent (root-based) structures, as outlined in their introduction to *A Thousand Plateaus: Capitalism and Schizophrenia*, 1–27. Unlike root-based systems, rhizomes have no beginning or end, no definitive structure or hierarchy.

44 Emmanuel Macron, 'COVID-19', *Le Point* (2020), 13 March 2020, <https://www.youtube.com/watch?v=raNtAGmAo68>, accessed 17 June 2020.

new ways to exercise within restrictive spaces that proved tensely testing for everyone's mental as well as physical wellbeing.

On the other hand, this crisis reflected the arbitrary nature of borders between national and familial bodies. Brexit, and the bourgeoning Frexit movement across the waters, took on a highly incongruous – if not completely risible – tone in the face of such international angst and cross-collaboration. Some family units also found themselves fragmented owing to domestic frictions, and people the world over were re-evaluating whereabouts they could truly call 'home'. To return to Deleuze and Guattari's theory, the crisis instigated multiple 'lines of flight' away from structured institutions and clearly defined centres – a figurative term that carried a painfully ironic undertone for those individuals unable to fly back to families in other states or countries.[45] While our bodies were materially curtailed, moreover, we rapidly learned to communicate and express ourselves in a meaningful way via virtual platforms. This introduced us to interesting and productive alternatives to face-to-face contact, but also highlighted the impossibility of responding appropriately to body language outside of 'real-time', since *affective* relationships rely largely on a biological body to be *effective*.

Beyond personal bodily identities and relationships, the health crisis carried contradictory consequences from a political perspective too. The corona virus was galvanized by governments to control the behaviour of its citizens, through attempts to collect and consolidate large swathes of personal data to track the health and location of bodies, that led to widespread fear about what the judicial ramifications would be once 'normality' resumed. Citizens' legal right to democratic protest was likewise jeopardized by the state control of bodily presence and contact in public, under the pretext of saving lives. The notion of the body politic has never been so plainly illustrated.

And yet, this international situation shone a revelatory light on glaring disparities between and within different countries in terms of bodily health and quality of life. Studies indicated that people from a BAME background were at a higher risk of dying from the infection in many countries, calling

45 Deleuze and Guattari, *A Thousand Plateaus: Capitalism and Schizophrenia*, 63.

into question the structural inequalities underlying such figures, and Black Lives Matter action during this period instigated serious and much-needed discussion about how to redress systemic racism.[46] Furthermore, the onus of lockdown was on protecting people over sixty and with underlying health conditions, which drew attention to at-risk individuals in our societies requiring additional support, and of the need to reorganize our ableist social spaces that frequently render these groups doubly vulnerable. Bodies in danger within and outside the home-space were brought to the forefront of social consciousness too: the enforced lockdown necessitated urgent consideration for victims of domestic violence who were unable to escape their abusers, and the issue of homelessness could no longer be ignored by politicians at a time when all citizens were being asked to stay indoors. Gendered imbalances were another glaring issue. Across the world, most paid carers and nurses are female, and the majority of unpaid childcare and caring for relatives is undertaken by women. As such, women's labour increased exponentially during this period, and juggling caring responsibilities alongside employment meant that women were at a higher risk of losing their jobs, or at the very least were less likely to excel in the workplace.[47]

46 Clive Cookson and Richard Milne mention Norway, the UK and the US specifically, in 'Nations Look into Why Coronavirus Hits Ethnic Minorities So Hard: Studies Focus on Bame Groups Who Are Over-represented in Covid-19 Cases', *Financial Times* (29 April 2020), <https://www.ft.com/content/5fd6ab18-be4a-48de-b887-8478a391dd72>, accessed 14 July 2020. Interestingly, they note that statistics in France cannot be compiled based on ethnicity.

47 Rosamund Hutt, 'The Coronavirus Fallout May be Worse for Women than Men. Here's Why', *World Economic Forum* (12 March 2020), <https://www.weforum.org/agenda/2020/03/the-coronavirus-fallout-may-be-worse-for-women-than-men-heres-why/>, accessed 18 June 2020; Helen Lewis, 'The Coronavirus Is a Disaster for Feminism: Pandemics Affect Men and Women Differently', *The Atlantic* (19 March 2020), <https://www.theatlantic.com/international/archive/2020/03/feminism-womens-rights-coronavirus-covid19/608302/>, accessed 26 June 2020; Alexandra Villarreal, 'Coronavirus Pandemic Exacerbates Inequalities for Women, UN Warns', *The Guardian* (11 April 2020), <https://www.theguardian.com/world/2020/apr/11/un-coronavirus-pandemic-gender-inequalities-women>, accessed 26 June 2020; Anna Fazackerley, 'Women's Research Plummets During Lockdown – But Articles from Men Increase', *The*

In short, the COVID-19 pandemic placed unprecedented emphasis on the importance of bodily health and identity, and on thinking about marginalized bodies within our communities. It showed us in dramatically new ways how bodily expression and movement are curtailed by biological forces, but all the more so by governmental, judicial and social order. It also taught us that it is possible to define the body beyond purely biological terms, and in terms of its connections to other bodies and of its potentialities (the horror of the virus stems from what the body may *become* once infected).[48] This volume responds to this timely and international re-evaluation of bodily identity, but it also indicates that such ideas have been at the heart of queer thinking and culture since its origins. By opting for a queer and querying approach we are de facto reaching beyond singular and normative definitions of bodily identity. In addition, the notion of bodily pain and political protest shored up by this crisis is a historically palpable one for the LGBTQ+ community. In response to the 1970s breast cancer awareness campaigns in the USA and the UK, for instance, Sedgwick explained that the prospect of death was not a novel one to her and other queer subjects. She asserted that she and others had already lost loved ones to AIDS, and that her experiences as a breast cancer patient were largely informed by 'the politics of homophobia and of queer assertiveness' that were proper to that epidemic.[49] Today there is still a great deal of stigma attached to a positive HIV diagnosis, as trans sex worker activist Giovanna

---

Guardian (12 May 2020), <https://www.theguardian.com/education/2020/may/12/womens-research-plummets-during-lockdown-but-articles-from-men-increase>, accessed 26 June 2020.

48 In keeping with Deleuze and Guattari's theory of becoming, Deleuze and Guattari argue that entities in a state of becoming cannot be defined by what they were or will be, but by the process in-between, and that that process cannot be defined in terms of similarities, regression, evolution or other linear ontological terms: 'Becoming is certainly not imitating, or identifying with something; neither is it regressing-progressing; neither is it corresponding, establishing corresponding relations; neither is it producing, producing a filiation or producing through filiation. Becoming is a verb with a consistency all its own […].' Deleuze and Guattari, *A Thousand Plateaus: Capitalism and Schizophrenia*, 279.

49 Sedgwick, *Tendencies*, 13–14.

Murillo Rincon makes abundantly clear. Rincon is committed to publicly denouncing the forms of mistreatment and injustices that she and other QTIPOC (Queer, Transgender and Intersex People of Colour) experience at the hands of authority figures in France and elsewhere.[50] Chief among these are sexual assault by prison guards and being blamed for the HIV-AIDS epidemic by medical professionals.[51]

These testimonies are stark reminders of the importance of defending the bodily rights of trans and queer persons. One has only to remember the recent demonstrations conducted to the slogan *Liberté, Egalité, Paternité*, against France's bioethics bill passed in 2019 to grant lesbians and single mothers access to IVF treatment (known as PMA, Procréation Médicalement Anonyme). Gay marriage has also only been legalized in four francophone countries – Belgium, Canada, France and Luxembourg, with the last two as late as 2013 and 2015 – and same-sex relations still constitute a criminal act in several member states, including Morocco, Tunisia, Senegal, Cameroon and Mauritania. Suffice it to say that queer bodily relations are very far from being the norm across the francophone world, and it is this type of institutional and cultural prejudice that this volume seeks to counteract, by queer(y)ing those norms that cause stigmatization and oppression.

This also partly explains why the body is such a central issue in French queer writing, as Evans establishes in their monograph on queer 'permeability'. Through a study of the theoretical and artistic work of Paul B. Preciado, Monique Wittig and ORLAN, Evans presents the body as a fundamental component of French queer thought and activism (with HIV, pharmaceuticals and surgical intervention playing a key part in many

50 Rincon established Acceptess-T (Actions Concrètes Conciliants: Education, Prévention, Travail, Equité, Santé et Sport pour les Transgenres), a not-for-profit organization which supports the most vulnerable of trans subjects such as trans sex workers. She is also a leading member of STRASS (Syndicat du TRAvail Sexuel) and CoreVIH, two staunchly intersectional organizations which work to support sex workers and to fight against the transmission of HIV respectively.

51 Countries mentioned include France, Brazil and Portgual. Rincon in Marianne Chargois, dir. *EMPOWER: Perspectives de travailleuses du sexe*. Art Whore Connection, 2018.

queer subjects' lives), and explains that, thanks to its prevailing political engagement, French queer thought has been much more virulent than the watered down efforts in the anglophone world.[52] This volume responds to this trend in French queer thought identified by Evans, by positing the body as central to queer study, and by conceiving of queer corpo-cultural expression as containing political agency.

Rincon and others' accounts also remind us that the stigmatization of queer and trans subjects is frequently experienced in tandem with additional forms of marginalization, such as racist or nationalist attitudes, or precarious citizenship, that limits their bodily freedoms. In a film directed by sex worker and activist Marianne Chargois, *EMPOWER: Perspectives de travailleuses du sexe*, a segment presented by Rincon is included alongside two more by Mylène Juste, a sex worker and performer who lives in a communal space with queer and/or migrant sex workers, and Aying, a Chinese-born sex worker who narrates how, as an illegal immigrant in France, she fears both violence from clients (given that they must work as incognito as possible) and repatriation as a woman *sans papiers*.[53] This is just one example of how queer representation can involve and give way to discussion about additional forms of bodily oppression. In the same vein, this volume adopts an investigative queer lens to query other corporeal issues that fall outside of normative categories in the francophone world, relating to nationality, race, class and physical ability.

At the most extreme end, the sources studied in this volume question the category of the human body itself, questioning how far our bodily identity defines who we are. What differentiates 'us' from the avatars that represent us, via dating apps, social media profiles and cloning? What dangers and benefits can we identify within posthuman forms of corporeal expression and communication? And how is this impacted by, and how will this impact on, queer subjects and relationships, and on those whose identity is defined along similarly non-normative lines? If queer bodies have historically been associated with anti-capitalist and dominant ideology (in so far as queer identity deviates

52 Evans, *The Body in French Queer Thought from Wittig to Preciado: Queer Permeability*, 3–4.

53 Mylène Juste and Aying in *EMPOWER*.

inherently from linear models of re/production, and is defined as a transgressive mode of being),[54] to what extent does this hold true in a postmodern age (when gay dating apps, for instance, generate large amounts of capital for a select few)? And how can this fluid approach to being be adopted by other marginalized groups? This volume thus situates the body as a primary object of queer study and vice versa, in keeping with French philosophical tradition and as a jumping board to broader queries about bodily norms.

This agenda is not only a resistant one (resistant to intolerant beliefs and behaviours), and interrogative (interrogating what we mean by the body and the human), but so too is it a celebratory one. We hope to reflect a diversity of bodily identities, experiences and desires as a means of indicating that, while restrictive bodily norms might not be easily erased, we need not be absolutely beholden to them, and that pushing back against bodily norms to varying degrees entails productive possibilities from a feminist, social, political, personal, legal, technological, scientific and cultural standpoint. More than anything, reflecting diverse bodily 'norms' can enable us to come to terms with our own bodies and our own 'normal'. This is particularly important during a time when humans the world over are acutely conscious of their own bodies, not just because of COVID-19, but subsequent to the increase in images of the body circulated in the media, as noted extensively by a range of social commentators.[55] The proliferation of a one-size-fits-all model of beauty has increased anxiety about bodily identity across the world, as people of manifold shapes and appearances invest inordinate amounts of time, money and energy to meet what philosopher Heather Widdows calls 'the beauty ideal'.[56] As the numbers of people with

54 Lee Edelmann articulates this particularly clearly through his case against 'reproductive futurism' in *No Future: Queer Theory and the Death Drive* (Durham, NC: Duke University Press, 2004), 3.

55 Recent examples include: Susan Orbach, *Bodies* (London: Profile Books, 2019); Heather Widdows, *Perfect Me: Beauty as an Ethical Ideal* (Oxford: Princeton University Press, 2018); Gabrielle Deydier, *On ne naît pas grosse on le devient* (Paris: Goutte d'or, 2017). We provide a brief overview of some of the overarching concerns in our introduction to 'Challenging Normative Spaces and Gazes: The Body in Twentieth- and Twenty-First-Century Francophone Culture', a special issue with *L'Esprit Créateur*, 60/1 (2020), 1–12.

56 Widdows, *Perfect Me*, 49.

anorexia, bulimia and body dysmorphia rises, so too do the profits within cosmetic, surgical and fashion sectors, who capitalize on people being deeply and dangerously uncomfortable in their own skin. In opposition to these hegemonic forces, celebrating a multitude of bodily identities and experiences is a way of accepting diverse body types and norms so that, to quote Susie Orbach, 'we can then take leave of them'.[57]

In short, this volume aims to extend the tradition of French thought and culture to consider queer ideology and identity from the perspective of the body foremost and, conversely, to explore how transgressive depictions of the body can represent and support a multiplicity of queer and otherwise marginalized subjects. In so doing, this volume mounts a challenge to the less progressive aspect of French and francophone tradition, namely reactionary views that undermine political progress and personal liberties in relation to the body.

Chapter Summaries

The volume is organized in four thematic sections which reflect the key themes and concerns tackled by each author, and each section takes a transmedial approach to allow us to compare how different media and genre queer(y) problematic bodily norms. The cultural production under analysis spans the twentieth and twenty-first centuries and originates from a cross-section of francophone spaces. While the cultural contexts under examination are clearly not representative of the francophone world in its entirety, the volume seeks to decentre Queer French Studies by incorporating material from beyond Hexagonal France.

In Part I, 'Queering the Body', the authors engage with key debates in queer studies to investigate how social and sexual norms are inscribed on the body, and how francophone digital media, literature and film endeavour to challenge and transcend these norms. Firstly, Brian Troth looks

57 Orbach, *Bodies*, 157.

at the homosexual male body in digital spaces in contemporary France, arguing that digital bodies created on online dating apps queer traditional understandings of bodily desire. Engaging with Deleuze and Guattari's concept of the 'Body without Organs', Troth studies the digital gay body through Arthur Cahn's novel *Les Vacances du petit Renard* [*The Little Fox's Vacation*] (2018) alongside his own auto-ethnographic reflections, concluding that the digital realm is a safe space which allows gay men to reject the heteronormative society in which they live. Adina Stroia continues to highlight the resistance towards heteronormativity in French culture in her exploration of lesbian representation in contemporary French women's writing. Analysing the works of French novelist Marie Nimier which explicitly feature same-sex relationships between women, she argues that the figure of the double appears as a site for the displacement of the sexual charge, an empowering space which privileges the postmodern fluid self and where queer identities can be negotiated and renegotiated. Ray Balstad closes this section by exploring the staging of heterotopias in Alain Berliner's *Ma Vie en rose* [*My Life in Pink*] (1997) and Céline Sciamma's *Tomboy* (2011); two films that depict the gendered and spatial (re)orientations of two children, and how these compare with the bourgeois domestic expectations of family and friends. Drawing on the spatial theory of Michel Foucault, Sara Ahmed and others, Balstad argues the case for several 'counter-sites' in these films, which serve to simultaneously mirror and disrupt 'real' heteronormative sites and the power structures which underlie them.

Part II, 'Rethinking Gendered Bodily Norms', groups together chapters which examine how gender debates are portrayed in fiction, theatre and film from a range of geographical spaces and cultural contexts. Kathleen Rizy queries normative definitions of motherhood through her examination of Marie Darrieussecq's short story 'Mon mari le clone' ['My Cloned Husband'] (2006). In this text, which is set in the 2020s, the narrator describes the gruelling process of IVF, the death of her husband whilst he is donating his sperm, and her subsequent cloning of him. By examining female agency in reproduction, cryogenics and cloning, Rizy reframes and feminizes a traditional androcentric conceptualization of technology. Through a study of plays by Martinican women writers Ina Césaire and

Suzanne Dracius, Vanessa Lee explores postcolonial theatre's potential for challenging contemporary stereotypes and marginalization of women, and for reclaiming historical narratives about French Caribbean subjects, such as the Insurrection of 1870. Lee presents bodily expression as a particularly rich tool for asserting female subjectivity and reappropriation of social spaces, and as a means of merging collective History with personal narratives. Finally, Seth Compaoré examines the embodiment of masculinity in Andre Téchiné's cinematic corpus. In his close analysis of *Quand on a 17 ans* [*Being 17*] (2016), a film which depicts the violent coming-of-age of its two male protagonists, he demonstrates how the film presents the male body's poetic by using a dramatic landscape as the backdrop and by foregrounding physical combat between the two men through Téchiné's photographic style of cinema. For Compaoré, Téchiné's film is a powerful deconstruction of both social and cinematic norms which dictate how the male body is configured in contemporary society.

Part III, 'Hybrid and Dysfunctional Bodies', interrogates the very definition of the body through an analysis of hybrid, transgressive, dysfunctional and unusual bodies in literature and film. Cristina Onesta provides a visceral account of countering bodily norms and gazes in Ananda Devi's novel *Manger l'autre* [*Eating the Other*] (2018) and Isabelle Boni-Claverie's short film, *Le Génie d'Abou* [*Abou's Genius*] (1998), from a gendered and racial perspective. Through this study Onesta explains how the obese body throws new light on ideal and abject bodies alike, and reinstates the importance of flesh and blood for sexual desire. Onesta also explores contemporary perceptions of disability, city-living and entertainment, and concludes that the studied works encourage critical reflection on our increasingly consumerist societies and art's respective responsibility. The novel *14* [*1914*] (2012) by Jean Echenoz is the subject of Sara Bédard-Goulet's chapter. In *14*, five characters from Vendée are mobilized to fight in the First World War. The text gives agency to both nonhuman entities (such as weapons and insects) as well as human bodies. Bédard-Goulet explores the concept of agency and emphasizes the value and potential of examining bodies through a non-binary lens. She investigates the bodily norms and boundaries which inform our conceptualization of 'human' and 'nonhuman' bodies. Kate Foster closes this section with her analysis of Gaston Leroux's *La Poupée sanglante* [*The Kiss that Killed*] and *La Machine à assassiner* [*The Machine to Kill*] (1924). Drawing on Haraway's notion of the cyborg, Foster argues that in these texts, Gabriel's cyborg body (composed of man and machine) constantly disrupts and queries fixed definitions of the corporeal body, enabling him to resist and reject the rigid identities imposed on him by others.

The final part, 'Bodies in Flux', queries how bodies are transformed through different forms of movement. Movement here is understood as both enforced and voluntary; conscious and subconscious; and a decision borne out of necessity and for pleasure. Using Ahmed's *Queer Phenomenology* (2006) as a theoretical framework, Loren K. Wolfe examines how, in the later writings of Hervé Guibert, sexuality is positioned in terms of repeated actions. The chapter focuses on how Guibert queries his homosexuality towards the end of his life and how his identity is profoundly inflected by his female heroines. Wolfe argues that these female characters escape normative definitions of heterosexuality and homosexuality as they powerfully urge the reader to echo their dedication to keeping Guibert's corpus alive. Jennifer Boum Make's chapter explores Emile Ollivier's novel, *Passages* (1991), which tells the story of two generations of Haitian exiles. Boum Make examines the role of testimony and Othered bodies in this polyphonic narrative. As Boum Make underlines, the media has desensitized audiences towards the struggles of migrants and refugees. Boum Make's chapter disrupts this norm by reflecting on how Ollivier's depiction of the Haitian Othered bodies can help us to develop a greater sensitivity towards the plight of migrants and refugees. Kathryn Chaffee's study aligns with Deleuze's theorization of movement as a dialectic process that occurs *between* multiple instances and bodies. Chaffee presents dance as a form of encounter in the cinematic *œuvre* of Claire Denis, examining the movements of individual bodies and their interactions with others around them, often in ways that disturb social, racial, historical, representational and heterosexual boundaries. Chaffee also elucidates how Denis' dance scenes involve the viewer more intimately with the diegesis.

The chapters in the volume thus redefine corporeal limitations by questioning defiantly what is meant by the body in the first place. The publication reveals that evaluating the bodily norms depicted in a wide array of francophone cultural production through a queer and querying lens allows us to fragment often oppressive and restrictive norms, and ultimately transform them.

Bibliography

Beauvoir, Simone de, *Le Deuxième sexe tome I: les faits et les mythes* (Paris: Gallimard, 1986).

—— *Le Deuxième sexe tome II: l'expérience vécue* (Paris: Gallimard, 1949).

Bessette, Jean, 'An Archive of Anecdotes: Raising Lesbian Consciousness after the Daughters of Bilitis', *Rhetoric Society Quarterly* 43/1 (2013), 22–45.

Boisclair, Isabelle, and Lori Saint-Martin, 'Les Conceptions de l'identité sexuelle, le postmodernisme et les textes littéraires', *Recherches féministes* 19/2 (2006), 5–27.

Boyle, Claire, 'Post-Queer (Un)Made in France?', *Queer Theory's Return to France*, *Paragraph* 35/2 (2012), 265–80.

Butler, Judith, *Gender Trouble: Feminism and the Subversion of Identity* (New York and London: Routledge, 1990); *Trouble dans le genre: le féminisme et la subversion de l'identité*, trans. Cynthia Kraus (Paris: La Découverte, 2005).

—— 'Sex and Gender in Simone de Beauvoir's Second Sex', *Yale French Studies* 72 (1986), 35–49.

Cameron, Debbie, and Joan Scanlon, 'Talking about Gender', *Trouble and Strife* (2010), <https://www.troubleandstrife.org/new-articles/talking-about-gender/>, accessed 24 June 2020.

Carbajal, Alberto Fernández, 'On Being Queer and Postcolonial: Reading Zadie Smith's *NW* through Virginia Woolf's *Mrs Dalloway*', *Journal of Commonwealth Literature* 51/1 (2016), 76–91.

Chargois, Marianne, dir. *EMPOWER: Perspectives de travailleuses du sexe.* Art Whore Connection, 2018.

Cookson, Clive, and Richard Milne, 'Nations Look into Why Coronavirus Hits Ethnic Minorities So Hard: Studies Focus on Bame Groups Who Are Over-represented in Covid-19 Cases', *Financial Times* (29 April 2020), <https://www.ft.com/content/5fd6ab18-be4a-48de-b887-8478a391dd72>, accessed 14 July 2020.

Curzon, Anne, *Fixing English: Prescriptivism and Language History* (Cambridge: Cambridge University Press, 2014).

Davis, Oliver, and Hector Kollias, 'Introduction', *Queer Theory's Return to France, Paragraph* 35/2 (2012), 139–43.

Dean, Tim, 'Queer', in Rachel Adams, Benjamin Reiss, David Serlin, eds, *Keywords for Disability Studies* (New York: NYU Press, 2015), 143–5.

Deleuze, Gilles, and Félix Guattari, *A Thousand Plateaus: Capitalism and Schizophernia*, trans. and intro. Brian Massumi (London: Bloomsbury, 2013), 173–93.

Deydier, Gabrielle, *On ne naît pas grosse on le devient* (Paris: Goutte d'or, 2017).

Duchen, Claire, *Feminism in France: From May '68 to Mitterrand* (London: Routledge and Kegan Paul, 1986).

Edelmann, Lee, *No Future: Queer Theory and the Death Drive* (Durham, NC: Duke University Press, 2004).

Evans, Elliot, *The Body in French Queer Thought from Wittig to Preciado: Queer Permeability* (Abingdon and New York: Routledge, 2020).

Galis, Polly, Maria Tomlinson, and Antonia Wimbush, 'Introduction', *L'Esprit Créateur, Special Issue, Challenging Normative Spaces and Gazes: The Body in Twentieth- and Twenty-First-Century Francophone Culture* 60/1 (2020), 1–12.

Hawley, John, and Dennis Altman, *Postcolonial, Queer: Theoretical Intersections* (New York: SUNY Press, 2001).

Hutt, Rosamund, 'The Coronavirus Fallout May be Worse for Women than Men. Here's Why', *World Economic Forum* (12 March 2020), <https://www.weforum.org/agenda/2020/03/the-coronavirus-fallout-may-be-worse-for-women-than-men-heres-why/>, accessed 18 June 2020.

Irigaray, Luce, *Ce sexe qui n'en est pas un* (Paris: Minuit, 1977).

—— *Éthique de la différence sexuelle* (Paris: Minuit, 1984).

Lewis, Helen, 'The Coronavirus Is a Disaster for Feminism: Pandemics Affect Men and Women Differently', *The Atlantic* (19 March 2020), <https://www.theatlantic.com/international/archive/2020/03/feminism-womens-rights-coronavirus-covid19/608302/>, accessed 26 June 2020.

Lorde, Audre, *Your Silence Will Not Protect You* (London: Silver Press, 2017).

Navarro-Ayala, Luis, *Queering Transcultural Encounters: Bodies, Image, and Frenchness in Latin America and North Africa* (Cham, Switzerland: Palgrave Macmillan, 2019).

Macron, Emmanuel, 'COVID-19', *Le Point* (2020), 13 March 2020, <https://www.youtube.com/watch?v=raNtAGmAo68>, accessed 17 June 2020.

Orbach, Susan, *Bodies* (London: Profile Books, 2019).

Partridge, Eric, *The World of Words: An Introduction to Language in General and to English and American In Particular* (London: Routledge, 2015).

Perreau, Bruno, 'The Queer Mind through the Transatlantic Looking Glass', *Contemporary France and Francophone Studies* 18/1 (2014), 75–85.

Rich, Adrienne, 'Compulsory Heterosexuality and Lesbian Existence', *Signs: Journal of Women in Culture and Society* 5/4 (1980), 631–60.

Robcis, Camille, 'How the Symbolic Became French: Kinship and Republicanism in the PACS Debates', *Discourse: Journal for Theoretical Studies in Media and Culture* 26/3 (2004), 110–35.

Sedgewick, Eve Kosofsky, *Epistemology of the Closet* (Berkeley and Los Angeles, CA: University of California Press, 1990); *Epistémologie du placard*, trans. Maxime Cervulle (Paris: Amsterdam, 2018).

—— *Tendencies* (Durham, NC: Duke University Press, 1993).

Sibalis, Michael, 'The Gay Liberation Movement in France', in Gert Hekma and Alain Giami, eds, *Sexual Revolutions* (Basingstoke: Palgrave Macmillan, 2014), 188–202.

Villarreal, Alexandra, 'Coronavirus Pandemic Exacerbates Inequalities for Women, UN Warns', *The Guardian* (11 April 2020), <https://www.theguardian.com/world/2020/apr/11/un-coronavirus-pandemic-gender-inequalities-women>, accessed 26 June 2020.

Widdows, Heather, *Perfect Me: Beauty as an Ethical Ideal* (Oxford: Princeton University Press, 2018).

Witting, Monique, 'The Straight Mind', *Feminist Issues* 1 (1980), 103–111.

Young, Iris Marion, *On Female Body Experience: 'Throwing Like a Girl' and Other Essays* (New York: Oxford University Press, 2005).

PART I

Queering the Body

BRIAN TROTH

1 Hookups: Social Networking and Digital Bodies in Twenty-First-Century France

What form(s) does the human body take? The easiest iteration of the human body to understand, perhaps, is that of a mass of bones, blood and organs. Yet in 2020, the human body is also conceptualized as a collection of intangible digital files. Almost everyone in the 'Global North' seems to be in possession of a digital body and many of us interact with them on a daily basis. In this chapter, I propose an analysis of the digital gay male body and the spaces he inhabits. I theorize that digital bodies queer traditional conceptions of bodily desire and inhabit digital spaces that will serve as loci for understanding the gay male body in the twenty-first century. In making the digital gay body the focus of the analysis, I invite the reader to consider how the digital body resists a more traditional view of corporeality. By first defining the digital body as a modern iteration of Gilles Deleuze and Félix Guattari's 'Corps sans Organes', or 'Body without Organs' (BwO), I argue that the digital body is a site of desire production that maintains gay male sexuality. By reading the digital gay body through Arthur Cahn's *Les Vacances du petit Renard* [*The Little Fox's Vacation*] (2018),[1] nuanced by auto-ethnographic observations, this study demonstrates the ways in which gay men use their digital bodies to navigate a digital space that assures their existence and allows them to reject heteronormativity.

Amongst current debates about the body, it is evident that some bodies are treated as if they have significantly more value than others. The unborn foetus seems to take primacy over its mother's bodily autonomy; bodies of colour are more often victims of police violence than privileged white

1 Arthur Cahn, *Les Vacances du petit Renard* (Paris: Seuil, 2018).

bodies; bodies that flee their home countries are treated as if they were diseases that must be eradicated; transgender bodies are being attacked for daring to urinate in public. In an age when the body is already going through considerable change and scrutiny, the time seems ripe to talk about the digital body too.

There are at least two reasons why we should talk about the digital body and the digital body in a French space in particular. The digital body has firmly taken hold in contemporary society. At 30 years old, I remember a time when many of my friends did not have social media, let alone my parents. The proliferation of social media apps, dating websites, interest- and hobby-based websites such as Pinterest and the myriad shopping apps and sites available combine to create someone's digital persona or avatar. The rise of digital technology has therefore shaped our identities. France offers a particularly compelling case study in the field of medical humanities and the digital body. The Paris-based HIV/AIDS activist group 'Aides' runs a Facebook group called Prep'Dial. Prep'Dial is dedicated to the discussion of PrEP, the name given to a method of HIV prevention by which users begin a Truvada regimen that builds immunity to the virus that causes AIDS. In August 2019, Prep'Dial had over 11,400 users. This is impressive when one considers that PrEPWatch estimates that between 13,000 and 14,000 people use PrEP in France. Of course, not every member of Prep'Dial is a PrEP user. However, for comparison, there are approximately 130,000 to 135,000 PrEP users in the United States, while the Facebook group PrEP Facts counts only 21,000+ users. The discrepancy in the ratios between the French-based PrEP'Dial and the USA-based PrEP Facts shows, for one reason or another, that the digital body is a particularly privileged actor in the French context. We cannot overlook other possible factors that may contribute to this discrepancy such as more localized spaces for conversation (such as city-based support groups) or reluctance to talk online about medical issues in the United States. Nevertheless, the digital body is an important factor to consider in how information about healthcare is transmitted.

For my purposes, I define the digital body as the non-physical profile(s) that people create within the World Wide Web. The most recognizable digital body is perhaps the one that is tied to dating apps. Yet, any part of our online existence can be considered an aspect of the digital body. Inasmuch as readers are clearly physical beings, it can be difficult to accept a digital body as a *body* – that the profiles on smartphone screens are both representations and re-presentations of something that a person might consider 'real'. I argue that we should consider the digital body as a modern iteration of Deleuze and Guattari's 'Body Without Organs', and that by their nature, digital bodies manufacture desire. Insofar as production is the linchpin of a capitalist society, the digital body's production of desire is the linchpin of modern society.[2]

In *Capitalisme et schizophrénie 1: l'anti-œdipe* [*Capitalism and Schizophrenia 1: Anti-Œdipus*] (1972), Deleuze and Guattari posit that capitalist society is imbued with binaries, not the least of which is the 'productive' and its complement, the 'non-productive': 'The body without organs is non-productive, sterile, inconceivable, unconsumable,' they write of the BwO.[3] This view of the BwO aligns with popular critiques of online interactions: do we ever really know who the other person is? Or, for the person hoping to find sex and love online, what if these digital interactions never produce physical ones? Although the BwO itself does not produce anything, it is the plane upon which desire can be produced:

> The body without organs, the non-productive, the unconsumable, is a surface on which the process of producing desire is recorded, so well that desiring-machines seem to come from him in the apparent, objective movement that brings them back to it.[4]

Take, for example, the protagonist of Arthur Cahn's *Les Vacances du petit Renard*. Paul Renard is on vacation with his family when he is gifted a new smartphone, which is capable of downloading Grindr (a gay-focused social networking app often used for a mix of dating, sex and networking

2 Modernity, here, is understood in Jean Baudrillard's terms whereby technological advances have reached the point where the future is uncertain. Defining characteristics of modernity for Baudrillard are the free, uninhibited movement of information, which I believe is assured by the digital bodies that form the basis of this chapter. Jean Baudrillard, *La Transparence du mal* (Paris: Galilée, 1990).

3 Gilles Deleuze and Félix Guattari, *Capitalisme et schizophrénie 1: l'anti-œdipe* (Paris: Minuit, 1972), 16. All translations are my own unless otherwise noted.

4 Deleuze and Guattari, *Capitalisme et schizophrénie: l'anti-œdipe*, 19.

between men). The 14-year-old, infatuated with Hervé, his aunt's 45-year-old best friend, turns to the creation of several fake Grindr profiles to interact with Hervé. In one exchange, the two share explicit photos of penises and buttocks, but with an unsatisfactory ending:

> – Jolie! Tu peux recevoir?
>
> – Non et toi?
>
> – Pas là.
>
> – Dommage.
>
> – Oui, je suis sûr que j'aurais kiffé me faire limer la gueule et le cul par un mec de ton genre.
>
> – Héhé, next time.
>
> Hervé lui envoie des photos de lui les fesses en l'air. Il éteint son téléphone. Il soupire.
>
> [– Pretty! Can you host?
>
> – No, you?
>
> – Not here.
>
> – Too bad.
>
> – Yes, I'm sure I would have loved having a man like you in my mouth and ass.
>
> – Haha, next time.
>
> Hervé sends him photos of himself with his butt in the air. He turns off his phone. He sighs. (169)]

Paul has created a fake account. For this particular encounter, he has chosen a dark-skinned man of the same age as Hervé. After the exchange of the photo of an anonymous penis, Hervé invites Paul (alias Mekamek – 'man to man') to come over for a hook-up. Paul being neither the person he claims to be, nor of age, obligatorily turns Hervé down, turns his phone off, and sighs, disappointed by his unrealized desires.

His disappointment points to a reality of online dating that Emily Witt notes in her book, *Future Sex* (2016), where she claims that 'until the bodies were introduced, seduction was only provisional'.[5] This calls into

5 Emily Witt, *Future Sex* (New York: Farrar, Strauss and Giroux, 2016), 21.

question a conflict between the profiles which go unread and the digital body which is supposed to re-present a physical body that users desire. The digital body that Paul crafted – quite literally, by piecing together seemingly random photos he has found online like a web-based Dr Frankenstein – serves only as the locus upon which Hervé's desire is inscribed. Hervé is physically attracted to the body that is re-presented on Grindr and it is this physical attraction that drives the interaction. Since the attraction is to a digital body that does not re-present the person to whom Hervé is speaking, norms of bodily desire are disrupted. The transcription of their conversation shows that no time is wasted on pleasantries, instead focusing immediately on whether Hervé is in the mood to hook up. Hervé's response to discovering that neither of them can host (and therefore will not hook up), further reveals the limitations of a BwO that is not productive: his use of the conditional past ('would have loved') shows that a physical encounter was perhaps the goal, but that its outcome was never a *fait accompli*. One may even wonder, because Hervé sends a photo of his 'butt' even after he knows that there will be no meeting, if the production of desire was not more important than the production of a physical encounter the entire time.

If the BwO is the surface on which desire can be created, the BwO is proof of the traceability of desire production. Enda McCaffrey's 'From Homographies of Invisibility to Hypervisibility' (2013), employs Derridean notions of trace (namely, that trace is the result of the disappearance of something: in his case, the origin of self or knowledge) to argue that gayness became hypervisible at the very moment that gay lifestyles could be recorded and policed.[6] I push McCaffrey's line of thought further by introducing the element of the digital body. The digital body – in this instance Mekamek and RV (Hervé's Grindr alias) – is a re-presentation of

6 McCaffrey is speaking of how gay rights laws and closed-circuit TV made gayness hypervisible in 1980s and 90s Belfast, driving a wedge between the gay men who were not ready for visibility and those men who eschewed certain behaviours because of their visibility. McCaffrey's argument is that the traces of gay lifestyles before hypervisbility is proof of their existence. See Enda McCaffrey, 'From Homographies of Invisibility to Hypervisibility: Queering and De-Queering City Centre Space', in Kathleen O'Mara and Liz Morrish, eds, *Queering Paradigms III* (Bern: Peter Lang, 2013), 33–61.

a physical body. Even if a physical encounter does not, did not, or could not, occur, the digital body is proof that the physical encounter exists, existed, or could exist.

The digital body, particularly in the case of social networking apps like Grindr which are conceived to facilitate physical connections (it is quite common for users of Grindr to mock the idea of using Grindr for anything other than sex), is more than proof of a physical presence. It is also the promise of a physical presence. I, like Deleuze and Guattari, employ the metaphor of an egg to illustrate this point. They write that:

> The Body without Organs is an egg: it is crossed by axes and thresholds; by latitudes, longitudes and geodesics, it is crossed by gradients that mark what it will become and the paths it will take, the destinations of that which is developing inside.[7]

The egg is a particularly adept analogy of the digital body. As an object, the egg is a physical thing that exists on its own: most of us need no proof of that. Yet the egg itself carries very little value; its worth is based predominantly on the potentialities within, of what it can become, and where it will go. The egg would have no value without the possibility of it being fertilized and becoming a living creature, or at the very least, an ingredient in a delicious omelette or baked good.

The egg, like the BwO, nonetheless accrues value that can be attributed to its potential. Similarly to how trace reveals the presence of something through its absence, the egg's existence is proof of something that does not yet exist. Even if the egg never produces its potential, the egg may take on the valuation of its product. A cursory glance at (anti-)abortionist stances reveals, for example, that an unborn foetus may draw more concern than the fully realized human being that is carrying it. The digital bodies, such as those found on Grindr, further illustrate the same phenomenon.

Grindr is but one of many examples of social networking apps that are aimed at men who have sex with men.[8] The basic premise is the same for all

7 Deleuze and Guattari, *Capitalisme et schizophrénie: l'anti-œdipe*, 28.

8 Others include Scruff and Hornet. While not specifically aimed at gay men, OkCupid and Tinder are other alternatives, though interestingly, they tend to be taken more 'seriously' than the former apps. That is, OkCupid and Tinder are used more frequently for dating than hooking up.

the apps: users download the app to their phone, create an account with an email address and curate their profiles; they create the digital bodies that then appear in a grid. The user's own profile is the first in the grid, and the rest are ordered by distance from the user who becomes the epicentre of his digital world. Features of how Grindr functions reveal to what extent the digital body and its physical counterpart occupy prime position in the app's use. Grindr encourages users to add a photo to their profile and allows users to identify the 'tribe' to which they belong and to which they are most attracted. These often refer to body types: sporty, smooth (clean shaven) or bears (heavier, hairy men). A user must make a conscious effort to read profiles, yet the screen is inundated with bodies from the moment he logs on. This fact recalls Witt's apt observation that 'until the bodies were introduced, seduction [is] only provisional'.[9]

In the digital world, no one polices the creation of digital bodies (aside from rules that state users may not publicly display nude images). A user is free to create any digital body he sees fit: Paul Renard in *Les Vacances du petit Renard*, for example, creates multiple profiles in order to communicate with Hervé, none of which are actual re-presentations of Paul himself. Even if users are more honest than Paul, a lot of work can go into the creation of a profile: the photo selected is one that the user thinks is most likely to catch someone's eye. Is it the best angle? Not too blurry? Perhaps the left nipple instead of the right?

With that in mind, we might evaluate if it is worth our time to interact with profiles that may or may not accurately represent the person who created them. Indeed, Paul's deceptive use of others' photographs raises questions as to whether the men on the other side are 'real'. Based on the ways in which we interact with the digital body, however, it is clear that we *should* treat these bodies as real and accept the digital body as transforming how we define real. In many ways, we already do by ignoring the possibility of deception in favour of the outcomes users hope to gain from engaging with apps.

To illustrate this, we must focus on the ideas of potential and desire, which are central to the framework that Deleuze and Guattari lay out in

9 Witt, *Future Sex*, 21.

their theorization of the BwO. Gay men would not spend time on their apps if they did not expect or hope to gain something from them. Indeed, it is important to emphasize that these digital encounters are designed to facilitate their physical counterparts. Gay men use social networking apps because they are ripe with potentiality. They are willing to invest that time because they fully believe that there is a physical person on the other side of their messages.

Of course, gay men are not the only population that makes use of the digital body. Yet, apps that specifically target gay men share characteristics that make them unique when compared to apps that target straight populations. Witt describes the need for dating apps to be perceived as clean so that women would not feel too embarrassed to engage with them. The model for gay men, however, was different:

> The founders of Manhunt, which transitioned from a phone chat line to a website in 2001 and became one of the most popular early dating sites for gay men, quickly recognized that in the world of men interested in meeting men, what job the person had or where he went to college were secondary questions. Sexual attraction and explicitly sexual communication tended to come first.[10]

Features of Grindr respond to popular notions that gay men are more interested in sex than in romance and dating. For example, users have the opportunity to send emojis that are included in the app, most of which are sexual in nature: peach and eggplant emojis (representing the butt and penis) in various skin tones, arrows pointing up (for the top, the insertive partner in anal sex) or down (for the bottom, the receptive partner), or an impish devil used to indicate arousal.

The manner in which Grindr interfaces with its users is further proof of Grindr responding to the stereotypical image of the promiscuous, sex-driven gay man. Witt states that 'Grindr introduced the theory that one could look at a picture of someone's abdomen and soon be having sex with a neighbour, and the theory became a question.'[11] The digital body compels us to question the acceptability of treating it as a re-presentation of a

10 Witt, *Future Sex*, 26.

11 Witt, *Future Sex*, 27.

body that could participate in a physical, sexual encounter. Through the geolocalization of its users and its making their locations such a salient feature, Grindr emphasizes proximity and one's ability to meet neighbours quickly and easily. This differs from other dating apps such as OkCupid, whose distinguishing feature is the compatibility calculator whereby users answer a series of questions to determine how likely they are to get along with or agree with possible matches. Even Tinder, whose swipe-right-for-yes-left-for-no *modus operandi* encourages decisions based on appearance, removes explicit reference to sexuality from the equation. Tinder had to take Grindr's model and make it a clean, well-lit space in order to succeed for straight people.[12]

One result of this interface is that gay dating apps tend to resemble digital versions of cruising grounds. This is significant, I would argue, because gay men are more dependent on their ability to navigate a digital space than straight people because gay men have historically been dependent on spaces in general. Scholars have extensively discussed this point for decades. To cite but a few examples: Lauren Berlant and Michael Warner argue that space is crucial to the creation of gay identity in 'Sex in Public';[13] Sébastien Chauvin and Arnaud Lerch claim that the history of gay men is indissociable from the history of their spaces;[14] Laud Humphreys's *Tearoom Trade* reminds its readers of the cultural importance of (semi-public) cruising grounds,[15] some of which achieve almost storied, legendary reputations such as the Quai d'Austerlitz in Paris, immortalized in Cyril Collard's 1985 *Les Nuits fauves* [*Savage Nights*].

We must recognize that gay men make use of spaces such as cruising grounds, bars and gay neighbourhoods because they have few ways of finding other gay men. In the 'Global North', spaces default to the hegemony of heteronormativity. The same may be said for the digital spaces, which, as we enter the third decade of the twenty-first century, are becoming more

12 Witt, *Future Sex*, 28.

13 Lauren Berlant and Michael Warner, 'Sex in Public', *Critical Inquiry* 24/2 (1998), 547–66.

14 Sébastien Chauvin and Arnaud Lerch, *Sociologie de l'homosexualité* (Paris: La Découverte, 2013).

15 Laud Humphrey, *Tearoom Trade* (Chicago: Aldine, 1971).

important for the maintenance of modernity and the guarantee of unrestricted circulation.

The AIDS epidemic prompted sexual health experts to call for the restriction of sexual partners and the closing-off of flow. In 'Prophylaxie et Virulence', the French philosopher Jean Baudrillard argues that the interruption of circulation goes against the promises of modernity: 'Yet this contradicts all of modernity's commandments: sex, money, information must freely circulate. Everything must be fluid, acceleration with no return.'[16] The fluidity of circulation may allow us to consider the ways in which gay men depend on spaces to maintain a free market of gay sexuality. Evelyn Hooker theorizes the gay bar as one of the 'most important of the public gathering places' that gay men appropriate for their use.[17] She argues further that gay men use the bar as a market in two senses of the term: an establishment in the business of providing drinks and services, and an establishment where sexual exchanges can be negotiated. She notes that heterosexual couples are not exempt from participating in a sexual market, but that certain features of gay spaces, such as the lack of women, the removal of societal norms and the veil of secrecy, allow for a certain sexuality to take place.[18]

We can further refine this understanding of the sexual market and its importance through the work laid out by Warner and Berlant in 'Sex in Public'. Berlant and Warner suggest that gay men are reliant upon spaces for the creation of their identity and, in ways that are less familiar to heterosexual people, the creation of these spaces is intimately connected to sex. They use Christopher Street in New York as an example: once a location gains a reputation as a cruising ground, commerce that caters to the 'sleazy' establishes itself and eventually attracts more 'respectable' business such as supermarkets and trendy stores.

These 'respectable' businesses owe their existence to the 'sleazy' subculture that preceded them. Berlant and Warner argue that:

16 Baudrillard, 'Prophylaxie et Virulence', *La Transparence du mal,* 72.

17 Evelyn Hooker, 'Male Homosexuals and their "Worlds."', in Judd Marmor, ed., *Sexual Inversion: The Multiple Roots of Homosexuality* (New York: Basic Books, 1965), 94.

18 Hooker, 'Male Homosexuals and their "Worlds"', 98.

> Respectable gays like to think that they owe nothing to the sexual subculture they think of as sleazy. But their success, their way of living, their political rights, and their very identities would never have been possible but for the existence of the public sexual culture they now despise. Extinguish it, and almost all *out* gay or queer culture will wither on the vine.[19]

Grindr and other similar apps may be seen as catering to 'sleazy' sexuality by facilitating promiscuous behaviour and anonymous sex. Yet by providing the space where a necessary component of gay sexuality can thrive, they will play a primordial role against the threat of extinguishing a public sexual culture. Proof of this can be seen in rereading Hooker's estimation of gay culture through the lens of the twenty-first century. She writes of the compartmentalization of one's private gay life and one's public straight life, that the consequence is the 'majority of homosexuals do not participate in the activities that go on in "public" institutions, facilities, or areas'.[20] Hooker wrote this in 1965. Since then, gay men in the West have become much more visible, with gay men rising to positions of power, being represented on television and in film, and being granted access to public institutions previously barred to them, such as institutionalized marriage throughout North America and the European Union.

If gay men are no longer necessarily relegated to the dark, underground corners of our cities as they once were in the 1960s, then they must find new ways of experiencing their sexuality. Enter the digital spaces: a modern iteration of the gay bar. Mirroring the 'sleazy' bars about which Berlant and Warner write, Grindr and company promote a certain type of sexuality that is frowned upon by the hegemonic norms of society (and, as we have seen, could not exist within the norms of a society looking for a 'cleaner' backdrop against which to find love).

The digital body and the digital spaces that they navigate are not without criticism, and here I address two concerns that arise with the creation of digital spaces: the first being that digital bodies contribute to a potentially problematic commodification of the body and that the digital spaces are responsible for the downfall of physical spaces. In response,

19 Berlant and Warner, 'Sex in Public', 561–2.
20 Hooker, 'Male Homosexuals and their "Worlds"', 94.

I propose that in our free market and especially a market where sexual exchanges occur, commodification *must* be permitted, and that apps allow this exchange to happen. Furthermore, I argue that the digital spaces do not threaten the health of physical ones, but rather provide an alternative, fill a gap, or democratize the process of accessing spaces.

As we see with Baudrillard's conceptualization of modernity, there must be a free flow of information. This echoes Julian L. Koplin's libertarian definition of the market economy whereby anything should be subject to the market economy so long as the participants are consenting adults.[21] The market created by digital dating resembles the market described by Hooker in her recollection of gay bars in the 1960s. Everyone has the right to participate in the free market of a gay bar if they have the means. Grindr et al. guarantee the democratic access to a digital version of this market: the apps cost nothing and are easy to access by any person with a smartphone and an email address.

The market is a stable feature of the gay world and the market attributes value to the 'goods' in it. Hooker notes that the value is not dependent on the 'genuine' self, but the 'cosmetic' self.[22] The bar culture placed emphasis on one's 'dress, manner, and body build'.[23] The market created by the digital body is not so different: gay men curate their online profiles, paying close attention to how they choose to re-present their bodies, or, in Paul's case in the novel, re-present a body he can pretend is his. A typical log-in screen on Grindr may show an equal number of stylized photos next to headless torsos that show off one's muscles:

> Sur Grindr, les hommes ressemblent aux personnages de *Qui est-ce?*. Leurs visages sont des caricatures grossières, quand visage il y a. Est-ce qu'il porte un Speedo bleu? Est-ce qu'il est un torse sans tête? Est-ce qu'il suce direct? Flap, flap, flap. Est-ce qu'il dit *no fem, no asiat, no gros, no vieux?* Est-ce que c'est Bisportversa?
>
> [On Grindr, men look like Guess Who characters. Their faces are coarse caricatures, if there's a face at all. Is he wearing a blue Speedo? Is he a headless torso? Does he

21 Julian J Koplin, 'Commodification and Human Interests', *Bioethical Inquiry* 15 (2018), 429.

22 Hooker, 'Male Homosexuals and their "Worlds"', 97.

23 Hooker, 'Male Homosexuals and their "Worlds"', 97.

suck right away? Flap, flap, flap. Does he say no femme, no Asians, no fatties, no old? Is it Vers Bi Sporty? (102)]

Such a market stresses how the digital body is curated and then commodified. Koplin warns us that this commodification is problematic. In part, this may be because it can prompt depression and feelings of malaise.[24] For Koplin, introducing bodies to a free market can cause us to start seeing bodies as mere commodities, and not so much as humans worthy of respect.[25] Demerits of such a system are beyond the scope of this article. It suffices to recognize that this system must be maintained because we live in a modern society wherein this market must be guaranteed. So long as gay men accept that a digital body is a prerequisite for participation in this digital world and that this digital world plays a large role in the creation of a gay identity in the twenty-first century, the market must exist.

The second point I address is that some are quick to criticize the digital spaces for killing gay bars, though the situation is far more complicated. As Western countries increasingly extend rights to the LGBTQ+ community, there is an erroneous notion that spaces specifically designed for queer people are no longer needed. It is perhaps less scandalous to see two men together in a sports bar and certainly gay men enjoy spending time with their heterosexual friends outside the confines of a traditional gay bar (whatever that may be). As I argued in 'Digital Geographies', however, digital spaces are not killing traditional physical spaces, but are filling a much-needed void as these other societal changes threaten the brick-and-mortar.[26] While I do enjoy and value physical encounters, it is not wholly problematic to consider a possible superiority of the digital space. Indeed, as argued in the Summer 2019 issue of *Têtu:*

24 In the Summer 2019 issue of *Têtu*, Anthony Fouet notes that 77 per cent of users report feelings of 'mal-être' and Grindr is among the worst apps for personal well-being according to Time Well Spent. Anthony Fouet, in Adrien Naselli, 'Faut-il brûler Grindr?', *Têtu* (Summer 2019), 76.

25 Koplin, 'Commodification and Human Interests', 439.

26 Brian Troth, 'Digital Geographies: Online Spaces and Gay Identity in 21st-Century France', *Contemporary French Civilization* 45/2 (2020), 229–45.

> Before, you had to go to a specific place, which is more costly in terms of time and money. You needed to have friends with whom to go, to be at ease with the codes of seduction, without accounting for the fact that some rejected the act of going to gay spaces. For most people, apps changed the way in which we approach physical encounters: they become a complement to the meeting. We keep going there (to physical spaces), but less so to stubbornly find a partner.[27]

The digital space is, in theory, far more democratic than the physical space: the most popular social networking apps are free to use and, since they are only as tethered to one location as one's cell phone is, they are accessible wherever one can access the internet.

Not everyone would agree that there is some superiority in digital bodies and social networking. In *Pride* (2017), Erik Rémès, who is perhaps best known in France for his condomless sex manifestos *Je bande donc je suis* [*I Get Hard Therefore I Am*] (1999) and *Serial Fucker* (2005), writes about gay life in France at the turn of the twenty-first century. On today's connected world, he writes that

> 'With smartphones and PNP (sex with drugs), orgies are becoming one of the only ways gay men socialize. In orgies, gay men spend more time on their phone than having sex. Barely have they found one partner, they are looking for the next. Our community is becoming autistic and psychotic with social media and drugs. It's very worrisome'.[28]

In a conversation between Paul and Arnaud in *Les Vacances du petit Renard*, Paul asks Arnaud if he is on Grindr. Arnaud laments that

> Tu vas rien trouver de beau. […] C'est quand même autre chose de rencontrer quelqu'un parce qu'il fait partie de ton monde d'une manière ou d'une autre. Tu vas me dire, être dans la même région c'est déjà un point commun. Mais je préfère rencontrer quelqu'un parce qu'on est allés au même concert, parce qu'on a des amis en commun ou un boulot dans le même domaine, plutôt que parce qu'il était à moins de huit cents mètres et qu'on était chauds au même moment. Parce que c'est comme ça que ça marche.

27 Fouet, in Adrien Naselli, 'Faut-il brûler Grindr ?', 77.

28 Erik Rémès, *Pride* (Paris: La Musadarine, 2017), 15.

> [You won't find anything beautiful. [...] It's a different thing to meet someone because he is part of your world in one way or another. You might tell me that being in the same place is already something you have in common. But I prefer to meet someone because we went to the same concert, because we have friends in common or a job in the same line of work, more so than because he was less than 800 meters away and we were horny at the same time. Because that's how it works. (105)]

Arnaud fetishizes finding love in an atmosphere that is not sexually charged, which would normally put him at odds with Erik Rémès, in whose literary world, sexual promiscuity and seropositivity are almost prerequisites for existence.[29] Yet, they may come to a point of agreement in their perception of the digital body: both seem to find it inferior to other ways in which gay men can create real connections, though neither one of them seems to have the same definition of what a real connection actually is.

Hooker's article reminds us that not only is the sexual market a stable feature of gay identity, but the system actively works against any other type of sexuality.[30] That is not to say that there is no other option. Reaching the end of his vacation in the countryside, Paul is sad that he will have to leave Hervé. In his mind, he compares himself to his sister and contemplates his decision to delete Grindr from his phone before he goes home:

> Elle a 8 ans, lui 14, et il se dit que, oui, certainement, elle perdra sa virginité avant lui. Quand elle aura 15 ans peut-être et lui, combien? 21 ans. Déjà. Demain. 21. Oui, peut-être qu'il en sera toujours là. À se branler en lisant *SAS* ou devant des vidéos de gens qui cachent des caméras dans leur chambre ou qui s'exhibent. Ce sont rarement des couples. Souvent des plans. D'ailleurs il va désinstaller Grindr. Ça n'a plus de sens. Il n'a pas envie de savoir, quand il sera à Paris, que son boulanger ou son voisin cherche à sucer now. Il n'a pas envie de ça, ou d'aller sur les parkings des aires d'autoroute. Il faudra attendre Hervé. Ou un autre Hervé. Il rêve d'un homme, il rêvera en attendant.

29 I paraphrase here Dr Daniel Maroun with whom I spoke on a panel on French HIV/AIDS film at the 2019 French and Francophone International Colloquium. Daniel Maroun, 'The French Response to HIV/AIDS: A Literary and Epidemiological Approach to Understanding the Past and Preventing Future Catastrophes', *20th and 21st Century French and Francophone Studies Colloquium* (Oklahoma City: 14–16 March 2019).

30 Hooker, 'Male Homosexuals and their "Worlds"', 101.

> [She's 8, he's 14 and he tells himself that she will certainly lose her virginity before him. When she's 15 perhaps and him, how old? 21. Already. Tomorrow. 21. Yes, maybe he'll still be there. Masturbating to pornographic books or videos of people who hide cameras or of exhibitionists. It's rarely couples. Often hookups. Anyway, he'll uninstall Grindr. It doesn't make sense anymore. He doesn't want to know when his baker or neighbour in Paris wants to suck now. He doesn't want that, or to go to the parking lots at highway rest areas. He'll have to wait for Hervé. Or another Hervé. He dreams of a man, he'll dream while he waits. (187–8)]

Paul, who lives in a very different world from his sister and others who fit heteronormative standards, represents the typical experience of gay men. While gay men today have more access to the same institutions within heteronormative society than did previous generations of gay men, they may still find it difficult to fully integrate. Gay men are not somehow predestined to a certain sexuality that requires promiscuity; yet there is a system in place that facilitates access to gay identity through this type of sexuality that is very much outside the norm.

Despite criticism that is brought against the digital body, Naselli notes in the Summer 2019 issue of *Têtu* that 'the mass return of gays to bars, saunas and other cruising spots is a sweet utopia'.[31] Though the use of the digital body is not without its problems, it is this shift in socialization that we must keep in mind as we conceptualize gay men and their bodies. By using a digital avatar to represent and re-present a physical body, the digital body questions heteronormative ideas about what a body is or is not. Bodies exist not only in physical form, but in a digital form that is ripe with potentiality. Though Paul and Hervé never engage in a physical relationship in Cahn's novel, their digital bodies interact. Not only does this interaction underlie the importance of bodily desire, it suggests that desire can be directed at a body that is not a body as has been traditionally conceived. In the twenty-first century and beyond, it is this digital form that will play the greatest role in our understanding of the gay male body and how it interacts with the world around it.

31 Naselli, 'Faut-il brûler Grindr ?', 79.

Bibliography

Baudrillard, Jean, *La Transparence du mal* (Paris: Galilée, 1990).

Berlant, Lauren, and Michael Warner, 'Sex in Public', *Critical Inquiry* 24/2 (1998), 547–66.

Cahn, Arthur, *Les Vacances du petit Renard* (Paris: Seuil, 2018).

Chauvin, Sébastien, and Arnaud Lerch, *Sociologie de l'homosexualité* (Paris: La Découverte, 2013).

Deleuze, Gilles, and Félix Guattari, *Capitalisme et schizophrénie 1: l'anti-œdipe* (Paris: Minuit, 1972).

Hooker, Evelyn, 'Male Homosexuals and Their "Worlds"', in Judd Marmor, ed., *Sexual Inversion: The Multiple Roots of Homosexuality* (New York: Basic Books, 1965), 83–107.

Humphreys, Laud, *Tearoom Trade* (Chicago: Aldine, 1971).

Koplin, Julian J., 'Commodification and Human Interests', *Bioethical Inquiry* 15 (2018), 429–40.

Maroun, Daniel, 'The French Response to HIV/AIDS: A Literary and Epidemiological Approach to Understanding the Past and Preventing Future Catastrophes', *20th and 21st Century French and Francophone Studies Colloquium* (Oklahoma City: 14–16 March 2019).

McCaffrey, Enda, 'From Homographies of Invisibility to Hypervisibility: Queering and De-Queering City Centre Space', in Kathleen O'Mara and Liz Morrish, eds, *Queering Paradigms III* (Oxford: Peter Lang, 2013), 33–61.

Naselli, Adrien, 'Faut-il brûler Grindr?', *Têtu* (Summer 2019), 74–9.

Rémès, Erik, *Pride* (Paris: La Musadarine, 2017).

Troth, Brian, 'Digital Geographies: Online Spaces and Gay Identity in 21st-Century France', *Contemporary French Civilization* 45/2 (2020), 229–45.

Witt, Emily, *Future Sex* (New York: Farrar, Straus and Giroux, 2016).

ADINA STROIA

2 Lesbian Selves: The Figure of the (Body) Double in Marie Nimier's Works

Cherchez la femme: The Lesbian Novel in French Literature

When one goes on a quest for the female-authored lesbian novel in French literature, it quickly becomes apparent that not only will the journey be long and solitary, but that the destination itself is to become more and more elusive. While the *extrême contemporarain* ('the contemporary extreme') has given women writers the chance to expose and explore transgressions done by and unto women in the form of their own sexual excesses, trauma, abortion, incest, rape and suicide, the very same authors remain corseted by the heteronormative matrix in the realm of sexual and romantic relationships. Such restrictive behaviour aligns with Judith Butler's understanding of the heterosexual logic 'that requires that identification and desire be mutually exclusive'.[1] This, she explains, 'is one of the most reductive of heterosexism's psychological instruments: if one identifies as a given gender, one must desire a different gender'.[2]

What follows on from this ubiquitousness of the heterosexual romance is a marked paucity of lesbian literature within the contemporary French canon. The *extrême contemporain* remains in the stranglehold of heteronormativity, despite its heterogeneous romantic and sexual configurations. Even Virginie Despentes, an author who has engaged with a range of sexually transgressive subjects and self-identifies as a lesbian following her relationship with high-profile trans author Paul B. Preciado (Beatrice at the time), has made few inroads into presenting a fully developed lesbian

1 Judith Butler, *Bodies That Matter: On the Discursive Limits of "Sex"* (New York and London: Routledge, 1993), 239.

2 Butler, *Bodies That Matter: On the Discursive Limits of "Sex"*, 239.

narrative. The author has instead contented herself with presenting her readers with 'lesbian awakenings' in her novels *Apocalypse bébé* [*Apocalypse Baby*] (2010) and the trilogy *Vernon Subutex* [*Vernon Subutex*] (2015–17). Despentes' lesbian representative is the recurring character la Hyène, whose strong sexual instincts are clearly signalled through the predatory overtones of her name. Under the 'guidance' of la Hyène, several heterosexually identified women discover the pleasures of Sapphic sex.

A further example would be author Anne F. Garréta, academic and self-identified lesbian, who is nonetheless far from being considered a 'lesbian writer'. This is perhaps largely due to her affiliation with the OuLiPo,[3] whereby the experimental textual constraints gain primacy over the narrative. Garréta's 1986 novel *Sphinx* [*Sphinx*] used Oulipian constraints to do away with gender altogether, a challenging and impressive achievement given the importance of gender in the linguistic construction of the French language. In her ungendered narrative, Garréta takes herself to task and delivers a story of sexual and romantic entanglements wherein the reader is unable to determine the gender of the protagonists. In *Pas un jour* [*Not One Day*] (2002), Garréta equally employs Oulipian constraints to highly visible effects. Using as a guiding force 'nul autre principe qu'écrire de mémoire' [no other principle than writing from memory],[4] the author provides us with a detailed catalogue of her lesbian sexual adventures, alphabetically ordered. Bearing the capitalized dedication 'À NULLE' [TO NO ONE],

3 Founded in 1960 by writer Raymond Queneau and mathematician François Le Lionnais, the Ouvroir de Littérature Potentielle (Workshop for Potential Literature) – better known by its acronym, OuLiPo – has at its core two tasks:

1. 'To invent structures, forms or new constraints, which would be conducive to the production of original works.

2. To work on past literary works in order to find the traces, – be they at times obvious and at other times more difficult to define/discover – of the use of structures, forms, or constraints.'

See <https://www.oulipo.net/fr/historique-de-loulipo>, accessed 30 June 2020, my translation. Among its notable members, the group counts novelists George Perec and Italo Calvino, poet/mathematician Jacques Roubaud and Anne F. Garréta.

4 Anne F. Garréta, *Pas un jour* (Paris: Grasset, 2002), 13. All translations are my own unless otherwise noted.

Garréta effectively voids any long-lasting lesbian coupling. These are but a few examples which serve to show that even among prolific writers who are anything but shy on the topic of sex, Sapphic eroticism has less currency that one would expect.

Equally illustrative of the scarcity of literary lesbian-centred texts is the academic interest they have generated. To date, Jennifer Waelti-Walters' *Damned Women: Lesbians in French Novels, 1796–1996* (2000) and Lucille Cairns' *Lesbian Desire in Post-1968 French Literature* (2002) remain the most representative academic studies on the subject. Waelti-Walters' study comes to the clear conclusion that after two hundred years of lesbians in French novels, 'the path that they have traced has remained almost invisible'.[5] Cairns' comprehensive study on lesbian representation within the French context recovers the figure of the lesbian from the clutches of the male imagination, but Sapphic representation by female authors remains nonetheless overwhelmingly underground. The mostly little-known texts presented by Cairns offer us an overview of lesbian-themed texts that is more often of sociological interest rather than of literary value, therefore indicating that representative visibility of the lesbian in literature remains an issue. Following on from Cairns' *Lesbian Desire*, this chapter operates within the discursive parameters set out in her study, for the clearly and comprehensively articulated definitional lines of the lesbian subject bear no further bending:

> The *sine qua non* of lesbianism is, I aver, erotic attraction between women. On the whole, then, my study deploys the word 'lesbian' to mean a woman/female human being who may not necessarily have had genital contact with, but whose erotic preference is for, other women/female human beings – at least in the (diegetic or actual) present, for I do not conceptualize sexual preference as a necessarily immutable, and certainly not as a congenital, property. I am thus closer to the constructionist than the essentialist position in the debate that has long raged in discourse on (particularly) homosexuality. Concomitantly, by 'lesbian-themed text', I designate a text inscribing sexual (and perhaps also, but not necessarily, affective) attraction between women/female human beings.[6]

5 Jennifer Waelti-Walters, *Damned Women: Lesbians in French Novels, 1796–1996* (Montreal: McGill-Queen's Press, 2000), 211.

6 Lucille Cairns, *Lesbian Desire in Post-1968 Literature* (Lewiston: Edwin Mellen Press, 2002), 11.

This chapter is therefore concerned with lesbian representations as penned by women writers. I started by asking myself what the positionality of the Sapphic subject is in French literature, for one must surely be able to find a more than appropriate abode in the much-lauded land of the erotic. My answer to this question forms the kernel of this chapter's ethos: a turn towards the self. Following on from Teresa de Lauretis' infamous dictum, 'it takes two women, not one, to become a lesbian',[7] this chapter interrogates the female resistance to literary representations of the lesbian Other through a doubling of the self.

My Lover, Myself

Doubles in literature have overwhelmingly been the province of the male writer and of his male protagonist. With fantastic overtones, the double's heyday dates back to the nineteenth century and its German Romantic period. The doppelgänger found its home in the works of E. T. A. Hoffman, Henrich Heine or Heinrich von Kleist, to name but the most representative writers. However, Dostoyevsky's aptly named novella, *The Double* (1846), in which a clerk vies for the attentions of a young woman only to be usurped by his double and eventually sent to a mental asylum, remains perhaps the best-known example of the ontologically threatening doppelgänger. As a figure indicative of deeper psychological trouble, the double is reprised in the canon of twentieth century literature by Vladimir Nabokov in his Russian-language 1936 novel *Despair*.[8] Albeit difficult to summarize owing to its numerous twists and turns, *Despair* is at its core the story of Hermann Karlovich, who uses his (perceived) double to commit the perfect murder – his own.

7 Teresa de Lauretis, *The Practice of Love: Lesbian Sexuality and Perverse Desire* (Bloomington and Indianapolis: Indiana University Press, 1994), 28.

8 *Despair* was revised and translated into English by Nabokov in a definitive second edition in 1965.

In this chapter, I contend that the trope of the double undergoes a queering through a reconfiguration of the relationship between the 'original' subject and its doppelgänger in female-centred narratives authored by women writers. I thus propose that the triangulation that exists within male narratives of the double insofar as two men are vying for the attention of a female love interest mutates into a dyadic scheme in female-double narratives. The male Other is cast aside in favour of magnetic Sapphic attraction. As Barbara Creed has suggested, this is where the lesbian is at its most threatening, as it 'suggests a perfectly sealed world of female desire from which man is excluded'.[9] Despite its clear queer resonances, the double in literature remains an unexplored category by writers and academics alike. This is partly due to the fact that visual media inarguably offer a more potent and immediate representation of the double. Otto Rank's seminal study, *The Double: A Psychonalytic Study* (1925), was inspired by *The Student of Prague*, an Expressionist film from 1913 directed by Stellen Rye and which recounts a tale of torment between a young man and his doppelgänger. This tendency extends to female doubles. As Lucy Fischer remarks, 'within the canon of texts on the female doppelgänger, however, perhaps the most interesting of all occurs not in literature but in the cinema'.[10] The female double often appears as a trope in visual representation, aided in no small part by the appeal that 'girl-on-girl' action – or simply its intimations – holds for the male gaze and which cannot and should not be underestimated. Even the most cursory of glances at a website specializing in pornography will quickly reveal lookalike women engaging in sexual activity, not to mention the domain's strange fascination with twins. But one must not even go scouring the oftentimes gritty corners of the Internet in order to reveal the pervasive nature of identical multiplication and of the sexual power it holds. Through its wide appeal and ubiquitousness in public space, fashion photography furnishes us with a poignant example, as Creed remarks:

9 Barbara Creed, 'Lesbian Bodies: Tribades, Tomboys and Tarts' in Elisabeth Grosz and Elspeth Probyn, eds, *Sexy Bodies: The Strange Carnalities of Feminism* (London and New York: Routledge, 1995), 86–103, 100.

10 Lucy Fischer, 'Two-Faced Women: The "Double" in Women's Melodrama of the 1940s', *Cinema Journal* 23/1 (1983), 24–43, 25.

> Fashion photography which displays the look-alike bodies of female models, often in an embrace, draws on the notion of the narcissistic female double to sell clothes and titillate the spectator with suggestions of auto-erotic, anorexic lesbian desire. Much pornography, intended for heterosexual male consumption, displays an obligatory scenario of nubile female bodies engaged in sexual acts. In pornography the body of the lesbian is constructed as insatiable – a monstrous quicksand of desire.[11]

Since pornography plays a crucial role in representations of the female double, it seems more than apt that the present chapter will first focus on Marie Nimier's *La Nouvelle pornographie* [*The New Pornography*] (2000).[12] Published on the cusp of a new millennium, *La Nouvelle pornographie* gently and playfully, albeit intentionally, mocks the wave of hardcore sex-oriented writing with which women made their mark in the 1990s, most notably Despentes' rape-revenge narrative, *Baise-moi* [*Rape Me*] (1994), or Christine Angot's *Inceste* [*Incest*] (1999), which references the author's supposed incestuous relationship with her estranged father. Shirley Jordan advises that 'French women writers' intensive focus on sex is one of the most striking features of the literary world in the 1990s and beyond'.[13] The motivations of a lay reader picking up a book entitled *La Nouvelle pornographie* might not be hard to guess, but the novel eskews such categorizations. Playing with readers' expectations and skilfully employing pornographic tropes, *La Nouvelle pornographie* stages the relationship between the character-narrator Marie Nimier, her editor Gabriel Tournon and her housemate Aline. The author is commissioned to write a volume of pornographic short stories (*nouvelles pornographiques*) which bring a feminist twist to the genre. Her attraction to her housemate Aline is interwoven throughout the text as Marie is writing her *nouvelles*. When Marie finds out that Aline is in turn having an affair with her editor, she has a fainting spell. Upon regaining consciousness, she declares that she is in fact … Aline. In the second text I will be analysing, *Photo-photo* [*Photo-Photo*] (2010),[14] the intervening 'editorial' voice is that of Karl Lagerfeld who informs Marie

11 Creed, 'Lesbian Bodies: Tribades, Tomboys and Tarts', 86.

12 Marie Nimier, *La Nouvelle pornographie* (Paris: Gallimard, 2002).

13 Shirley Jordan, *Contemporary French Women's Writing: Visions, Women's Voices, Women's Lives* (Oxford: Peter Lang, 2004), 54.

14 Marie Nimier, *Photo-photo* (Paris: Gallimard, 2010).

Nimier that she has a dead ringer by the name of Frederika who lives in Baden-Baden, Germany. Nimier's meeting with Frederika culminates in a sexual encounter, thus making explicit what was only alluded to in *La Nouvelle pornographie*.

This chapter proposes that the elusive location of the queer subject expressed through the figure of the double provides a pertinent vantage point from which to investigate contemporary notions of female subjectivity and bodily identity. Through the works of Nimier which intimate as well as overtly narrativize same-sex relationships, I argue that the figure of the double appears as a site for the displacement of the sexual charge, a terrain where ambiguities and issues of identity are played out and interrogated. The double in Nimier appears as a manifestation of the postmodern fluid self and is marked by a distinct queer sensibility which is diffusely present. The existence of porous borders between the (body) doubles exposes the mechanisms of repressed desire through the impossibility of the female-centred encounter, which in its extreme manifestation stages the metamorphosis into the Other, thus engendering the dissolution of ontological barriers.

Marie Nimier: New Pornographies

In an oft-quoted interview with Jeanne Sarah de Larquier dating from 2004, Marie Nimier confesses to a fascination with liminality, foundational to her own being. This liminality infuses her writing:

> I am born out of [this] marginality, which is to say that I have never felt at ease in the centre. [...]. In the margins, one is able to breathe. There is room. And from that vantage point, one undoubtedly has a sharper perception of the centre.[15]

On the French literary scene, Nimier occupies a peculiar position. Rather than be caught up in the literary currents, she has imposed herself as one

15 Jeanne Sarah de Larquier, 'Entretien avec Marie Nimier', *The French Review* 78 (2004), 340–53, 347.

of the most eclectic writers in France, not only through the hybrid character of her work, but through a constant repositioning of her textual universe which destabilizes and challenges fixed perceptions. Her works are imbued with a ludic sense. With a manifest penchant towards linguistic acrobatics, the *double entendres* and homonyms are at home in her writing. Fixity is exchanged with fluidity and the cohabitation of seemingly contradictory terms carves out a new space which seeks to escape a much-abhorred normative core. Words, sentences, narratives and identities are part of a larger strategy which seeks to destabilize and queer a fixed centre. The double as a figure moving away from the magnetic force of a centre has been present in her work from the first novel *Sirène* [*Siren*] (1985), which introduced us to the hybrid figure of the mermaid, central to Nimier's writing. With the figure of the mermaid, the splitting and doubling is located within the self, hinting at an internal schism, an intrinsic identity tension. However, while building on the doubling present in her work, I will direct my attention towards an externalized, yet resonant, decentring mechanism: same-sex desire. The presence of Sapphic attraction is an aspect which has received little attention in the field of academic inquiry surrounding Nimier's writings, especially given the recurrent insertion and precision of such episodes.

A genealogy of same-sex desire which I trace back to *Domino* [*Domino*] (1998) has been taking shape within Nimier's *œuvre*.[16] Part detective story, love story and a writer's story, the novel abounds in tales of the scandalous with overt references to incest and prostitution. Among this amalgam of 'perversions', one deviance almost escapes unobserved: the slight shift into the territory of same-sex desire. The eponymous character, playfully named Domino (short for Dominique), encounters her lover's friend in whose house they (Domino and her lover) shared their sexual tryst:

> Elle se présenta, Kristen Shift, et s'avança pour me serrer la main. J'aimais bien sa voix, son accent, la façon dont elle relevait ses cheveux [...]. Le tissu léger glissait, découvrant ses jambes. [...] Elle me proposa de la suivre dans la cuisine. Tout était beau en elle, voluptueux. [...] Je frissonnais. J'avais envie que cette histoire de cabas

16 Marie Nimier, *Domino* (Paris: Gallimard, 1998).

> ne finisse jamais, j'avais envie de me greffer dans la vie de Kristen, oui, je voulais être son greffon.
>
> [She introduced herself as Kristen Shift and took a step towards me to shake my hand. I took a liking to her voice, her accent, her way of putting up her hair. […] The light fabric was sliding off, revealing her legs. […] She suggested I follow her to the kitchen. Everything about her was beautiful, voluptuous. […] I shuddered. I never wanted this whole basket kerfuffle to end. I wanted to graft myself onto Kristen's life. Yes, I wanted to be her graft. (45)]

Enter Kristen Shift, who with her English-sounding name is introduced as the Other who fleetingly attracts the protagonist's sexual attention. Her surname indicates the shifting nature of sexual attraction, the gliding present in articulations of desire *chez* Nimier, thus sketching the double which will take shape in various forms in *La Nouvelle pornographie* and *Photo-photo*.

As her writing has become more assured, Nimier has dared to project the self into exteriority through characters that mirror a series of anxieties, most poignantly sexual, creating a space where the conundrums which plague the characters can be exposed and worked through. In *La Nouvelle pornographie*, Nimier proposes a spellbinding chain of associations between Marie Nimier as author and as character. Through complex layering these associations seek to both bring closer and distance the character from the real-life referent. The self is further extended into to figure of Aline onto whom Nimier transfers the 'burden' of 'la nouvelle pornographie'. Whilst the Nimier character is pondering the significance of the term and trying to produce it according to the guidelines provided by her editor, it is Aline who seems to embody it. In *Photo-photo*, however, the double is not merely alluded to, but is firmly set up through the character of Frederika, her doppelgänger.

The female double is born out of a particular set of cultural and textual circumstances. Nathalie Morello and Catherine Rodgers note that 'it has become clear that psychoanalysis, postmodernism and the different forms of deconstructionism have marked this generation: many of its subjects are doubled, shattered or ill-defined'.[17] The figure of the double seems to be particularly germane to discussions of *autofictional* selves. I propose that

17 Nathalie Morello and Catherine Rodgers, *Nouvelles écrivaines: nouvelles voix?* (Amsterdam: Rodopi, 2004), 28.

by extending the self into the figure of the double, Nimier captures and distils Isabelle Grell's view of *autofiction* who argues that 'the author is involved in a process of unveiling a clearly contoured world, wherein truth is anchored in an extension of the self unto the Other and is an expression of *being-in-the-world* in its lived fragmentation'.[18]

Yet, of course, our author further complicates such developments and additionally infuses *La Nouvelle pornographie* with a distinct postfeminist character. Through the two female figures, the eponymous Marie Nimier (to whom I will refer as Marie in order to avoid confusion) and the character of Aline, Nimier places at the centre a post-feminist subject and its dual facets. Thus, two stances of post-feminist legacy oppose each other through the female figures: Aline, a liberated young woman who fully embraces her sexuality; and Marie, torn and attempting to reconcile her emotional side with her sexuality in the wake of a harsh feminism that relinquished traditional feminine attributes as signs of weakness. Nimier stages the fragility and the restlessness of the contemporary female subject, the product of a feminism which has not quite succeeded nor quite failed. As Victoria Best and Martin Crowley note, 'far from attempting a resolution of this complexity, Nimier's text portrays the complexity itself as an accurate account of postmodern sexuality for women'.[19] Marie is stuck in the rift between the entrapment of traditional female gender roles and the liberated, sexually insouciant woman. Nimier astutely stages the state of confusion of the contemporary woman, who would like to embrace sexuality, but who is not yet ready to give up on her romantic projects either: 'il fallait toujours que je m'invente une histoire d'amour. Même dans les situations les plus scabreuses, je trouvais un alibi romantique' [I always needed to invent a love story. Even in the grittiest of situations, I found myself a romantic alibi. (43)]

The differences between Marie and Aline are referred to on the same page, as she follows on to describe her friend: 'elle avait besoin d'amour gratuit, sans contribution sentimentale' [she needed a no-frills type of love,

18 Isabelle Grell, *L'Autofiction* (Paris: Armand Colin, 2014), 106.

19 Victoria Best and Martin Crowley, *The New Pornographies: Explicit Sex in Recent French Fiction and Film* (Manchester: Manchester University Press, 2007), 36.

no feelings involved (43)]. Comparatively, Marie has difficulties moulding 'new pornographies' and abandoning her own dreams and desires: 'Aline me connaissait bien. Elle savait que mon fantasme le plus tenace n'était pas de violer un sapeur-pompier, avec ou sans casque, mais, comme toutes les fillettes nourries aux contes de fées, de me marier, d'être heureuse, et, par conséquent, d'avoir beaucoup d'enfants' [Aline knew me well. She was aware that my deepest-seated fantasy wasn't to rape a fireman (with or without his helmet). Like all the other girls nourished by fairytales, I wanted to get married, be happy, and in turn have a lot of children (45)]. It is love which Marie reads as transgressive: 'aimer, voilà l'audace' [to love, therein lies the dare! (165)]. Her roommate however is an explorer of the porousness of borders, a shifter in her own right: 'Aline avait appris à être souple, elle passait d'un univers à l'autre sans problème apparent [...] elle était incapable de choisir, elle ne pouvait que glisser' [Aline had learned how to be flexible. She would pass from one world to the other without apparent difficulty. [...] She was incapable of choosing, she could only slink out (36)]. This reflects Cathy Wardle's view that: 'Nimier's writing posits an otherness which is radically unsettling, hard to pin down, impossible to define, as rather than merely reversing the hierarchy of binary oppositions, she shifts the foundations upon which binary difference stands, celebrating the pleasures of the ambiguous and the indecidable.'[20] To this effect, her editor Gabriel Tournon remarks upon Marie's predilection for displacing established categories: 'vous êtes diabolique, avait-il dit avec un large sourire, vous ne laissez jamais les choses exactement où elles sont, il faut toujours que vous affûtiez un détail qui déplace les certitudes' [you are diabolical, he said with a broad smile. You never let things stay put. You always have to add a detail that pushes certainty away. (98)]

Our protagonist Marie engages in acts of precarious balance on the dividing line between fully affirmed heterosexuality and homosexuality, inscribing a distinct queer dimension to her sexual and emotional cartography. The first chapter plunges the reader into the narrator's imagination and creative ambitions, Marie's first attempt at a *nouvelle pornographique*.

20 Cathy Wardle, 'Ce qui n'est pas moi: Writing the Self, Desiring the Other in *La Nouvelle pornographie*', *Cincinatti Romance Review*, 23 (2004), 273–84, 275.

We are privy to a domestic sexual fantasy involving a domestic appliance, namely an ironing table. The passage which ends this first chapter, however, betrays the narrator's attraction to her roommate, Aline:

> Ses gestes étaient lents, chargés de rêves. Une certaine mollesse dans la lèvre inférieure, une moue, une nonchalance laissaient à penser qu'elle avait envie de faire l'amour. Elle dormait avec un vieux T-shirt de mon frère. Je me sentais vide et sale. Lorsqu'elle se dressa sur la pointe des pieds pour prendre les tasses, je vis sa touffe noire se dessiner en transparence. Elle tenait le bas du T-shirt coincé entre les jambes, et c'était douloureux, ce tissu prêt à lâcher – j'avais tellement besoin de tendresse.
>
> [Her gestures were slow, laden with dreams. A certain looseness in her lower lip, a *moue*, a nonchalance, which put together made one think that she was in the mood to make love. She slept in one of my brother's old T-shirts. I felt empty and dirty. As she reached for the cups on the tips of her toes, I saw the dark tuft of her pubic hair appear through the transparent fabric. She was holding down the hem of her T-shirt between her thighs, and it was painful to watch this piece of fabric about to give way and rip – I badly needed tenderness. (24)]

Hiding under the veil of fictionality – as part of an imagined ménage à trois scenario which is supposedly yet another short story – Marie gives textual flesh to her desire for Aline:

> Aline plongea sa main entre mes cuisses, par-derrière, et, avec l'habileté d'un prestidigitateur, y fit disparaitre ses doigts. Son index me caressait, le gras de son index qui jouait avec mon clitoris. [...] Je soupirai. La peau d'Aline était douce et chaude, j'aimais son odeur moelleuse, sa précision.
>
> [From behind, Aline dove her hand between my thighs and, with the agility of a magician, made her fingers disappear therein. Her index finger was caressing me, its very tip was playing with my clitoris. [...] I let out a gasp. Alice's skin was soft and warm. I loved her sweet scent, her precision. (86)]

Such short and explicit outpourings of same-sex desire punctuate the text. Earlier on in the first chapter, as she is caught up in the creative process, navigating the corridors of memory and fiction, thoughts of other women intrude upon the various sexual scenarios she is fictitiously attempting to devise. Thinking back to her school days as a possible source of inspiration, she remembers her classmate Solange:

> Parfois Solange – disons qu'elle s'appelait Solange – portait son index à sa bouche. Elle constituait un réservoir de salive tout près de sa lèvre inférieure, ainsi n'était-elle pas obligée d'enfoncer le doigt. J'avais honte de la regarder, d'ailleurs je ne la regardais pas: je la voyais. Je m'asseyais en biais, appuyé contre le mur, dédoublant, oui, je dédoublais.
>
> [Sometimes Solange, (let's just say her name was Solange), would put her index finger to her mouth. She would make a little pool of saliva on the very inside of her lower lip so that she would not have to push her finger in. I felt shame watching her, no, I was not watching her: I saw her. I would sit across from her at an angle, against the wall, splitting my self in two, yes, I would split my self in two. (14)]

Although the hesitations of her desire are linguistically and semantically marked through repetition, punctuation and negation, the scopic drive wins out: Marie cannot look away. The narrator further confers powerful attributes to such desire, as she seems to be suggesting that not only is the double the Other on whom one projects sexual feelings, but that same sex desire can in turn cause doubling. Best and Crowley note the processual flux at work: 'The erotic subjectivity displayed by the narrator is [...] unstable, uncertain and represented as engaged in a perpetual process of becoming.'[21]

The *dénouement* of the novel does not offer a well-defined resolution. Instead it ties further knots, fusing together the strands of subjectivity. Just as there were different points of entry into the text – as confusing as they were through the multiplication of layers of fictionality – and suggested ways of reading, the final scene of the novel too offers different points of exit, either heteronormative or with queer overtures. In a tale of reversal which contradicts classical narratives of traditional male doublings, it is not the double which annihilates the self, but the subject itself which assimilates the double. An onomastic exchange takes place following Marie's sudden malaise. This final scene is a manifestation of 'ce trouble du double qui vous surprend, du double qui vous pénètre sans demander l'autorisation' [this ambiguity of the double that takes you by surprise, of the double who

21 Best and Crowley, *The New Pornographies: Explicit Sex in Recent French Fiction and Film*, 36.

penetrates you without asking for permission (91)]. When prompted for her name by the fireman, Marie declares that she is called Aline:

> Il me demanda mon nom et je compris que je m'étais trompée de personnage, dès le début de l'histoire, une erreur d'aiguillage, facile à corriger avec les moyens modernes, une erreur de distribution. [...] On me demandait encore comment je m'appelais en surveillant ma tension. Des mots sortirent de ma bouche, je les répétais pour m'en convaincre. Oui, Aline, j'ai bien entendu, nota le pompier assis sur le côté, mais votre nom de famille. Le brouillard se dissipa. La première fois que j'ai vu un sexe de femme, je l'ai trouvé très sombre.
>
> [He asked me for my name and I understood that I had mistaken the characters from the very beginning of the story, a calibration error, easy to correct with modern means, a simple distribution error [...]. I was yet again prompted for my name while having my blood pressure taken. Words left my mouth, words that I had to repeat in order to convince myself. Aline, yes, that I already got, wrote down the fireman lying on his side, but what is your family name? The fog dissipated. The first time I ever saw a woman's vagina, I found it very dark. (181)]

One could read this as a metamorphosis which would then transform Marie into the source of interest of Gabriel's romantic and sexual attention, but I propose that the nuances of the passage allow for a non-normative, queer(ing) reading. Through a coupling which is signalled onomastically, Marie finally effaces the border between the two characters – of subjectivity and of repressed desire. The double does not outperform. Instead, the double allows the subject to perform itself. Wardle suggests that 'in her final words then, it could be argued that Marie is finally facing up to her transgressive desire, recognizing the attraction of an otherness which does not rely upon gender as the primary marker of difference'.[22] The reference to the 'sexe de femme' further strengthens such a reading and its phrasing, its undecidability gestures towards futurity: whether or not Marie has changed her opinion produces an opening in meaning which is coherent with queer practices.

22 Wardle, 'Ce qui n'est pas moi: Writing the Self, Desiring the Other in *La Nouvelle pornographie*', 282.

Photo-photo: Finding Your/Self

However optimistically I would like to read such signs, I must now turn my attention to *Photo-photo*, for although a tense sexual thread runs through *La Nouvelle pornographie*, it is in this later novel that Nimier gives free rein to the sexual energy contained in the figure of the double, as it culminates in a sexual encounter between the narrator and her doppelgänger. Same-sex interest thus reaches full expression in *Photo-photo* in absence of the male romantic interest but guided by the spectral figure of Karl Lagerfeld, who alerts her to the existence of her double:

> Vous savez que vous avez un sosie? me demanda-t-il d'un air mystérieux. Une femme extraordinaire, une amie. Elle s'appelle Frederika, c'est beau Frederika, ça vous irait comme un gant. Elle travaille aux Thermes de Caracalla, à Baden-Baden.
>
> [Do you know that you have a doppelgänger?, he asked me rather mysteriously. She is an extraordinary woman, a friend of mine. Her name is Frederika. Frederika is a beautiful name, it would fit you like a glove. She works at the thermal baths of Caracalla, in Baden-Baden. (34)]

Thereafter, in *Photo-photo*, the double is constructed through a textual game of 'connect the dots' and it is *through* and *in* the text that the double surfaces. Their actual encounter only happens towards the end and is very briefly described (see 203–4). In contrast with *La Nouvelle pornographie*, the double is not simply alluded to but is set up as doppelgänger in the figure of Frederika. The doubling is intricately embroidered at a linguistic and narrative level. Through various elements which are paired or mirrored, the portrait of the double emerges:

> Quand tu mets en scène tous ces éléments qui marchent par deux (paire de chaussures, paire de lunettes, Otto et Toto, les jumelles, jusqu'au *n* manquant de la mention *Personel*, sur l'enveloppe d'Huguette Malo), j'ai l'impression de voir se dessiner le portrait de cette femme, cette Allemande qui anime un atelier de dessin pour les enfants, celle qui te ressemble tant.
>
> [When you set up all these elements that only work in pairs (pair of shoes, pair of glasses, Otto and Toto, the twins, all the way to the missing *s* of 'addressee only' on Huguette Malo's envelope), I am under the impression that a portrait of this woman

is being sketched out, this German woman who leads a drawing workshop for children, the one who resembles you so closely. (124)]

Despite the seemingly neat doubling which permeates the text, a sense of uncanniness remains pervasive: 'il y avait trop de differénces, ou trop de similitudes, pour ne pas se sentir mal à l'aise' [there were too many differences, or too many similarities, for one not to feel ill at ease (72)]. Thus, a particular fluidity which plays with notions of similarity and difference persists in Nimier's writing, particularly in the realms of gender and desire. I would like now to focus on an episode which is key to understanding the author's position on gender normativity. When the narrator visits Frederika in Baden-Baden, she brings with her a very special memento, a drawing she had made when she was 8 years old and which gave birth to controversy among her school-age peers. Asked to draw a *bonhomme* by the schoolteacher, the young narrator produces a drawing of a little girl:

> Quand elle affichera les autres propositions, je comprendrai ce qu'elle a voulu dire. Tous les personnages ont une pipe ou un chapeau, une moustache, un marteau, une cravate pour évoquer cette chose un peu mystérieuse qui pend entre leurs jambes et que l'on ne voit pas [...] Qu'est-ce qu'il a de drôle, mon dessin? Qu'est-ce qu'il a de risible? Car tous rient maintenant qu'il est exposé dans la classe, ils rient parce que c'est une fille, et qu'une fille parmi tous ces messieurs, c'est rigolo, voilà.
>
> [When she put up the other drawings, I understood what she had meant. All the drawn people have either a pipe or a hat, a moustache, a hammer, or a tie, a something that makes one think of that rather mysterious thing that hangs between their legs and that we never see. [...] What's so funny about my own drawing? What's so laughable about it? They are all laughing now that it has been pinned up for all the class to see. They are laughing because it's a girl, and a girl, among all of these men, it's funny, there you go. (143)]

Issues of female representation and projections of self are astutely staged in this scene, which, through the figure of the 'bonhomme', challenges the idea of man as standard referentor neutral point of reference. Self-representation seems to take on obscene qualities, though one cannot but wonder what reaction would an anatomically correct drawing of a bonhomme have elicited? Toril Moi remarks that: 'The pleasure of self-representation, of her desire for the same, is denied woman: she is cut off from any kind of pleasure that might be specific to her.'[23] The situation is nonetheless paradoxical for the narrator because, by offering a representation of her own female self, she too is Othered. She is thus berated for daring to perform her own gender in a specular relationship since this performance opposes the patriarchal norm. Through a transgression of linguistic and figurative categories 'the invisible normativity of heterosexual culture' is exposed;[24] the discursive gestures of power are revealed through acts of resistance:

> J'explique qu'il y a des bonshommes masculins et des bonshommes féminins, cela va de soi, non ? Pour la fillette de huit ans que je suis, admettons que j'ai huit ans, ça va de soi, mais le problème est ailleurs. [...]. Ce qui fait de la peine, c'est le décalage. L'incompréhension. L'aveuglement.
>
> [I explain that there are male human figures and female human figures, and that that goes without saying, right ? For the eight-year old that I am at that moment, let's just keep in mind that I am eight-years old, that goes without saying, but that is not where the problem lies. [...]. What pains me is the knowledge gap. The incomprehension. The blindness. (144)]

As a child, Ana de Medeiros notes, the narrator 'does not spontaneously "think" through gender'.[25] This initial intuition, however, remains valid throughout Nimier's works as her desire is marked by an attraction that is neither driven by gender nor remains unencumbered by it. For the narrator, the magnetic undertones exerted by women precede the age of adult sexuality, as revealed by the memory of her reaction to the drawing of a little girl: 'je suis fière de moi, de mon travail. Décidément, cette petite fille me plaît. Ou plus exactement, elle m'attire' [I am proud of myself, of my work. I like this girl. Definitely. Or, to be more precise, I am attracted

23 Toril Moi, *Sexual/Textual Politics*: *Feminist Literary Theory* (London: Routledge, 2002), 133.

24 Lauren Berlant and Michael Warner, 'What Does Queer Theory Teach us about *X*', *PMLA* 110/3 (1995), 343–9, 347.

25 Ana de Medeiros, 'Now I See Me, Now You Don't' Working with/Against Paternal Influence in Marie Nimier's *Photo-Photo*', in Thomas Baldwin, James Fowler and Ana de Medeiros, eds, *Questions of Influence in Modern French Literature* (London and New York: Palgrave Macmillan, 2013), 194–207, 202.

to her (130)]. If we are to view the drawing as a figurative double, the seed for same-sex desire is planted through the desire for self-representation.

Nimier plays with the dividing line, persistently effacing borders within and between subjectivity. The encounters with the doubles display the material practices of such erasures: 'Frederika gomme mes jambes, mes épaules, mes bras [...]. Elle m'efface, frotte encore, comme si elle voulait entrer en moi' [Frederika is rubbing my legs, my shoulders, my arms [...] She is erasing me, scrubbing yet again, as if she wanted to enter me (174)]. This passage strikes a resonant chord with readers of *La Nouvelle pornographie* – this is a scene between Marie and Aline: 'je ne sais pas ce qui nous arrivait, ce qu'elle voulait effacer en se frottant contre mon corps, comme si j'étais une gomme'. [I did not know what was happening to us, what she wanted to erase by rubbing herself against my body as if I were an eraser (115)].

To conclude, Nimier extends the self into the figure of the double through a dissolution of borders, staging the displacement that is at the core of self-identity: 'pour moi, ça pouvait se formuler ainsi: comment ressembler à quelqu'un qui vous ressemble quand on ne se ressemble pas à soi-même?' [I could formulate the question like this: how to resemble someone who resembles you when you do not resemble yourself? (170)], the narrator of *Photo-photo* asks. Tales of incoherence haunt the notion of subjectivity itself as contemporary literature has dispensed with the idea of finding yourself. As Jordan astutely remarks, 'postmodern thought has rendered the idea of recovering a lost (pre-existent) self redundant'.[26] The encounter between self and 'other' in the form of the double is a manifestation of contemporary modes of being, as critically understood. As explored in this chapter, the double is based on modes of interrogation and quest, has fluid and porous borders and is coherent with queer practices as evidenced through its display of Sapphic potentiality. The double in Nimier's works therefore has a distinctly postmodern flavour, dispensing with the neat contours of a self and its mirrored image. By projecting herself in *La Nouvelle Pornographie* and in *Photo-photo*, Nimier shows us that the self

26 Jordan, *Contemporary French Women's Writing: Visions, Women's Voices, Women's Lives*, 19.

remains opaque more often to itself, as it undergoes a constant process of evolution. Unmoored and undefined, the self is free to queer itself.

Bibliography

Berlant, Lauren, and Michael Warner, 'What Does Queer Theory Teach us about *X*', *PMLA* 110/3 (1995), 343–9.

Best, Victoria, and Martin Crowley, *The New Pornographies: Explicit Sex in Recent French Fiction and Film* (Manchester: Manchester University Press, 2007).

Butler, Judith, *Bodies That Matter: On the Discursive Limits of "Sex"* (New York and London: Routledge, 1993).

Cairns, Lucille, *Lesbian Desire in Post-1968 Literature* (Lewiston: Edwin Mellen Press, 2002).

Creed, Barbara, 'Lesbian Bodies: Tribades, Tomboys and Tarts' in Elisabeth Grosz and Elspeth Probyn, eds, *Sexy Bodies: The Strange Carnalities of Feminism* (London and New York: Routledge, 1995), 86–103.

Fischer, Lucy, 'Two-Faced Women: The "Double" in Women's Melodrama of the 1940s', *Cinema Journal* 23/1 (1983), 24–43.

Garréta, Anne F., *Pas un jour* (Paris: Grasset, 2002).

Grell, Isabelle, *L'Autofiction* (Paris: Armand Colin, 2014).

Jordan, Shirley, *Contemporary French Women's Writing: Visions, Women's Voices, Women's Lives* (Oxford: Peter Lang, 2004).

Larquier, Sarah, 'Entretien avec Marie Nimier', *The French Review* 78 (2004), 340–53.

De Lauretis, Teresa, *The Practice of Love: Lesbian Sexuality and Perverse Desire* (Bloomington and Indianapolis: Indiana University Press, 1994).

De Medeiros, Ana, 'Now I See Me, Now You Don't' Working with/against Paternal Influence in Marie Nimier's *Photo-photo*', in Thomas Baldwin, James Fowler and Ana de Medeiros, eds, *Questions of Influence in Modern French Literature* (London and New York: Palgrave Macmillan, 2013), 194–207.

Moi, Toril, *Sexual/Textual Politics*: *Feminist Literary Theory* (London: Routledge, 1985).

Morello, Nathalie, and Catherine Rodgers, *Nouvelles écrivaines: nouvelles voix?* (Amsterdam: Rodopi, 2004).

Nimier, Marie, *Domino* (Paris: Gallimard, 1998).

—— *La Nouvelle pornographie* (Paris: Gallimard, 2000).

—— *Photo-photo* (Paris: Gallimard, 2010).
—— *Sirène* (Paris: Gallimard, 1985).
Waelti-Walters, Jennifer, *Damned Women: Lesbians in French Novels, 1796–1996* (Montreal: McGill-Queen's Press, 2000).
Wardle, Cathy, 'Ce qui n'est pas moi: Writing the Self, Desiring the Other in *La Nouvelle pornographie*', *Cincinatti Romance Review* 23 (2004), 273–84.

RAY BALSTAD

3 Children Out of Line: Gender (Dis)Orientations and Paths of Queer Resistance in the Heterotopia

Space is profoundly material. So too is the experience of space, rendering it is also fundamentally phenomenological. Rather than empty or neutral, space is valent. Imbued with directional fields that suggest we move in one way or another, it both produces and is produced by gravitational economies of desire.[1] Some lines are concrete and intentional, such as roads. Others, perhaps, are more abstract, for example, those that guide our decisions, such as whether to take this road or that. A certain degree of freedom remains: we *can* deviate from these routes, or we *can* go against our better judgment in our decision-making. Those valencies, while charged with varied intensity, are ultimately mutable. Sara Ahmed calls on 'desire lines' as an architectural phenomenon determined by the traffic of pathways.[2] While often the 'desire line' would be the shortest possible path to any destination, we might think instead of these directives as paths of least resistance, determined by the nature of the impetus to reach that destination. In this sense, space and the objects that inhabit it inflect one another. My (repeated) motion along the path of least resistance is what determines it as such. In the same way, the path of least resistance also serves to guide my movement along that path, revealing the hegemony intrinsic to the 'desire line'.[3] These desire lines guide our orientation towards the objects in front of, along and outside these paths. While Ahmed explores this thematic

1 I use 'desire' in a larger sense, evoking not just sexual desire, but desire as the guiding lines for our orientation towards or away from objects.

2 Sara Ahmed, *Queer Phenomenology: Objects, Orientations, and Others* (Durham, NC: Duke University Press, 2006).

3 Indeed, 'hegemony' is derived from the Greek *hēgeisthai*, meaning 'to lead'.

explicitly within the cadre of sexuality, I expound on and extrapolate these ideas to a discussion of gender in the films *Ma Vie en rose* [*My Life in Pink*] (1997)[4] and *Tomboy* (2011).[5] I will further elaborate this along with Michel Foucault's *heterotopia*, which conceptualizes alternative worlds in which these desire lines and orientations might be contorted, inverted, or perturbed. Through these films, I examine the point at which space, sexuality and gender come together, a space in which we re-orientate ourselves around sexuality and gender to envision what a queer world – a heterotopia – might be like.

In *The Production of Space* (1974), Henri Lefebvre attempts to delineate these hegemonic gravities, tracing the ways in which space is *produced*.[6] Returning to the aforementioned example of roads and paths: the design and construction of a road is generally enacted by a governing agency, which determines the most productive ways its subjects do, or should, move through that space. Though perhaps different subjects move differently through that space, these roads will likely be designed by and for dominant populations. Decisions about how to move through a space (e.g. to take road A or B) are likewise determined by what route is most 'productive' or which path will be of least resistance to dominant populations. As a result, the creation of these pathways is driven more concretely by a governing body, and more abstractly by a logic of neoliberal capitalism through which that governing body operates. This logic seeks to make 'productive' every possible gesture, articulation and movement of the body. Within this framework, the reproduction of the neoliberal capitalist subject is grounded in the efficient reproduction of the species, predicated on the efficacious production of *heterosexual* space, which is sculpted by and encourages heterosexual modes of discourse, gesture and behaviour as paths of least resistance. The production of *queer* space then serves not only as a counter to heteronormative ways of being, but also as a site which may contest the nature of the (re)productive neoliberal capital

4 Alain Berliner, dir. *Ma Vie en rose*. Canal+, 1997.

5 Céline Sciamma, dir. *Tomboy*, Hold Up Films, 2011.

6 Henri Lefebvre, trans. Donald Nicholson-Smith, *The Production of Space* (Oxford: Blackwell, 1958).

subject itself, opening the possibility to new pathways that may orient our subject positions differently.

As Ahmed points out, 'queer' in its etymology indicates a 'twist' or a 'turn'. Deviation is likewise to 'turn away' or 'turn out of the way'. In a broad sense, it is 'queer' to occupy or move through space against these directives. In a more restricted manner, 'queer' space might refer to concrete spaces such as cruise spots, queer bars, or queer activist organizations. The interrelations and coming together of a group of queer people can manifest queer space, but what power over space might be exercised at the level of the individual? Can an individual's deviation from a path render space 'queer'? If a character within a film can manifest queer space, can the film itself and the action of viewing it both present and produce queer space as well? If so, what might be the topology, the function, or the parameters of these 'other spaces'?

Foucault proposed the heterotopia, or 'other space' in a 1967 lecture[7] as a mode of conceptualizing the social structure of space, looking at the placement, localization and relations among sites – whether concrete or abstract – that we inhabit in our daily lives. For example, the train is at once a unified and confined space, which is simultaneously connected to, and disconnected from, every site along its tracks. The set of relations between the train and cities, stations, farms, the countryside or a cargo-loading dock is ever-changing, and the nature of that relation governs movement through those spaces. More abstractly, Foucault speaks of relations such as those between sites of leisure and relaxation (such as the theatre or the park) or sites of rest (including the home and the bed). However, these seemingly unified and untroubled relations are of less interest to Foucault. This quasi-unity obscures the network of political and economic structures at play in guiding bodies through space. By inverting or perverting this relation, we may unearth the structures underlying these spaces and sites.

Foucault introduces two ways of conceptualizing this perturbation of space: the utopia and the heterotopia. The utopia, he advocates, is an

7 The lecture was later transcribed and published in *Architecture/Mouvement/Continuité* in October 1984 and was then translated to English and published in *Diacritics* in 1986. As Foucault did not review this text, it is not a part of his official body of work.

ultimately unreal and unrealizable space, a site 'with no real place'.[8] The very fact of imagining an ideal, inverted, or unattainable space has the power to lay bare the social, economic and political relations undergirding 'real', material spaces. Gaston Bachelard notes in *The Poetics of Space* (1958), 'Representation is dominated by Imagination. Representation becomes nothing but a body of expressions with which to communicate our images to others.'[9] Departing from the realm of the imaginary, the heterotopia by contrast is enacted through this work of representation. Foucault conceives of heterotopias as 'counter-sites' or 'effectively enacted utopia in which [...] real sites [...] are simultaneously represented, contested, and inverted'.[10] The heterotopia, as a necessarily material 'counter-site' must remain separate from the site(s) through which it is formed, and it is through this uncanny distantiation that it becomes illuminated.[11] What may be revealed should these sites inflect into one another, or, against their very nature, rupture or collide?

In his theorization of the heterotopia, Foucault delineates several principles that parameterize the emergence and existence of an 'other space':

1. *Ubiquity*: Heterotopias can exist in any culture or society.
2. *Purpose*: A heterotopia must have a well-defined function, though that function is ultimately mutable as the socio-cultural conditions of its counter-site may shift.
3. *Hetero-spatiality*: The heterotopia can transpose within it otherwise disparate sites (e.g. a theatre, cinema or garden).

8 Michael Foucault, 'Of Other Spaces', *Diacritics* 16/1 (1986), 22–7, 24.

9 Gaston Bachelard, *The Poetics of Space,* trans. Marie Jolas (Boston: Beacon Press, 1969), 150.

10 Foucault, 'Of Other Spaces', 23.

11 Playwright Bertolt Brecht theorized this as *Verfremdungseffekt* [translated by the *estrangement effect, defamiliarization effect* or *distancing effect*]. Brecht used the term to describe the relation between theatrical representation and audience. *Distantiation* is the process by which the audience is made aware of its own gaze and positioning within the theatrical space. This effectively denatures 'performance' as such and serves to impede the audience's facile identification with that which is represented, such as when performers directly address the audience. In this way, the work of estrangement allows the performance to occur on the plane of the conscious rather than that of the subconscious. For more information see: Bertolt Brecht, 'On Chinese Acting', *The Tulane Drama Review* 6/1 (1961), 130–6.

4. *Heterochrony*: Heterotopias warp the conventional temporality of their counter-sites.
5. *Opening and Closing*: The heterotopia must be open to entry, though barriers to entry (membership, performance rituals, etc.) may exist.
6. *Contingency*: The heterotopia functions only in relation to its counter-site. Its function may be either 'illusory' (to reveal the illusory nature of its 'real' counter-sites) or 'compensatory' (to provide a counter-site that is as organized and well-manicured in every way that its real counterpart is not).

Foucault insists on the materiality of the heterotopia (distinct from the utopia only in its tangibility) and thus he invokes the importance of the problematic of space. In *Queer Phenomenology: Orientations, Objects, Others* (2006), Ahmed situates the experience of space within queer theory, detailing the ways in which objects carry histories forged in hegemony, thus both affecting and effecting our orientations to them in the space we/they inhabit. Power guides our orientations towards objects[12] and the paths that we follow in relation to them. Ahmed does the work of asking what it could mean to 'queer' our orientations, our paths, our relationships with objects, to reconsider the way in which the space around us has been formed to orient us as productive heterosexual, cisgender bourgeois subjects. Both *Ma Vie en rose* and *Tomboy* tell the story of a child who has 'turned away' from the sex assigned at birth. Or, perhaps, the child has 'turned away' from the paths designated by, as well as towards, that assignment, reorienting themselves in gender and reorienting gender in space. As these children deviate from that path, the question of space becomes crucial to their narratives. Through these films, the child's notions of place dictates how it orients itself, and these (re)orientations may manifest heterotopias, revelatory sites of resistance.

Ma Vie en rose by Alain Berliner[13] is the story of Ludo Fabre, a young child assigned male at birth. She/he[14] is the youngest child of a white

12 Ahmed employs the word 'object' so as to refer to anything that is not 'subject'; thus, 'object' can be animate or inanimate, human or inhuman, concrete or conceptual.

13 Alain Berliner is a Belgian director best known for *Ma Vie en rose*. Berliner co-wrote the film with Chris Vander Stappen, a Belgian screenwriter and director whose *œuvre* deals with topics of gender and queer sexualities more explicitly than that of Berliner.

14 The question of which pronoun(s) to employ in referring to this character is, indeed, sticky. While Ludo presents (or expresses the desire to present) in a feminine way

Christian middle class family who has just moved to a chic new neighbourhood, thereby creating an injunction to the rites of performance that permit membership to the bourgeois suburb. Ludo displays her/his predilection for clothing, gestures and objects normally relegated to the realm of 'girlhood'. In the beginning of the film, Ludo is introduced wearing a princess dress and costume jewellery. She/he is seen applying make-up. When she/he debuts at the family's housewarming party, the audience applauds at the presentation of the Fabre family's supposed daughter. Ludo's father anxiously announces that Ludo is not his daughter but his *son*, the '*fort en farce*' [a jokester]. Ludo continues to pursue these transgressive gender orientations over the course of the film. These gender orientations catalyse family tension, and exacerbate the rift between a family of newcomers and the rest of the neighbourhood. This neighbourhood views Ludo's steadfast predilection for the feminine as a sexual perversion and thus a threat to the dominant heterosexual order. The film is complex in its framing of Ludo's transgressions; family, neighbours and schoolmates repeatedly interpret Ludo's conduct as a sign of her/his homosexuality. However, the focus of the film is instead on Ludo's experience and 'working-out' of gender, further confounding the already fraught distinction between gender and sexuality. The portrayal of Ludo's orientations around gender rather than her/his fondness for Jérôme, a classmate, leads us to believe the Ludo is likely not gay, but rather is oriented towards gender differently than what is taken to be 'natural'.

Unlike many films that reckon with gender performance, this revelatory rupture between assigned gender and gender performance occurs within the first few minutes of the film. This early episode avoids the tired fetishization of the 'gender reveal' as the film's climactic spectacle, a trope which positions the primary polemic of gender in the interstice between

---

and is attracted to stereotypically feminine realms of play, to ascribe a set of pronouns could, perhaps, be to ascribe a vocabulary and an identity that the film leaves unclear. Neither wanting to impose an identity, nor imply that to pursue traditionally feminine gender presentation is analogous to girlhood, the feminine pronoun 'she' seems inappropriate. At one point in the film, Ludo claims the term *garçon-fille* (boy-girl). I will thus use the composite 'she/he' and its iterations in reference to Ludo.

biology and determinism.[15] These gender 'spectacles' conceive gender as inherently biological by categorizing it according to the appearance of one's genitals, and deterministic insofar as that appearance implies a certain set of underlying behavioural ciphers.

Tomboy is a semi-autobiographical film informed by director Céline Sciamma's own tomboyish childhood as it unfolds through the film's main character Laure. Like Ludo, Laure has just moved to a new neighbourhood. As she[16] explores her environs, she crosses paths with a young female neighbour called Lisa, who assumes Laure to be a boy.[17] Without correcting Lisa, Laure introduces herself as Mickaël. Outside this minor interaction, gendered language is entirely absent in the first fifteen minutes of the film. Only when Laure exits the bath is it revealed that the masculine persona assumed by both Lisa and the viewer is a deviation from the gender Laure was assigned at birth.[18] Unbeknownst to her family throughout most of the film, Laure cultivates a space in the neighbourhood under this assumed masculine identity.[19] Her identity is thus split into inside and outside. Within

15 Biological essentialism asserts that certain social concepts and behaviors (ex. intelligence, personality, gender, sexuality) are biologically encoded rather than socially constructed. Applicable in many areas outside of gender, biological essentialism is often associated with fields such as phrenology or scientific racism. With respect to gender, biological essentialism typically posits that (1) there are two genders (male/female), and (2) qualities ascribed to masculinity or femininity are endemic to the biological distinction of male/female. For further reading on biological essentialism and social construction of gender, see Simone de Beauvoir, *Le Deuxième sexe* (1949); Christine Delphy, 'Un féminisme matérialiste est possible' (1982); Judith Butler, *Gender Trouble* (1990).

16 While Laure assumes a masculine persona at points in the film, the film is ultimately centered around the figure of the *tomboy*, whose appearance, interests, gestures, etc. may be read as masculine. However, the *tomboy* remains a fundamentally female figure.

17 This assumption is clear in Lisa's use of a masculine *nouveau* as she asks Laure: 'tu es nouveau?' [are you new here?].

18 While the title of the film is perhaps a giveaway in this respect, a French audience may not be acquainted with the meaning of the word 'tomboy' and thus its implications may be not be readily apparent.

19 There is an important distinction to be made here between 'identity' as a mode of subjectivity (such as that of a queer identity or trans identity) and identity as an

the home, while Laure's masculine gender presentation is tolerated, she frequently receives subtle directives from her mother that encourage even the most minute or ephemeral manifestations of femininity.[20] Outside the home, Laure is Mickaël, a somewhat reserved and sensitive boy new to the neighbourhood. While this split is known to the viewer throughout the majority of the film, the narrative culminates in a public collision of these two identities, forcing Laure's family and friends to confront this cognitive dissonance.

Docile Orientations

Normative spaces and ways of being are mutually constitutive and react in volatile ways to the kind of cognitive dissonance exhibited by Laure's and Ludo's ability or inability to 'pass'. This dissonance incites a distantiation that illuminates the paradigm of the heterosexual bourgeois subject. These norms are maintained simultaneously through their reproducibility, inducing a feedback loop that carves out and cements paths of gender and sexual orientation that will effectively perpetuate the paradigm. This process is effectuated precisely through the erasure of the normative as an 'oriented' position in the first place. Laure's mother does not see herself as 'oriented' towards the feminine or towards motherhood just as Ludo's brothers do not see themselves as 'oriented' towards masculinity because these are the ways in which their bodies have long been conditioned. Juxtaposed with Ludo and Laure, these secondary actors highlight the process of orienting as one that both guides and conditions the body.

---

assumed persona. In this case, I use the word 'identity' in reference to Laure's performance as Mickaël.

20 This can be seen, for example, when Laure's mother expresses pleasant surprise on hearing that Laure has made friends with the neighbour girl, Lisa, since Laure typically befriends young boys and gravitates towards masculine modes of play. Later, Laure's mother further compliments her after she returns home sporting costume makeup after playing with Lisa.

In *Surveiller et punir: la naissance de la prison [Discipline and Punish: The Birth of the Prison]* (1975), Foucault introduces the notion of a 'docile body', evoking the way in which a soldier's bodily movements are coercively syncopated in time and space to carry out certain tasks with near automatic efficiency. The 'docile body' is one upon which discipline has been enacted so as to 'dissociate power from the body'.[21] In this way, externally enacted power is billed instead as 'aptitude' or 'capacity', and is conceived as internal to the body. Discipline interrupts the inertia of the body, from which any internal power might arise, acting then as a self-effacing, external force which 'establishes in the body the constricting link between an increased aptitude and an increased domination'.[22] The internalization of discipline begets the docile body, whose orientations and paths through space and time become naturalized through this dissociation of power and body. In the films, disciplinary actions, varying in scale and intensity, serve as reactions to perceived ineptitudes or 'misorientations'; these actions range from the subtle directives of Laure's mother, to the violent shearing of Ludo's hair at the climax of the film. These actions, whether suggestive or forceful, are the disciplinary cogs that drive the process of (re)orienting, so that these orientations may be carried out with optimum efficiency.

Ahmed draws attention to the notion of 'orientation' as a mechanism which elucidates the directional flow of subjects and objects in social space and the pathways or 'desire lines' that are carved out in order to encourage a subject to move in particular ways through that space. Ahmed reminds us that '[f]or a life to count as a good life, then it must return the debt of its life by taking on the direction promised as a social good, which means imagining one's futurity in terms of reaching certain points along a life course'.[23] Foucault invokes the docile body to refer specifically to the power arm of the state as it enforces both political and economic discipline on bodies so as to produce both obedient and productive subjects. Ahmed, however, extrapolates the notion of external power placed upon a body to illustrate the way that this power not only shapes the body, but the very

21 Michel Foucault, *Discipline and Punish: The Birth of the Prison* (New York: Random House, 1995), 138.

22 Foucault, *Discipline and Punish: The Birth of the Prison*, 138.

23 Ahmed, *Queer Phenomenology: Objects, Orientations, and Others*, 21.

structure of space-time. The mechanisms about which Ahmed speaks are perhaps, in a larger sense, less precise than the finely calibrated dictates to which the soldier's body must respond. Nonetheless, in order for the mechanisms of power enacted on bodies to produce politically docile and economically productive subjects, these mechanisms must also extend to the home.

To produce both docile and productive subjects, we take the model of the heterosexual bourgeois household. The heterosexual couple must produce at least two children (one male, one female), who will then be formed too as heterosexual workers, who, through recursion, may maintain stability and secure the future of the nation-state. The moulding of the heterosexual, bourgeois family, however, happens through the laying out of the networks and pathways meant to guide subjects from birth, orienting them towards objects associated with the gender assigned to them. Young girls are encouraged to play *within* the home. They are given kitchen playsets, baby dolls, and encouraged to consume media that marries femininity and domesticity by presenting them with the feminine ideal as wife and mother. Their realms of play limit movement and circumscribe 'feminine space' purely within the home. Likewise, boys are encouraged to play *outside* the home. They are directed towards objects that galvanize them to exercise power over an infinite domain, demonstrated by Laure's interactions on the football pitch, where she is invited to play (as Mickaël) while Lisa is relegated to the side-lines since girls are not permitted to play.

The feminine ego ideal is exemplified in Ludo's play experience throughout the film. This model for Ludo is Pam, a Barbie-style doll who is featured in Ludo's favourite television show *Le Monde de Pam* ['Pam's World']. White with blonde hair, blue eyes and a classic hourglass figure, Pam is the ideal wife and homemaker. Pam serves as Ludo's guardian angel and spiritual guide throughout the film. She intervenes in moments of crisis such as when Ludo's mother slaps her/him at a party after she/he exchanges costumes with a girl. As the film progresses, it becomes clear that Western bourgeois family values which promote hetero- and cis-normative ways of being are projected onto, and carried out through, Ludo. Even her/his spaces of open gender play (such as her/his play marriage to Jérôme) mimic those of heteronormative spaces through structures such as gendered domestic labour and aesthetics and heterosexual nuptials.

The film is organized in a series of episodes in which Ludo's exploration of 'girly' orientations are met with hostility and attempts to reorient her/him towards objects and movements through space aligned with the gender assigned to her/him at birth. Many queer texts ground deviations from gender and sexual norms in childhood (resulting from trauma, 'mistakes' in child-rearing, etc.), thus producing a causatory narrative of queerness, often born of folly. Ludo's narrative stands in opposition to this trope as her/his turn towards the feminine appears without antecedent, and this appears not to be a 'turn' at all. 'Je serai une fille!' [I will be a girl!][24] she/he says, indicating that her/his ultimate orientation is away from manhood and towards womanhood. However, her/his mother responds: 'tu es un garçon et tu resteras un garçon toute ta vie! Quel têtu, hein? Tu bien faisais ta mère, toi.' [you are a boy and you always will be! You're so stubborn. Just like your mother.] This moment simultaneously negates and affirms her/his orientation, confirming Ludo's likeness to her/his mother, while also negating the very possibility of that orientation, ultimately resulting in gender disorientation. Attempts to course-correct Ludo's tendency towards feminine gender performance range from the puzzled and judgmental gaze of neighbours and classmates, to homophobic epithets and threats of physical violence or eternal damnation.

Without grounding queerness in a particular event, the *tabula rasa* purity of the figure of the child narrativizes queerness as part of the child's ethos, as if to imply that one is 'born' gay or transgender. Ludo's several half-hearted attempts to 'butch-up' at her/his family's behest always result in a return to the feminine, as if this were in fact Ludo's natural orientation.[25] Classmates ostracize Ludo for her/his fondness for dolls and her/his affinity for Jérôme, who asks to be seated elsewhere because he does not want to go to hell. Jérôme too risks ridicule, and thus initiates a turn away from Ludo in order to be perceived as 'correctly' oriented. Conditioned to

24 All translations are my own unless otherwise noted.

25 This narrative risks yet another sticky biologically essentialist trope, implying that queerness is somehow genetically or deterministically encoded.

avoid punishment and derision, Ludo observes her/his brothers and male schoolmates in their behaviours, in repeated attempts to reorient towards masculinity. In one instance, Ludo glimpses a male classmate kissing an unconsenting female classmate, to which someone responds: 'ça, c'est un mec en vrai!' [now that's a real man!] Ludo smiles, having been presented with concrete action that could reorient her/him towards masculine identity, as well as reorienting others towards Ludo. For example, Jérôme's orientation towards Ludo as a romantic interest must fundamentally change should Ludo reorient her/himself towards the masculine identity to which she/he has been relegated. Furthermore, Ludo's reorientation towards the masculine is routinely at the behest of others who wish for her/him to orient differently. In meeting this request, Ludo is attempting to 'fall in line' by enacting masculine behaviours. While playing after school, Ludo turns towards a female classmate and attempts to kiss her. She scoffs and rebuffs Ludo, pushing her/him down to the ground, replying with a smirk that 'j'embrasse pas les filles!' [I don't kiss girls!] Ludo here is caught in a double-bind, her/his girlhood and boyhood dually denied, leaving Ludo gender-disoriented once again.

Contrary to Ludo, Laure's masculine identity is not naturalized. While she has a boyish gender presentation, she does not shy away from playing with her little sister, nor is her masculinity threatened when Lisa describes her as 'pas comme les autres' [not like other boys]. As Mickaël, Laure is reserved and kind, and she doesn't mind sitting on the side-lines of the football game with Lisa. Laure's embrace of masculine identity is a way of experimenting with gaze. The film exposes the process of making legible the rites, gestures and orientations that constitute membership to masculine identity. In one such sequence, Laure sits on the side-lines of the football match. What follows is a series of shot/reverse shots as Laure observes the football pitch. Her gaze follows the neighbourhood boys as they spit on the ground, remove their shirts and flex their prepubescent muscles as they run back and forth across the pitch. These are behaviours that Laure later replicates in the mirror at home. Whereas before, the bathroom is the revelatory site of Laure's biologically assigned gender, the bathroom mirror reproduces a perfectly crystallized 'inverted' image of herself. Before the mirror, Laure removes her shirt, flexes and spits into the sink. The next time we see her on the football pitch, she joins in the game, during which she will reproduce these same behaviours, reinforcing her 'boy' persona.

Ahmed remarks that '[w]hat bodies "tend to do" are effects of histories rather than being originary'.[26] Having been historically oriented towards gender in a particular way, Laure's gender (re)orientation requires that she 'face' others differently, by (re)orienting herself towards others in her gesture, comportment and expression, altering her movement through space. Nevertheless, for Laure to 'pass', she must invisibilize these turns. This process arrives through the gestural conditioning so as to create a 'history' that habituates the body to particular orientations. In this way, orientation becomes docile, even automatic or naturalized. Ludo, on the other hand, never manages to fully assimilate her/his masculine orientations, and thus Ludo's perceived turn towards the feminine becomes a site of public resistance, whereas for Laure these turns remain interior. To her friends, it appears that Laure has not 'turned away', but is, in fact, 'in line' while the visibility of Ludo's turns renders her/him 'out of line'.

Heterotopic Play

The heterotopia can manifest itself only through its relation and/or opposition to a real space. Thus, the play space has a natural propensity for heterotopia, as many play spaces are designed as microcosms, miniatures, or representations produced by 'real' spaces. These 'other worlds' are queer in the sense that their bodies and the movement of those bodies through space can be used to manipulate the gaze of other characters. The alternate realities imagined by these characters serve as counterspaces which, in and of themselves, materialize within the film as 'real space'. Ludo constructs the heterotopia through the enactment of gendered rituals in sites of play, such as the marriage ceremony with Jérôme. Ludo approximates the Western, Christian, heterosexual rite in the bedroom of Jérôme's deceased sister. Donning one of his sister's dresses, Ludo walks

26 Ahmed, *Queer Phenomenology: Objects, Orientations, and Others*, 56.

down the aisle hand in hand with Jérôme. The path to the altar is lined with stuffed animals and, at the end, sits a teddy bear which masquerades as vicar. However, the film creates a fundamental rupture between these separate spaces in which the audience is made aware of the ways in which these characters are reorienting themselves with respect to the worlds in which they live. In the marriage ceremony, due to Ludo's assigned gender, she/he is ultimately incapable of fully embodying the feminine role. However, in the heterotopic world of play, this reorienting away from the gender assigned Ludo at birth poses no problem. The two are discovered by Jérôme's mother moments before the nuptial kiss that would officiate Ludo and Jérôme's marriage. This ruptures the heterotopic imaginary, thwarting Ludo from achieving the feminine ego ideal and leaving the heterosexual matrix underdetermined.

Within the film, Ludo's repeatedly attempts to fall 'in line' with the feminine ideal by donning princess garb, letting her/his hair grow and play-acting a marriage with her/his neighbour Jérôme. The illusory nature of this feminine ideal is revealed in part through its exposition of the same pathways with which its audience should be familiar: those of bourgeois compulsory heterosexuality, motivated and undergirded by a biologically essentialist model of gender. The question of social space and sexual difference is established straightaway in the opening scenes of the film, parodically exhibiting the gendered rites in which women, their families and their homes are embroiled and networked.

The film opens on the interior of a garishly decorated dollhouse. The grandiose bedroom and living room furnishings are made in hyper-saturated blues, purples and pinks, and their shapes are exaggerated with arabesque finishings. We are immediately plunged into the microcosmic realm of domestic hyperbole that characterizes the dollhouse. Bachelard notes that it is in miniaturizing the world that we may better possess it, and yet in so doing 'values become condensed and enriched'.[27] To 'possess' the home is to actualize the paragon of femininity, or, in other words, to distil the otherwise complex dynamics of the household into traditionally gendered tasks such as cooking, decorating and child-rearing. This process then reduces

27 Bachelard, *The Poetics of Space*, 150.

feminine spaces to the gendered division of labour. The imperfect reproductions of these dynamics will ultimately render these paradigms and the characters who effectuate them insufficient.

While in French we might refer to a character such as Laure as a *garçon manqué* [a tomboy or a boy 'lacking'][28] the opposing term, a *fille manquée* [girl 'lacking'] is employed rarely, if ever. While a *garçon manqué* is anatomically 'lacking', the term *fille manquée* cannot be understood in the same phallogocentric system. A *fille manquée* might refer instead to an empty or unfulfilled feminine role, the adjective *manqué* also referring to the failure to fulfil an expectation. Ludo repeatedly attempts to assume spaces traditionally occupied by girls, but is only afforded the opportunity to do so in the quite real case of a 'girl lacking'. Indeed, when Ludo debuts at the beginning of the film, she/he assumes the place of her older sister. Ludo's play marriage takes place in the room of Jérôme's deceased sister whose dress Ludo dons for the ceremony. In Ludo's imaginary, she/he takes the place of Pam in the dollhouse. When Ludo's parents take her/him to see a psychologist, they confess that, during the pregnancy, they were hoping to have a girl. Lastly, in a school play, Ludo pursues the young girl starring as Snow White, stealing her costume and assuming her role in the play. Nonetheless, Ludo's attempts to fill the roles of 'missing girls' are ultimately futile. Reacting to this displacement, she/he constructs situational heterotopias in which she/he is permitted to fill these spaces in ways not afforded by the 'real' space of the film.

Filmic Heterotopias: Affect and the Queer Child

In Foucault's third principle of the heterotopia, he specifically cites cinema as a source of this essential heterotopic contradiction. *Ma Vie en rose* brings together spaces that are fundamentally material, but whose

28 The term *garcon manqué* is marked by the idea of a 'lack' or a 'deficiency', which betrays the term's moralizing connotations, denoting the orientation as non-normative and 'less-than'.

two-dimensional projection of a three-dimensional space on the screen unites them with the otherwise discontinuous space of the cinema. The heterotopia thus has the capacity to 'juxtapose in a single real place several spaces, several sites that are in themselves incompatible'.[29] The world portrayed in the film necessarily cannot exist in the same spatio-temporal location as that which is shown in the theatre. While I have discussed the presence of heterotopias *within* these two films, Foucault's proposition of the performative space as heterotopic merits further examination.

Perhaps the most important function of the heterotopia is its revelatory feature. In *In a Queer Time and Place: Transgender Bodies Subcultural Lives* (2005), Jack Halberstam asserts that '[e]ntertainment, in many ways, is the name we give to fantasies of difference that erupt on the screen only to give way to the reproduction of sameness'.[30] So too was Adorno and Horkheimer's critique of narrative cinema as an emerging linchpin of the culture industry. However, Halberstam opens the 'fantasy of difference' to the possibility of the reproduction of difference as well. The filmic heterotopia has the ability to mobilize the reproduction of sameness to potentially subversive ends. While, under a certain lens, the children in these films fulfil roles that presume the reinforcement of a dominant heterosexual order (Ludo through her/his attachment to Jérôme and Laure through her adolescent romance with Lisa), the framing of this reproduction of sameness is crucial.

To understand this framing, we may borrow from Giuliana Bruno's invocation of the touristic gaze as it relates to spatiality. She advocates that 'the touristic gaze involves (a simulation of) being there, the experience of being-in-space, calling on physical involvement from the part of the "consumer" of space'.[31] The touristic gaze is 'not only a gaze embedded in corporeality but also a gaze that *incorporates*'.[32] The film creates a site within the space of the screen, which then interpellates the audience, encouraging

29 Foucault, 'Of Other Spaces: Utopias and Heterotopias', 6.

30 Judith Halberstam, *In a Queer Time and Place: Transgender Bodies, Subcultural Lives* (New York: New York University Press, 2005), 84.

31 Giuliana Bruno, 'Bodily Architectures', *Assemblage* 19 (1992), 107.

32 Bruno, 'Bodily Architectures', 107.

a (distanced) engagement with the filmic world. The 'fantasy of difference' invites the touristic gaze and, in so doing, incorporates the body of the viewer. Halberstam's critique of mainstream film's illusory claim to apprehension of difference is directed particularly at narratives that reinforce norms and fetishize non-normative bodies through normative gazes and modes of storytelling. Halberstam cites Kimberly Peirce's *Boys Don't Cry* (1999) as a film that 'opens the door to a nonfetishistic mode of seeing the transgender body – a mode that looks with, rather than at, the transgender body and cultivates the multidimensionality of an indisputably transgender gaze'.[33]

While I have been careful not to brand these films or their protagonists as 'transgender', Halberstam's invocation of 'looking with' is a mechanism of reorientation. The fact that Bruno's touristic gaze incorporates the body of the film viewer in and of itself does not necessarily constitute a 'looking with'. The audience's compulsory orientation positions the viewer across from the screen, leading uncritical filmic gazes to invite the viewer only to 'look at'. However, through manipulations of the filmic gaze, the viewer can be invited instead to look 'with'.

At the diegetic level, both films engage Ludo and Laure in practices of 'looking at' in their observations of their peers, but with the ultimate goal of reorienting themselves so that they may instead be able to 'look with' and thus apprehend and internalize difference. By asking the viewer to engage with the protagonists' transitions from 'looking at' to 'looking with', the viewer is afforded the same opportunity for transformation. Halberstam further argues that the ability to 'look with' relies on 'the successful solicitation of affect – whether it be revulsion, sympathy, or empathy – [...] in any reorientation of the audience's gaze'.[34]

These affects can only be intensified in the representation of the queer child, for whom the sympathy of the audience is already heightened. We cannot fault the child that has not yet learned to 'correctly' orient itself to the same degree as we might fault an adult. Hostile responses to any

33 Halberstam, *In a Queer Time and Place: Transgender Bodies, Subcultural Lives*, 92.

34 Halberstam, *In a Queer Time and Place: Transgender Bodies, Subcultural Lives*, 77.

failed attempt to orient 'correctly' elicit an intensified sympathetic affective response when seen through the child's eyes. Further, children's play spaces form naturally occurring heterotopias as they come into being through the child's attempt to orient itself in an adult world. Play warps the sense of time and place, transposing elements of the adult world onto the experience of the child who must experiment with how to orient itself towards and away from objects within the space, and how those orientations dictate the 'desire lines' along which they must travel. The attempts of the child to orient and reorient in that space denaturalize our own orientations within spaces to which heterotopias serve as counter-sites. Moments of gendered dissonance or gender disorientations bring to light the marking of the heterotopic space. The queer child, then, is uniquely positioned to mobilize affect in such a way that its (dis)orientations invite the viewer to both 'look with' and to become disoriented in gender, space and time.

Ahmed crucially observes that our orientations and pathways are shaped by power. This has the effect not only of creating a gravitational pull towards the normative, but also affects what objects, desires and outcomes are reachable as we move through these spaces. If the act of 'turning' denaturalizes our proximities to, and propensities for, certain objects, gestures, paths and movements through space, it also denaturalizes the apparatuses of power at play in orienting bodies in such a way. The breaking of the 'docile' body must involve reorienting ourselves towards, and within, the apparatus. To emancipate the docile body, one must externalize interiorized exercises of power. Ludo achieves this through repeated resistance to reorientation, while Laure observes and replicates exercises that allow her to manipulate the gaze of others. Finally, the films themselves as heterotopic spaces denature the process of orientation as such. If the heterotopia seeks to reveal the structure of powers at play through its representation of uncanny sameness or uncanny ideal, the heterotopia (and the filmic heterotopia in particular) may serve as a site – or, rather, a counter-site – which both illuminates, and celebrates, the liberatory phenomenology of difference.

Bibliography

Ahmed, Sara, *Queer Phenomenology: Objects, Orientations, and Others* (Durham, NC: Duke University Press, 2006).

Bachelard, Gaston, *La Poétique de l'espace* (Paris: Presses Universitaires de France, 1958); *The Poetics of Space*, trans. Maria Jolas Bachtrans (Boston: Beacon Press, 1969).

Beauvoir, Simone de, *Le Deuxième sexe* (Paris: Gallimard, 1949).

Berliner, Alain, dir. *Ma Vie en rose*. Haut et Court, 1997.

Brecht, Bertolt, trans. Eric Bentley, 'On Chinese Acting', *The Tulane Drama Review* 6/1 (1961), 130–6.

Bruno, Giuliana, 'Bodily Architectures', *Assemblage* 19 (1992), 106–11.

Butler, Judith, *Gender Trouble: Feminism and the Subversion of Identity* (New York: Routledge, 1990).

Delphy, Christine, 'Un féminisme matérialiste est possible', *Nouvelles Questions Féministes* 4 (1982), 50–86.

Foucault, Michel, 'Des espaces autres', *Empan* 54/2 (2004), 12–19.

—— *Discipline and Punish: The Birth of the Prison*, trans. Alain Sheridan (New York: Random House, 1995).

—— 'Of Other Spaces: Utopias and Heterotopias', *Diacritics* 16/1 (1986), 22–7.

—— *Surveiller et punir: la naissance de la prison* (Paris: Gallimard, 1975).

Halberstam, Jack, *In a Queer Time and Place: Transgender Bodies, Subcultural Lives* (New York: New York University Press, 2005).

Lefebvre, Henri, trans. Donald Nicholson-Smith, *The Production of Space* (Oxford: Blackwell, 1958).

Sciamma, Céline, dir. *Tomboy*. Hold Up Films, 2011.

Bibliography

[illegible]

PART II

Rethinking Gendered Bodily Norms

KATHLEEN RIZY

4 Motherhood Reconceived: The Posthuman Future Is Female in 'Mon mari le clone' by Marie Darrieussecq

The 'Roaring Twenties' was a decade of economic growth and prosperity. Inversely, our current decade is beginning with a crash instead of a roar. The 2020s has ushered in uncertainty and fear as a pandemic has gripped the global economy and forced many into isolation. The fragility of human life has therefore taken centre stage. In an effort to limit movement and the consequent spread of the virus, doctors have been forced to prioritize patients. Physicians have subsequently postponed the treatment of infertility, despite the American Society for Reproductive Medicine (ASRM) COVID-19 Task Force's announcements concerning infertility treatment: 'Infertility is a disease, and treatment of infertility is medically necessary. [...] We know that other important non-emergency treatments are also being postponed during this pandemic. Fertility treatment is not being singled out.'[1]

What is the role of literature during such a tumultuous period of human history? For the French author Marie Darrieussecq, literature is a place where 'everything is yet to be discovered, to be heard, to be seen'.[2] In her first novel *Truismes* [*Pig Tails*] (1996), set in a dystopic France of the near future, the protagonist narrator undergoes a physical transformation from a woman to a sow.[3] While the title of one of her short stories 'Mon mari

1 ASRM and SART, 'FAQS for Patients Related to COVID-19' (9 April 2020), <https://www.asrm.org/news-and-publications/news-and-research/announcements/FAQs-Related-to-COVID-19/>, accessed 9 April 2020.

2 John Lambeth and Marie Darrieussecq, 'Entretien avec Marie Darrieussecq', *The French Review* 79/4 (2006), 806–18, 809.

3 Marie Darrieussecq, *Truismes* (Paris: P.O.L., 1996).

le clone' ['My Cloned Husband'] from the collection entitled *Zoo* (2006) sounds more like an episode of *The Twilight Zone*, it is no less illuminating than the award winning *Truismes*. There are fifteen short stories in *Zoo*, of which two treat the theme of cloning ('Quand je me sens très fatiguée le soir' [When I Feel Very Tired at Night] and 'Mon mari le clone') and five talk about motherhood or the relationship between mother and daughter ('Juergen, gendre idéal' [Juergen, Ideal Gender], 'On ne se brode pas tous les jours les jambes' [One Doesn't Stitch One's Legs Every Day], 'Noël parmi nous' [Christmas Together], 'Mon mari le clone' and 'Encore là' [There Again]). Therefore, 'Mon mari le clone' is the only story in the collection that follows a protagonist who becomes a mother through cloning. While the protagonist narrator of 'Mon mari le clone' does not undergo outright metamorphosis, moreover, her own body is nonetheless the focus.

'Mon mari le clone' is told by a first-person narrator in the 2020s. She describes her personal journey with reproductive technology. She and her husband struggle with infertility, and during sperm collection for the fourth attempt at in vitro fertilization, her husband dies suddenly from a heart attack. His body is transferred to the Body Bank, a cryogenics facility. After twenty years, doctors propose cloning her husband after failed attempts to thaw bodies preserved by cryogenics. After she signs some papers to allow the cloning company to extract some cells from her husband, she buries him and holds a small funeral for his family. Finally, she prepares over nine months for the 'birth' of her husband's clone, Jean-Jacques.

Francesca Ferrando argues that 'the body as the norm in biological and medical sciences has been unequivocally male'.[4] However, in this short story, when a scientific journal contacts the protagonist narrator to inquire about her marriage and presumably her reproductive health, she agrees to recount her story only after being told that it will help with women's research. She lives in the 2020s, but her reproductive journey began at the end of the previous century (a mere thirty years prior, in the 1990s), when women still needed sperm to reproduce.[5] The narrator provides insight about her

4 Francesca Ferrando, 'The Body', in Robert Ranisch and Stefan Lorenz Sorgner, eds, *Post- and Transhumanism: An Introduction* (Frankfurt am Main: Peter Lang, 2014), 149–62, 153.

5 Marie Darrieussecq, 'Mon mari le clone', in *Zoo* (Paris: P.O.L., 2006), 221.

own well-being as it relates to reproductive technology without the clinical sterility often associated with medical research, and her account is a form of enquiry which challenges the male body as the norm and also presents the female body as a locus of inquiry into what it means to be a mother.

The androcentric perception of the human body has inhibited women from engaging with technology. In his *Basic Writings* (1977), Martin Heidegger suggests that we can develop a free relationship with technology only if we 'recover the essence of technology as something other than the anthropocentric will to power'.[6] I propose that we look at reproductive technology in particular as something other than the androcentric will to power, or the centring of men's bodies and interests which render women's experiences inferior, to examine how the female body challenges the man/woman dualism through the re-conception of motherhood. 'Mon mari le clone' exemplifies how, in this posthuman future, women may gain physical agency alongside reproductive technology by querying conventions of the female body and by redefining the maternal body as more than a vessel used to fulfil a biological imperative or gender norms. Instead, 'Mon mari le clone' celebrates a non-normative conceptualization of the maternal body and informs the way the female body interacts with the machine body of reproductive technology.

Reproductive technology intervenes to provide options to infertile individuals who wish to conceive, and the narrator and her husband choose in vitro fertilization. Pregnancy is divided into three trimesters, with each one bringing different issues and concerns. While the protagonist of 'Mon mari le clone' does not become pregnant, she does become a mother to her cloned husband through three stages which lead to her embodiment of motherhood: masculine absence, interconnectedness, and nine months of maternal preparation. The death of her husband during their fourth attempt to conceive via IVF marks the beginning, or first trimester, of the narrator's story:

> Il est vrai que tout en étant soulagée (au moment même de sa mort) d'échapper aux FIV, aux traitements hormonaux et autres triturations, me gagnait peu à peu un

6 Anna Yeatman, 'Feminism and the Technological Age', *Australian Feminist Studies* 29/79 (2014), 85–100, 86.

sentiment d'absence, vague et sans crise, mais que je n'avais jamais éprouvé même à l'annonce de ma stérilité.

[It is true that while I was relieved (at the moment of his death) to escape IVF, hormone treatments and more triturations, I was overwhelmed little by little by a feeling of absence, vague and free of turmoil, but it was a feeling I had never felt when I was told I was sterile. (223)][7]

She reveals her suffering during IVF treatments, the complexity of which Robyn Rowland describes in explaining that 'the practical experience of IVF is more complicated. Women who have usually undergone the exhaustive procedures of fertility testing, followed by the invasive procedures of IVF, talk about the frustration and irritation of the constant testing process'.[8] The protagonist 'escapes' IVF rather than quits, abandons, or stops the procedure. The end of this procedure, during which her egg and his sperm would be put together in a Petri dish, and the death of her husband underline the masculine absence. This is notably without crisis, which allows her to reconstruct her relationship to reproductive technology as one in which she is no longer in a dualistic construction.

In regards to her own infertility our narrator says, 'pour bien saisir les aspects les plus délicats de notre histoire, il faut se replonger dans le contexte de la fin du siècle précèdent, à l'époque où nous, femmes, avions encore besoin de semence masculine pour nous reproduire' [to understand the most delicate aspects of our story, it is necessary to return to the previous century, at the time when we women still needed male sperm to reproduce (221)]. The choice of the word 'semence' [sperm] reinforces the man/woman dualism, since it does not suffice to explain the new, technological reality in which the protagonist is currently living. Instead, it is followed by the adjective 'masculine' [male] to differentiate between the male and female bodies, and to reflect the traditional view of maternity that this narrative rejects: that of maternity being biologically linked to masculine presence. She explains that he died from a heart attack 'dans la salle de prélèvement où il procédait seul au recueil de ses gamètes' [in the semen collection room

7 All translations are my own unless otherwise noted.

8 Robyn Rowland, *Living Laboratories: Women and Reproductive Technologies* (Bloomington and Indianapolis: Indiana University Press, 1992), 19.

where he went alone to the collection of his gametes (222)]. This role reversal of sorts, during which the husband dies at a moment associated with virility, stamina and prowess, challenges the normative perception of male and female bodies. Now, weakness and fragility describe the male body in contrast to the female body which has already endured painful and invasive IVF treatments. Donna Haraway insists that we acknowledge that 'communications technologies and biotechnologies are the crucial tools recrafting our bodies. These tools embody and enforce new social relations for women worldwide'.[9] As the protagonist is no longer subjected to invasive and arduous IVF treatments, her body is recrafted, reconstructed as no longer in function of her male counterpart. The posthuman, maternal body is one which may not be dominated, sexually objectified or manipulated.

While raising her son, the clone of her dead husband, the narrator says, 'on m'a fait comprendre que mon témoignage pourrait aider la recherche féminine, et c'est, j'insiste, uniquement dans ce cadre – un rapport de cas – que j'accepte de m'étendre ainsi sur ma vie privée' [they explained to me that my account could help with women's research, and that is, I insist, only for this – a case report – that I accept to speak in detail about my private life (221)]. As her cloned husband plays beside her, with 'un avenir serein' [a peaceful future (221)], she begins describing her painful past, the most delicate aspects of her private life. During their many attempts at IVF, she was struck by 'stérilité psychologique' [psychological sterility (222)]. When the nurses announce her husband's death, '[elles] ont invoqué un malencontreux concours de circonstances, l'équinoxe de printemps, la conjugaison des poussés de sève – je n'ai pas voulu en savoir plus' [they alluded to an unfortunate set of circumstances, the spring equinox, the combination of vigorous thrusts (222)].

Her husband dies on 21 March 2001, on the vernal equinox, during which daytime and night-time are of equal duration. It also denotes the onset of spring. However, for the narrator and her husband, it is the opposite, as their union opposes the symbolic values which spring connotes, such as rebirth and fertility. With her husband's death, the narrator may

9 Donna Jeanne Haraway, *Simians, Cyborgs, and Women: The Reinvention of Nature* (New York: Routledge, 1991), 164.

no longer conceive a child with her husband's sperm. Is it truly a regrettable set of circumstances? For the narrator, it is most pointedly not: 'je n'ai certes pas, pendant ces vingt années, joué à la veuve éplorée' [During those twenty years, I certainly did not play the role of the grieving widow (222)]. While she and her husband may have been equally present on the morning of their final IVF treatment, the balance will shift following the equinox, the rebirth of our protagonist. Previously sterile, inside and out, she will become embodied during her journey to motherhood *in extenso* while her husband is disembodied and stored in 'la Banque des Corps' [the Body Bank]:

> Je n'étais pas triste, j'étais distraite et disponible, ni veuve, ni divorcée, ni vieille. Je me promenais dans les rues en rentrant du bureau, je longeais les quais, poussais la porte des musées et ressortais de suite, écoutais des demi-concerts et assistais à des premiers actes, quittant les théâtres et les cinémas à mi-course de ce qu'on y donnait.
>
> [I was not sad, I was distracted and free, neither widowed, divorced, nor old. I walked in the streets upon returning from work, I walked along the quays, pushed open museum doors and left immediately, listened to parts of concerts and attended first acts, leaving the theatres and cinemas halfway through what was being performed or shown. (223)]

Although this passage could be interpreted as restlessness on the part of the narrator, I argue that it marks a turning point whereby the narrator enters into a new coalition, as Haraway would refer to it, whereby '[n]ature and culture are reworked; the one can no longer be the resource for appropriation or incorporation by the other'.[10] Both the dependency on her husband's sperm and invasive fertility treatments call to mind ecofeminism. Françoise d'Eaubonne introduced the term in her novel *Feminism or Death* (1974), and in another novel, *Eco-Feminism: Revolution or Maturation?* (1978), in which she asserted that women, like nature, are victims of male domination and that the patriarchal system is founded upon the appropriation of procreation, fertility and the female body.[11] Of course, this calls to mind another type of appropriation of women; in the

10 Haraway, *Simians, Cyborgs, and Women: The Reinvention of Nature*, 150.

11 Françoise d'Eaubonne, *Le Féminisme ou la mort* (Paris: Pierre Horay, 1974).

Manifesto of the Communist Party (1848), Karl Marx and Frederick Engels argue that capitalism favours the nuclear family for (re)production,[12] and in *Das Kapital* [*Capital*] (1867), Marx maintains that the exploitation of workers and nature are linked.[13]

Martha E. Gimenez declares that 'women's liberation from male dominance is inextricably linked to women's and men's liberation from compulsory parenthood'.[14] I would expand on this assertion by engaging with ecofeminism and Marxist feminism to propose that: liberation of the labouring body – both the body that gives birth and the one that contributes economically to the household through child-rearing – is inextricably linked to women's liberation from compulsory, biological motherhood through questioning the restrictive norms of the maternal body and through co-operating with both nature and technology.

The posthuman narrative is one in which 'our understanding of what is human [expands] into areas which have traditionally been deemed the opposite of our constitution – namely, other species, such as animals or plants, and technological apparatuses such as machines'.[15] To embrace a feminist posthumanism, in light of the masculine absence, the narrator can rework her relationship to reproductive technology, fellow women, and her own maternal body as both natural and machine, a transformation which she experiences as empowering.

The narrator explains the next phase of her life, her second trimester in her journey to motherhood:

> On entrait doucement dans les années de soie, ces années de douceur où nous baignons, aujourd'hui, avec bonheur, grâce à la parité et à l'antidéterminisme biologique. Moi aussi, de mon temps, j'avais milité, marrainée par une amie qui s'inquiétait de mon veuvage. Il faut éliminer les différences entre les corps, différences sans issue, sources de tous les ennuis, de tous les débats, séparations, conflits, épurations et polémiques.

12 Karl Marx and Frederick Engels, *Manifesto of the Communist Party* (Chicago: Charles H. Kerr & Company, 1888), 33.

13 Karl Marx, *Capital* (New York: Vintage Books, 1977), 283.

14 Martha E. Giménez, *Marx, Women, and Capitalist Social Reproduction* (Leiden: Koninklijke, 2019), 162.

15 Michael Mack, *Contaminations: Beyond Dialectics in Modern Literature, Science and Film* (Edinburgh: Edinburgh University Press, 2016), 192.

> [We slowly made our entrance into the silk years, those soft years during which we happily do well, thanks to equality and biological anti-determinism. In my day, I had also campaigned, sponsored by a friend who worried about my widowhood. We must eliminate differences between bodies, dead-end differences, sources of all problems, all debates, conflicts, treatments and polemics. (224)]

This description of the 2020s recalls the 1920s, or 'les Années folles' ['The Roaring Twenties'], which gave birth to fertile social, political, artistic and cultural productions, and gave prominence to unbridled individualism. This passage recalls that same individualism, led by the feminist voice this time. There is strength in the individual to eliminate the divisive differences upheld by the patriarchy while still embracing the diversity of the female experience. In this instance, 'biological anti-determinism' pertains to the narrator's unconventional path to motherhood, without the cause and effect of fertility treatment. Rather, she insists that we must acknowledge the female body in all its forms: pregnant, infertile, pre-menopausal, post-menopausal, and so on and so forth. As she embraces her biological anti-determinism, she may become a mother on her own terms and embrace the independence of her newfound corporal freedom, a crucial aspect of individual liberty which did not exist in the 1920s. While the garçonne look, which obscured the bust and waistlines, proposed an elimination of differences between male and female bodies, abortion and contraception were outlawed in France in 1920 after the First World War.

The narrator does spend time with a feminist group, yet she also values her time alone:

> Mais surtout, je gardais le goût des promenades. Je rêvais, j'aimais être seule. Je lisais aussi, aux beaux jours, dans les jardins publics. J'aimais surtout observer les variations de la lumière: aux changements de saison, le flottement de la poussière dans les rayons, le pollen qui dérive … ou les rondes de feuilles mortes, et la brume près de la Seine, la patine des troncs et des pierres, le temps qui peu à peu se dépose, poli, lustré, au flanc des monuments.
>
> [More importantly, I still enjoyed walks. I dreamt, I loved being alone. I also read, on nice days, in the public gardens. I especially liked to watch the changes in the light: seasonal changes, the floating dust in the sunbeams, the drifting pollen … or the dancing fall leaves, and the mist next to the Seine, the patina of tree trunks and stones, the season deposited, burnished, shiny, on the side of the monuments.] (224)

In this passage, the interconnectedness between the narrator and the natural space of the park serve as a model of interaction that may, as David Foulkes explains, '[replace a model] … of vertical hierarchy', such as the traditional superiority of men over women.[16] The very procedure of in vitro fertilization requires the patient to be in a horizontal position. The protagonist's body was prostrate, manipulated by technology and injected with male sperm. Now, she stands upright and observes. She walks alongside the riverbank and exalts light and seasonal changes. For feminist post-humanities, 'it is beyond doubt today that we are as much in nature as nature is in us. […] Humans today are, after all, more obviously entangled in co-constitutive relationships with nature and the environment, with science and technology'.[17] Therefore, we see an alternative entanglement: while there is no vertical hierarchy, as the female narrator spends time with and in nature, this description of her time in nature precedes her transition to motherhood. Like nature, her body is changing. A pregnant woman can be juxtaposed with a fertile landscape, reminiscent of its insemination or 'masculine' intervention. Here, there is no masculine intervention, no fertile landscape. Instead, the pollen, or potential fertilization, drifts away. (Re)productive presence is arrived at through the entanglement of the feminine, the natural and the scientific. Our narrator will soon undergo changes alongside the reproductive technology of cloning as she embodies motherhood.

The beginning of the narrator's third trimester, or last step in her journey to motherhood, is marked by psychological illness. She has strange dreams, she struggles to follow conversations, and she often visits her husband's body to pass the time. In Darrieussecq's first novel, *Truismes*, dreams and sleep are essential elements of the narrator's transformation from woman to sow. While the narrator of 'Mon mari le clone' does not metamorphose into a sow, she does undergo a transformation and transition to motherhood. In *The Interpretation of Dreams* (1899), Sigmund Freud argues that

16 David Foulkes, *Dreaming: A Cognitive-psychological Analysis* (Hillsdale, NJ: L. Erlbaum Associates, 1985), 28.

17 Cecilia Åsberg, 'Feminist Posthumanities', in Rosi Braidotti and Maria Hlavajova, eds, *Posthuman Glossary* (New York and London: Bloomsbury Publishing, 2018), 157–60, 157.

we can better understand the unconscious mind through the analysis and interpretation of dreams. The concept of psychological displacement, or an unconscious defence mechanism whereby the mind substitutes either a new aim or a new object for goals felt in their original form to be dangerous or unacceptable, was particularly important in Freud's explanation of dreams. For Jean Laplanche and Jean-Bertrand Pontalis, Freud's analysis is significant because ['the comparison of the manifest content and latent dream thoughts bring a difference in focus'].[18] The reference to the narrator's dreams reveals her latent thoughts related to a progressive journey towards her own rebirth, a new stage in her womanhood which was previously unbearable and caused a psychological sterility.

Motherhood previously denoted a painful transformation for the narrator. Now, the new maternal body, unencumbered by these painful experiences, displaces the former maternal body. As Susan Squier explains, 'science and technology have so rearranged the boundary conditions for the reproduction of human identity that the choice is no longer between the natural body and the culturally constructed body, but between different fields of bodily (re)construction bearing different social and cultural implications'.[19] Therefore, alongside reproductive technology, maternity is reconstructed and reconceived as neither entirely natural nor cultural. It is no longer simply a biological imperative, and this passage acknowledges both physical and metaphysical aspects of fertility. It redirects the reader's focus to the maternal body rather than a potential foetus's body or the male body, as it is in fact dead.

While physical sterility indicates an inability to conceive naturally, to carry or give birth to a healthy and viable foetus, one could argue that psychological sterility indicates an inability to conceive of motherhood whether it be natural or not. Therefore, our protagonist needs to address her psychological health to embody motherhood. She leaves her job to go to an institution: 'ce n'est qu'ensuite, en 2022, que j'ai dû me retirer tout à

18 Jean Laplanche and Jean-Bertrand Pontalis, *Vocabulaire de la psychanalyse* (Paris: PUF, 1967), 118.

19 Susan M. Squier, 'Reproducing the Posthuman Body: Ectogenetic Fetus, Surrogate Mother, Pregnant Man', in Judith Halberstam and Ira Livingston, eds, *Posthuman Bodies* (Bloomington and Indianapolis: Indiana University Press, 1995), 113–32, 119.

fait de mon travail, pour me reposer dans une institution' [Only then in 2022 did I have to retire completely from my work to rest in an institution] (225). While it is unclear whether she chooses to go to the institution voluntarily, she never mentions her work again. The perinatal period is a moment of transition, and this passage indicates that the narrator undergoes the psychological change typical of women who experience pregnancy and childbirth. The narrator takes the role of motherhood seriously, and this in turn challenges the reader to reconceive of the maternal body as more than physical. 'Mon mari le clone' permits the reader to deconstruct the oppressive norm of the maternal body as only biological or physical and to rebuild it in a more holistic way.

When she leaves the institution, she describes her life in 2022: 'j'avais alors cinquante-trois ans. Les médecins, découragés par les progrès trop lents et les nombreux scandales liés aux décongélations ratées, m'ont rendu le corps, en m'adressant à une société de clonage' [I was then 53 years old. The doctors, discouraged by the progress taking too long and the numerous scandals linked to failed thawing, gave me the body while speaking to me about a cloning company] (225). The narrator carries out an intimate funeral with her husband's elderly mother, sister and a few close friends. Now, not only is absence masculine, presence is gynocentric as the female character is at the forefront, empowered and about to become a mother in spite of biological challenges.

The reproductive technology of cloning is also gynocentric. Glenn McGee remarks that '[i]t goes without saying that human cloning does not involve, or need to involve, sexual intercourse. As one probes the seeming asexuality of cloning, one is initially drawn to the metaphors that feed and follow the asexual nature of technology'.[20] Again, our protagonist is uncoupled, and cloning permits her to become a mother despite the lack of sexual reproduction. Furthermore, '[c]loning does not pose a unique challenge, but it has called attention to the vast array of new technologies that make new kinds of families whose parameters and relationships are neither pregiven nor socially sanctioned'.[21] Many feminists argue that

20 Glen McGee, 'Cloning, Sex, and New Kinds of Families', *The Journal of Sex Research* 37/3 (2000), 266–72, 266.

21 McGee, 'Cloning, Sex, and New Kinds of Families', 271.

various forms of reproductive technology, particularly in vitro fertilization, reinforce the definition of motherhood as a biological imperative rather a social relationship.[22] The protagonist's journey to motherhood contradicts this argument, as the reproductive technology of cloning enables her to become a single mother without conception and in spite of her age. 'Mon mari le clone' thus destabilizes normative models of motherhood as a biological relationship between mother and child carried out through a gendered division of parental labour at a 'natural' stage in life by a woman.

When her husband's clone is born, the protagonist's description reveals that it is as if he has been frozen in time while she has continued to age. The narrator describes seeing her husband's clone for the first time:

> Taillé dans ses trente ans comme dans du marbre, [...] il avait des paupières d'enfant, bleutées et translucides, et des lèvres roses que leur longue immobilité dotait d'une jeunesse surnaturelle; comme s'il n'avait ni trente ans, ni évidemment cinquante, mais aucun âge; comme si le gel l'avait retiré dans ces landes d'avant-naissance où l'on déambule, pensif, dans un corps d'air et de lumière.
>
> [Carved from his thirties like from marble, [...] he had the eyelids of a child, bluish and translucid, and pink lips whose lengthy inactivity provided a supernatural youth; as if he was neither thirty years old nor fifty years old, but ageless; as if the ice had pulled him out of the prenatal grasslands where one wanders, pensive, in a body of air and light] (225–6).

She insists on two things: his youth and his supernatural quality. His mother says that it seems like he will start speaking and will open his eyes, but what the reader discovers is that his body is merely a shell for a newborn version of the narrator's husband. He must start anew. '[L]'individu, à l'arrivée, est en bien meilleure santé, comme neuf, et prêt à repartir de zéro' [upon arrival, the individual was in better health, like new, and ready to start again from zero] (227). Her body ages, and perhaps she is not 'fertile' in the traditional sense, but she redefines fertility in becoming a mother post-menopause. The 'individu' [individual] could also refer to her, as her husband's rebirth parallels her own new beginning as a mother

22 Judy Wajcman, *Feminism Confronts Technology* (University Park: The Pennsylvania State University Press, 1991), 57.

with a new bodily landscape which may nurture and raise a child without being biologically pregnant.

Unlike the failings of cryogenics, the cloning and surrogacy processes are painless since the cloning company takes care of the following steps: 'choix d'une mère porteuse, frais médicaux, certificats, etc.' [choice of a surrogate, medical expenses, certificates, etc.] (226). Of course, this is not the case in the 2020s in France outside the literary world: 'Surrogacy is outlawed in France, however, because French law forbids persons to sell their body parts.'[23] In Darrieussecq's short story, the French government offers public assistance which allows each mother to 'y trouver son compte' [have her needs met] (226). The cloning company helps the narrator avoid the difficult administrative process of finding a surrogate mother and dealing with medical expenses. The narrator emphasizes the complexity of the cloning process, which has been perfected after progressing from analogical to digital DNA sequencing completed *in extenso* after many errors and the existing issue of the time difference. This means that mothers have the absolute certainty of ending up with the same individual in good health and like new based on the sheer intensity and length of the scientific process (226–7).

For the narrator, the situation is ideal, but she disagrees with one of her best friends who chooses to become pregnant with her own husband's clone. The narrator distinguishes between herself and her friend by clarifying that her friend is non-menopausal, but this choice bothers our narrator who normally considers herself to be open-minded. While she seeks to overcome binaries through her own experience with motherhood, she reinforces them by expressing her discomfort with her friend's pregnancy. She is unable to differentiate between hers and her friend's cloning experiences and instead posits her own experience as somehow more justified for reasons to do with her age. She loses contact with her friend. This recalls two questions posed by Ferrando regarding our perception of the human body in the posthuman era: 'Will gender, race, age and class among others,

23 Sandra Reineke, 'In Vitro Veritas: New Reproductive and Genetic Technologies and Women's Rights in Contemporary France', *International Journal of Feminist Approaches to Bioethics* 1/1 (2008), 91–125, 95.

represent significant categories of reformulation? More radically, from a futuristic perspective: will posthumans need any embodiment at all?'[24]

While these categories imply boundaries or dichotomies, such as old/young, menopausal/non-menopausal, pregnant/non-pregnant, 'Mon mari le clone' presents different definitions of the motherly body which transcend these restrictive bodily norms. Although, the narrator is not pregnant in the sense of carrying a developing child, she does undergo a pregnant moment in her life. The cloning incubation period lasts nine months, during which time the narrator says she has time to get used to the idea. During these nine months, the narrator researches classes on child development, looks for the best breast milk and a childcare centre (227). The narrator thus offers a different example of a motherly body, as an expectant mother who prepares her surroundings for the arrival of a child who, while not carried by her own body, will be her physical and emotional responsibility.

The narrator finishes her story by describing her husband/son's upbringing: 'aujourd'hui Jean-Jacques se porte bien. Il va sur ses huit ans. Il joue du piano, a commencé le tennis, travaille correctement à l'école. Nous nous promenons souvent au square' [today Jean-Jacques is doing well. He is going to be 8 years old. He plays piano, started playing tennis and works properly at school. We walk often to the square.] (227). The name 'Jean-Jacques' recalls Jean-Jacques Rousseau and his *Discours sur l'origine et les fondements de l'inégalité parmi les hommes* [*Discourse on the Origin and Basis of Ineqaulity Among Men*] (1754). Rousseau argued that it is society which corrupts Man, otherwise free, moral and uncorrupted by society while in the state of nature.

While one could argue that society, by means of the patriarchy and capitalism, manipulates and controls the female body through technology, 'Mon mari le clone' challenges this narrative that nature and culture are separate and that one should be placed above another, through a non-normalized representation of a maternal body. At first, the narrator tries to raise Jean-Jacques like his mother and sister suggest, but she disapproves of certain aspects of his original, bourgeois upbringing, such as voting for right-wing political parties. This recalls a hierarchical relationship, in

24 Ferrando, 'The Body', 149.

which men of the bourgeoisie achieved many of the political, educational and economic rights that women were still denied. She finds that raising him the same way as his mother did would contradict his views as a young man in his 20s, when they first met, when he also began voting leftist. She admits to feeling disoriented, as she met her husband after his formative years and has to guess the steps to his development and upbringing. She cannot reproduce exactly some of her husband's already lived experiences. Finally, she points out that no one can anticipate the long-term effects of cryogenics and cloning.

For the narrator, motherhood is a process, and through the creative process of writing, Darrieussecq reveals women as processes themselves. By exposing the supposed oppositions that exist, like femininity and masculinity, she does not rely on simple, traditional dualities. She shows the reader a female subject who is perpetually evolving, one who is not quantitative and evolves in tandem with another subject (her husband-turned child) as he also evolves.

'Mon mari le clone' challenges the reader to rethink their definitions of and attitudes towards motherhood, pregnancy and reproductive technology as they relate to the female body. The narrator gives us her own account of the events which led to motherhood *in extenso*, with cloning, and in spite of the limited definition of infertility before its implementation. One can question the role of natural conception, or conception at all, as essential to motherhood. In this vein, the female body of the narrator serves as a posthuman model, as it 'interrogat[es] what it means to be human in digital age' and 'doesn't necessarily want to leave the body behind'.[25] More specifically, it interrogates what it means to be a woman and a mother. How will the reader make use of what Darrieussecq calls our 'internal landscape' to act upon our ['external landscape']?[26] 'Mon mari le clone' enables the reader to imagine how the female body and motherhood are changing and *can* change to better represent the posthuman, female subject.

25 Kim Toffoletti, *Cyborgs and Barbie Dolls: Feminism, Popular Culture and the Posthuman Body* (New York and London: I.B. Tauris, 2007), 12–13.

26 Marie-Claire Barnet, Shirley Jordan and Marie Darrieussecq, 'Entretien avec Marie Darrieussecq', *Dalhousie French Studies* 93 (2010), 123–9, 127.

Bibliography

Åsberg, Cecilia, 'Feminist Posthumanities', in Rosi Braidotti and Maria Hlavajova, eds, *Posthuman Glossary* (New York and London: Bloomsbury, 2018), 157–60.

ASRM and SART, 'FAQS for Patients Related to COVID-19' (9 April 2020), <https://www.asrm.org/news-and-publications/news-and-research/announcements/FAQs-Related-to-COVID-19/>, accessed 9 April 2020.

Barnet, Marie-Claire, Shirley Jordan and Marie Darrieussecq, 'Entretien avec Marie Darrieussecq', *Dalhousie French Studies* 93 (2010), 123–9.

Darrieussecq, Marie, *Zoo* (Paris: P.O.L., 2006).

D'Eaubonne, Françoise, *Le Féminisme ou la mort* (Paris: Pierre Horay, 1974).

Ferrando, Francesca, 'The Body', in Robert Ranisch and Stefan Lorenz Sorgner, eds, *Post- and Transhumanism: An Introduction* (Frankfurt am Main: Peter Lang, 2014), 149–62.

Foulkes, David, *Dreaming: A Cognitive-Psychological Analysis* (Hillsdale, NJ: L. Erlbaum Associates, 1985).

Giménez, Martha E., *Marx, Women, and Capitalist Social Reproduction* (Leiden: Koninklijke, 2019).

Haraway, Donna Jeanne, *Simians, Cyborgs, and Women: The Reinvention of Nature* (New York: Routledge, 1991).

Lambeth, John, and Marie Darrieussecq, 'Entretien avec Marie Darrieussecq', *The French Review* 79/4 (2006), 806–18.

Laplanche, Jean, and Jean-Bertrand Pontalis, *Vocabulaire de la psychanalyse* (Paris: PUF, 1967).

Mack, Michael, *Contaminations: Beyond Dialetics in Modern Literature, Science and Film* (Edinburgh: Edinburgh University Press, 2016).

Marx, Karl, *Capital* (New York: Vintage Books, 1977).

Marx, Karl, and Frederick Engels, *Manifesto of the Communist Party* (Chicago: Charles H. Kerry & Company, 1888).

McGee, Glen, 'Cloning, Sex, and New Kinds of Families', *The Journal of Sex Research* 37/3 (2000), 266–72.

Reineke, Sandra, 'In Vitro Veritas: New Reproductive and Genetic Technologies and Women's Rights in Contemporary France', *International Journal of Feminist Approaches to Bioethics* 1/1 (2008), 91–125.

Rowland, Robyn, *Living Laboratories: Women and Reproductive Technologies* (Bloomington and Indianapolis: Indiana University Press, 1992).

Squier, Susan M., 'Reproducing the Posthuman Body: Ectogenetic Fetus, Surrogate Mother, Pregnant Man', in Judith Halberstam and Ira Livingston, eds,

Posthuman Bodies (Bloomington and Indianapolis: Indiana University Press, 1995), 113–32.

Toffoletti, Kim, *Cyborgs and Barbie Dolls: Feminism, Popular Culture and the Posthuman Body* (New York and London: I.B. Tauris, 2007).

Wajcman, Judy, *Feminism Confronts Technology* (University Park: The Pennsylvania State University Press, 1991).

Yeatman, Anna, 'Feminism and the Technological Age', *Australian Feminist Studies* 29/79 (2014), 85–100.

VANESSA LEE

5 The Female Body in the Plays of French Caribbean Women Writers

Introduction

In her work on gender and theatre, Alisa Solomon writes that:

> The mutability of human identity promised by theater [...] is precisely what makes theater the queerest art, perennially subject to railing by those with a stake in promoting the 'natural order' of the status quo.[1]

Postcolonial, and specifically Caribbean, theatre has at its core the objective to question the social and societal status quo. Postcolonial theatre, like other postcolonial arts and theory, revisits, interrogates and critiques the colonial past and postcolonial present. It may take the form of a rejection of former colonizers' theatrical conventions, an articulation of anticolonial thought, and even the merging of colonized and colonizer theatrical practices to create a new dramatic form.

In the context of Caribbean theatre, syncretic and pluralistic performance forms are often employed to question, critique, or even subvert social realities, historical events, and postcolonial and neo-colonial contexts. Although not 'postcolonial' in a literal, geopolitical sense, since they remain French possessions, the French overseas territories in the Caribbean are postcolonial in that they have experienced the colonialist moment and share with other postcolonial nations the trauma of slavery and colonialism, and a cultural, geographical and historical proximity to independent

1 Alisa Solomon, *Re-dressing the Canon: Essays on Theater and Gender* (London and New York: Routledge, 2005), 2.

Caribbean nations that has fostered a frequently defiant attitude towards the French metropole. French Caribbean authors have greatly contributed to the formation of postcolonial artistic genres, including theatre. The contribution of women writers to French Caribbean drama has been significant, even though the study of their works has been insufficient, leaving much to be developed.[2]

The question of the representation of the female colonized body has gained much traction over the past decade.[3] Combining gender studies and postcolonial theatre analysis can be particularly fruitful, as both disciplines question socially, historically and culturally established norms. As Helen Gilbert and Joanne Tompkins point out, '[f]or many postcolonial dramatists, particularly women, a parallel project is to recuperate female subjectivities while showing that gender is an ideology mapped across the body in and through representation.'[4] This chapter analyses the various dramatic devices employed by French Caribbean women writers to explore, criticize and re-articulate the representation of the female Caribbean body.

In the Caribbean context, women writers, including dramatists, regularly denounce the exoticization and eroticization of the Caribbean female body. These ways of seeing still shape and dominate the perception of women from former French colonies today, so much so, that these representations have been normalized both in former colonized and colonizer societies. Theatre is an ideal vector through which Caribbean women writers challenge such exotic and gendered stereotypes, as it permits not only the voicing, but also the embodiment of Caribbean women's experiences. The female body on stage is also shown as plural and changeable. Plural, because the plays depict a wide range of female characters. Changeable, since a character may move between different ages and

2 See the work of Stéphanie Bérard, Sylvie Chalaye, Françoise Kourilsky, Christiane Makward, Emily Sahakian, Alvina Ruprecht.

3 See studies by Pascal Blanchard, Jacqueline Couti, Félix Germain and Silyane Larcher.

4 Helen Gilbert and Joanne Tompkins, *Post-colonial Drama: Theory, Practice, Politics* (London and New York: Routledge, 1996), 212.

conditions, and actors may play characters younger and older than themselves, establishing a transgenerational link between spectator, actor and character that may underline common concerns shared by different generations of Caribbean women.

The authors analysed in this chapter are the Martinicans Ina Césaire and Suzanne Dracius. Born in 1942, Ina Césaire is an ethnographer by profession. Her anthropological training and research have inspired many of her writings. She is particularly interested in oral literatures and the transmission of cultural forms through orality. Her twenty-two plays cover a multitude of themes, spaces and timeframes related to Martinican local history, and there is an emphasis on women's issues, such as motherhood, sexuality, women's agency and women's position in society. Her works have been performed in the United States, the Caribbean and mainland France. Suzanne Dracius, born in 1951, is an equally well-established Martinican writer. Her literary creations include novels and poetry, and she has also written scholarly articles on French Caribbean writing and art. Excluding Aimé Césaire, she is the only Martinican to be made an honorary member of the American Association of Teachers of French (AATF). Her works focus on the female experience in the Caribbean, issues of Caribbean identity and the politics of diaspora.

This chapter investigates stereotypical representations and norms of Caribbean femininity as depicted in Césaire's *La Poupée ashanti* [*The Ashanti Doll*] (2008). It also analyses Dracius's *Lumina Sophie dite Surprise* [*Lumina Sophie Known As Surprise*] (1996), interrogating methods employed in historical theatre to reclaim and embody the experiences of female historical figures. The chapter also discusses Césaire's play *Mémoires d'île* [*Island Memories*] (1983), questioning how embodied remembrance facilitates the sharing of memories and experiences across different generations of Caribbean women, on and off stage. Each of these plays is an ideal example of the contestation and problematizing of bodily and gendered norms in contemporary society, historical narrative and transgenerational debate. There is also a heavy emphasis on physicality in each play, with a use of physical movement and performance forms to express the physical and mental emancipation of women and to create a link between women, actors and audiences of different generations.

Stereotypes of Caribbean Femininity on Stage in Ina Césaire's *La Poupée ashanti*

While many gendered stereotypes that still fuel Western and French metropolitan imaginaries about Caribbean women hark back to the colonial and slave pasts of Caribbean society, it has been argued that even local male intellectuals and artists perpetuate what Richard Price and Sally Price call the 'routine sexism of Martiniquan daily life':

> Men, backed by a relatively complicitous silence from most female Martiniquans, regularly relegate women to a non-productive domestic sphere, as mothers and sexual partners, by denying them entry into such areas of authority as historical knowledge, political power, cultural interpretation, or public literary creativity.[5]

'Mothers or sexual partners', or the matriarch and the seductress, are the two stereotyped categories into which Caribbean women fall. Both have their origins in colonial history. On the slave plantations, enslaved women were sexually coveted by the owners and overseers, and in colonial contexts more broadly female colonized bodies were sites of struggle between male colonizers and colonized. As Emily Sahakian puts it, 'the insult – that enslaved women chose white men and betrayed black men – is a common, albeit often unspoken trope in the French Caribbean', and has led to the perpetuation of the trope of the lascivious and traitorous seductress.[6] The figure of the steadfast long-suffering mother also developed in the slave plantation system, which forbade the formation of stable family units; men were sold off with the women left to raise children who could, in turn, be sold. From this developed the 'ubiquitous image of the courageous French Caribbean woman, who is devoted to her children whom she raises in the absence of a reliable father'.[7] These stereotypes continue

5 Richard Price and Sally Price, 'Shadow-boxing in the Mangrove', *Cultural Anthropology* 12/1 (1997), 3–36, 16.

6 Emily Sahakian, *Staging Creolization: Women's Theater and Performance from the French Caribbean* (Charlottesville: University of Virginia Press, 2017), 23.

7 Sahakian, *Staging Creolization: Women's Theater and Performance from the French Caribbean*, 24.

to underlie representations of black women in Caribbean and French societies as passive objects of desire or unfaltering sufferers.

Ina Césaire has written a number of plays that undermine residual stereotypes around Caribbean femininity. *La Poupée ashanti* is a work that merits particular focus since it deals directly with the seductress and the matriarch stereotypes. As of yet unperformed, but published in Christiane Makward's 2011 anthology of Césaire's plays, it tells the story of Edwige Magloire, a single mother who works as a prostitute, under the sobriquet Gloria, to pay for her daughter Victoire's medical school fees. Victoire is unaware of this, her mother making her believe she works as a cleaning lady in a hotel.[8]

La Poupée ashanti creates a 'critical engagement demanded of dramatic spectators [that] can trigger a parallel critical engagement with the world, and especially, women's place within in it'.[9] The play critically engages with the treatment of women in contemporary Martinican society. It therefore takes on a social dimension, since Edwige has limited choice in finding the means to raise her daughter as a working-class woman. She either has to remain home in the 'domestic' sphere as a mother, or fall into the role of the 'sexual partner' as a prostitute. The fact that Edwige hides her true profession from her daughter suggests she is ashamed of it, and so maintains this façade of the steadfast working-class mother. For financial reasons, however, Edwige is also obliged to prostitute herself to survive. But neither persona can ever be shown alongside the other, and so Edwige the mother, and Gloria the prostitute, are two separate performances she offers to two different audiences: her daughter and 'respectable' society on the one hand, and her clients and the group of marginals with whom she socializes on the other.

What is most intriguing about the fact that the same female character performs differing stereotypical roles associated with Caribbean femininity is that the transition between these two personas takes place on stage:

8 Ina Césaire, *La Poupée ashanti,* in Christiane P. Makward, ed., *Rosanie Soleil et autres textes dramatiques,* (Paris: Karthala, 2011), 347–69. All translations are my own unless otherwise noted.

9 Solomon, *Re-dressing the Canon: Essays on Theater and Gender*, 9.

> Elle ôte ses vertigineux escarpins et chausse de confortables sandales. [...] elle retire sa tenue et ses bijoux voyants, se démaquille, essuie toute trace de parfum et efface le vernis éclatant de ses ongles. [...] Elle enfile une ample blouse de ménagère et noue négligemment un foulard sombre sur ses cheveux déjà grisonnants. Elle termine sa transformation en enfilant d'épaisses lunettes d'écaille [...]
>
> [She removes her vertiginous heels and puts on comfortable sandals. She removes her outfit and garish jewellery, removes her makeup, and wipes off all trace of perfume and removes the bright varnish from her nails. She puts on an ample housecoat and nonchalantly wraps a dark scarf around her greying hair. She ends her transformation with a pair of thick horn-rimmed glasses.] (350)

Solomon argues that while some theatre 'may hide its artificiality from the audience', another kind seeks to explore the workings of femininity and 'just lets it hang out. And sometimes [...] brazenly parades around in its underwear'.[10] In *La Poupée ashanti*, Césaire lets it 'hang out', by having her protagonist undertake her transition between her two feminine personas on the stage. By showing the transition between personas, Césaire underlines the performativity, and therefore facticity, of each.

The move between the two personas is also a move between spaces. The gendered division of space often confines the female to inner and domestic spaces, while the male occupies outer and public domains. Edwige inhabits both inner and outer spaces, and as Mildred Mortimer describes it, moves 'toward empowerment by entering space from which indigenous patriarchs and European colonizers have excluded her, and establishing a new relationship to domestic space, characterized under patriarchy as a restrictive enclosure: she posits a liberating alternative space within it'.[11] The divide between domestic and public spaces is made apparent in *La Poupée ashanti* since it is coupled with specific representations of the type of 'woman' who inhabits each space. Edwige travels between spaces and does so in different guises. As Gloria, she frequents the 'Manicou bleu': '... bar miteux d'un quartier populaire de Fort de France' [a run-down bar in

10 Solomon, *Re-dressing the Canon: Essays on Theater and Gender*, 9.

11 Mildred Mortimer, *Writing from the Hearth: Public, Domestic, and Imaginative Space in Francophone Women's Fiction of Africa and the Caribbean* (Lanham and Plymouth: Lexington Books, 2007), x.

a working-class neighbourhood of Fort de France] (347). She even uses a room in the bar to change back into Edwige Magloire:

> … Gloria se dirige vers la petite salle attenante au bar. […] Devant une coiffeuse bancale surmontée d'un miroir éméché, très rapidement, elle retire sa tenue […] Elle se débarrasse de sa flamboyante chevelure postiche et range soigneusement le tout dans un placard mural.
>
> [Gloria moves over to the small room adjacent to the bar. At a lopsided dressing table upon which a scratched mirror, she very quickly removes her outfit. She takes off her garish wig and carefully stows everything away into a cupboard.] (350)

Edwige's other persona, the working mother, inhabits a very different, and domestic, space: 'maison d'Edwige Magloire. Elle pénètre sans hâte dans son salon désert […] Sur le buffet: un cadre photographique représentant un jeune couple souriant et leur petite fille'. [the house of Edwige Magloire. She enters slowly into a deserted living room. On the dresser: a photo frame containing the photograph of a young couple and their little girl.] (351).

Edwige's two personas allow her to inhabit these different spaces seamlessly. However, it is soon revealed that she is at ease in neither. The 'Manicou bleu' is at once familiar and unfamiliar. She has her place there, as much as the rest of the all-male clientele. Yet she does not interact with any of the other bar patrons. Gloria's fellow prostitute Shirley proffers the following explanation to this: 'nous autres, prostituées, nous sommes la classe la plus humiliée de la société. Même les pauvres nous méprisent, tandis que les riches marchent sur notre tête! [We prostitutes are the most humiliated group in society. Even the poor resent us, and the rich walk on our heads!]' (349) This antipathy towards prostitutes may be why none of the patrons ever spoke to Gloria before, and underlines the discriminations faced by women such as herself and Shirley as the most marginalized members of society.

The Edwige persona barely inhabits the home to which she returns each night. The housewife she plays is in itself a role that dissimulates her true character, her daughter not knowing anything about the real nature of her night work. Edwige's chameleonic travelling between different locations suggests that she may be free of her movements. She is neither fully herself, nor accepted for who she is, anywhere. The marginalization she experiences as a consequence of moving between spaces reveals the existence of such boundaries between public, professional and domestic, female and male space, and thus the increased agency she enjoys in crossing them.

Césaire foregrounds the complexities of the Martinican female condition in *La Poupée ashanti*. The female body is a canvas onto which different personas are projected, and thus interrogates the impermeability of stereotypes of Caribbean femininity. While the movement of the body between spaces subverts gendered binary oppositions relating to space, it also raises the question of female agency, for if Edwige can indeed move between spaces, she must do so in disguise. She remains marginalized, since she is not fully herself in either persona or space. The stage may be a 'liberating alternative space' in which to demonstrate the agency women gain by subverting stereotypes. However, this is not the case for Edwige. Edwige's difficult situation, despite her agency on stage, echoes the lived reality of contemporary Martinican women, who cannot escape such gendered discriminations. While stereotypes and spatial restrictions can be confounded on stage, much remains to be amended in social reality. Besides constituting a useful tool for the subversion and questioning of contemporary social norms, theatre has also been employed by Caribbean women writers to reassess historical narrative and reclaim women's voices from the past.

Staging the Historical Female Body in Suzanne Dracius's *Lumina Sophie dite Surprise* (1996)

Theatre is a particularly apt medium with which to explore history, and in particular silenced or marginalized histories. Indeed, in historical theatre not only is the past event performed 'live' on stage, but historical figures are also brought to life and put in a dialogue with the audience. This act is particularly important in a postcolonial context, and from a gender studies perspective, for theatre reclaims histories and experiences by representing them on stage. Theatre and performance are also contestatory media, which oppose, problematize and offer an alternative to the more 'prosaic' discipline of history seen from, and made in, the West.

Martinique and Guadeloupe, which are not constituted as independent nation-states, have to grapple with metropolitan history as well as their own, and thus theatre functions as a means of undermining the construct of the French state and its institutions. By using art forms born of what Édouard Glissant terms the 'tormented chronology' of the French Caribbean, French Caribbean theatre both questions official narratives as well as provides a voice for a community confined to the margins.[12] A number of Caribbean writers have written historical plays that reappraise the history of the Caribbean and other postcolonial nations.[13] While plays by female authors depict both female and male historical figures, the protagonists of historical works by male Caribbean authors have tended to be male.

In official local histories, there is little trace of the role women have played in the construction of the French Caribbean. This role is even less visible in the French national historical narrative. And yet, women did indeed play a major part in forging French Caribbean society. Women assumed key roles in Caribbean historical events such as the Insurrection of Southern Martinique in 1870 – the first major people's uprising since the abolition of slavery in 1848.

The event and the women involved in it inspired plays by both Césaire and Dracius.[14] Dracius's play *Lumina Sophie dite Surprise* (1996), recounts

12 Édouard Glissant, *Le Discours antillais* (Paris: Seuil, 1981), 133.

13 See, for example: Aimé Césaire's triptych of plays exploring the politics of decolonization: *La Tragédie du roi Christophe* (1963); *Une saison au Congo* (1966); *Une tempête* (1969).

Maryse Condé's *An Tan Révolysion: elle court, elle court, la liberté* (1989), relating events ranging from the French and Haitian revolutions to the first abolition, and then the reinstatement, of slavery in Guadeloupe.

Patrick Chamoiseau's *Man Dlo contre la Fée Carabosses* (1981), an allegory of slavery and colonialism told in the form of a *conte*.

Ina Césaire has also written several plays on local Caribbean history, see Makward's *Rosanie Soleil et autres textes dramatiques* (Paris: Karthala, 2011).

14 See also Ina Césaire's play *Rosanie Soleil* (1992). Its protagonist Rosanie Soleil also appears in *Lumina Sophie dite Surprise* under the name 'Rosalie'. Rosanie is presented alongside three other women: her twin sister Eïsanor, her mother Mme

the final days of its eponymous heroine. Born Marie-Philomène Roptus, Lumina was a 19-year-old pregnant seamstress who became the leader of a group of *pétroleuses*, female arsonists tasked with burning down plantations during the Insurrection. After the Insurrection was quelled, Lumina was arrested, tried and imprisoned in Saint-Laurent de Maroni in French Guyana where she died nine years later. Lumina has been the subject of popular songs, two secondary schools bear her name, one in Martinique and the other in French Guyana, while a skyscraper in Fort-de-France was also named after her.[15] She is defined by Dracius as the equivalent to, and the opposite of, the French metropolitan Joan of Arc: black and pregnant as opposed to white and virginal. The figure of Lumina thus represents another Martinican singularity differentiating the region from the metropole.

Lumina Sophie dite Surprise is significant in that it narrates the lives of women involved in the event. The play gives them more substance than do court transcripts and the occasional historical pamphlet on the Insurrection.[16] Above all, for Dracius, theatre allows a lost female historical figure to find her voice through her embodiment by a flesh-and-blood actress who resuscitates the character from 'the limbo of oblivion and misogynous denial'.[17] In resuscitating these women, Dracius above all confers on them personalities, individuality and subjecthood. Indeed, the lack of official historical information, which may be seen as an obstacle in portraying the historical character, is used here as grounds for invention exploited by Dracius to create complex and new characters.

Beyond the single historical figure of Lumina, in *Lumina Sophie dite Surprise* there is also an emphasis on the collective representation of the

---

Soleil, and their neighbour Voisine Fumée. Unlike Dracius's play, it is set in the days leading up to the Insurrection, and focusses on a smaller group of women.

15 Songs about Lumina Sophie: *Lumina* by Loriane Zacharie, and *Lumina Sophie* by Mizik Bo Kail.

The schools 'Lycée Polyvalent Lumina Sophie' in Saint-Laurent du Maroni, French Guyana and 'Lycée Professionnel Régional Lumina Sophie' in Martinique, bear her name. The 'Tour Lumina' in Fort-de-France was inaugurated in 2012.

16 See works by Lémy Lémane Coco, Gilbert Pago, Dominique Taffin, Muriel Descas-Ravoteur and Micheline Marlin-Godier.

17 Axel Artheron, 'Suzanne Dracius: le "carrefour" du théâtre pour se hisser au- dessus du magma de l'humaine marchandise', *Africultures* 80–81/1 (2010), 224–30, 224.

historical event. Lumina Sophie is, as Axel Artheron points out, a 'symbol of the female rebels, but also [...] a metonymy of that rebellion'.[18] Yet, to underline the significance of the role in the Insurrection of several women, rather than that of a single woman, and by extension the significance of women in society as a whole, particular importance is granted to the Chorus of *Pétroleuses*. This is one of several references to Ancient Greek drama and culture in the play. In Ancient Greek drama, the Chorus represents 'la voix du peuple, [et] la sagesse populaire, immémoriale [the voice of the people and popular, immemorial wisdom]', and is often made up of members of the protagonist's society, just as the Chorus in this play is made up of Lumina's fellow Insurgents, local women who bring with them the performance traditions of their local space, namely dance, singing and storytelling.[19]

In postcolonial theatre, the actor's 'body's ability to move, cover up, reveal itself, and even "fracture" on stage provides it with many possible sites for decolonization'.[20] This is made apparent in *Lumina Sophie dite Surprise* through the extensive usage of dancing and choral movement. Dance and choral movement perform multiple functions in the play. Dance is often performed as a defensive mechanism, with moves from traditional war dances *laghia* and *danmyé*. These dances, as Patrick Chamoiseau tells us, arose from the slaves' reclaiming of their bodies and their subjecthood: 'Through the rhythms, the person suffocated in the slave emerges.'[21] And so, the *Pétroleuses* demonstrate that they are capable of defending and expressing themselves through these dance sequences.

The *Pétroleuses*' use of movement contrasts with writing as record-keeping and conveyor of memory. Dracius's play proposes that there are other means of commemorating and recording historical figures, particularly those that have been marginalized and erased from official and colonial histories. This is made even more apparent in the play's final scene, which depicts a battle between the *Pétroleuses* and government militia. The *Pétroleuses* fall dead one by one, to then rise and stand on an 'autre scène

18 Axel Artheron, 'Propos liminaire' in Suzanne Dracius, *Lumina Sophie dite Surprise* (Paris: Idem, 2014), 21.

19 Dracius, interview with the author, Paris, 27 December 2015.

20 Gilbert and Tompkins, 204.

21 Patrick Chamoiseau, *Écrire en pays dominé* (Paris: Flammarion, 2002), 172.

de l'Histoire [another stage of History]' where the Muse, a supernatural being, proceeds to narrate the Epilogue that outlines the events following the Insurrection and Lumina's fate.[22] This 'other stage' is that of official history. The Muse's final, monotonous speech contrasts with the energy and liveliness exhibited by the *Pétroleuses* in the rest of the play, and also contrasts theatre with more didactic genres. Despite the monotony of the speech, Dracius reinstates the story of the *Pétroleuses* into official history. However, the author also reverses the roles of theatre and historical writing, and the more objective genre comes at the end of the play, as a complement. The play is not to be understood as a footnote to be added to the history of the Insurrection, but in its own right, as a free-standing account of the events. The *Pétroleuses* have inscribed their own subjectivity into historical narrative, just as 'the post-colonial body disrupts the constrained space and signification left to it by the colonizers and becomes a site for resistant inscription.'[23]

Individual voices emerge in Dracius's play from the collective Chorus. The Ancient Greek Chorus 'gradually gave form to individualized characters, after the leader of the chorus (*exarchôn*) had established the main actor, who gradually began to imitate an action.'[24] Thus, the use of a Chorus in *Lumina Sophie dite Surprise* also allows the individuation of other characters in addition to Lumina, who symbolize different types of women involved in the Insurrection. One such character is Simonise, who is also a *conteuse*, a storyteller, a role usually performed by a man in the Caribbean context. Despite the existence of a female-led tradition of *conte* in French literature, the oral storytelling tradition in the Caribbean is for the most part upheld by male practitioners. This negligence of the role of women is one of what Pascale de Souza describes as 'two antithetical sides of the Antillean *conte*'; the other being that the *conte* constitutes a means for 'an oppressed culture to express its need for autonomy, to oppose itself to

22 Suzanne Dracius, *Lumina Sophie dite Surprise* (Paris: Idem, 2014), 145.

23 Gilbert and Tompkins, 204.

24 Patrice Pavis, *Dictionary of the Theatre: Terms, Concepts, Analysis,* tr. Christine Shantz (Toronto and Buffalo: University of Toronto Press 1996), 53.

its colonial heritage of humility and endurance'.[25] This against-the-grain feminization of the *conte*'s narratorial voice in *Lumina Sophie dite Surprise* allows women who contributed to the Insurrection to participate directly in this traditional artistic form of social criticism.

Simonise's *contes* adhere to the genre's codes; opening and closing phrases, audience interaction, sound effects and movement. However, the format is reappropriated to relate women's experiences. Simonise narrates two *contes*, the first about abuses inflicted on female plantation workers by the white overseers, and the second about similar abuses perpetrated by men of the *Pétroleuses*'s own class. In the first *conte*, explicit gestures illustrate the trauma of physical abuse inflicted on female plantation workers. For instance, Simonise leads her fellow Chorus-members in a dance punctuated by hip thrusts. This dance, which accompanies her tale, symbolizes the violation of women's bodies by the overseers: 'il sait te flanquer du piquant à tout bout de champ. Un instant d'épuisement? PIQUANT! Tu essuies ta sueur? PIQUANT! Tu t'isoles pour uriner? PIQUANT! [he knows when to give you a good poking at all times. A moment of fatigue? POKE! Wiping off your sweat? POKE! Finding a quiet place to urinate? POKE?]' (75) The physical reality and violence of abuse are emphasized through these movements, which also permit the exorcizing of the trauma experienced by generations of women workers, including the characters portrayed on stage.

Each *conte* ends with these respective formulae 'tout ceci n'est pas un conte [all this is not a tale] and 'récit véridique: j'ai assisté à la scène. [true story: I witnessed the scene.]' (133) This technique is used by *conteurs* to certify their authority as narrator of the *conte*. Yet in the case of these *conte*, the statements can be taken at face value in order to highlight their veracity. Most *contes* in the French Caribbean are social critiques that relate the struggles of the storyteller's contemporaries or even of their ancestors during the colonial and slave periods. This often occurs through the use of allegory, with, for instance, the use of animals to represent different character types or the setting of the story in the fantasy world of the *conte*. The

25 Pascale De Souza, 'Discours carnavalesque chez Ina Césaire: déferler les *Mémoires d'Iles*', *Œuvres et critiques* 26.1 (2001), 122–33, 124.

narratives in *Lumina Sophie dite Surprise* do not make use of such devices and are thus troublingly realistic.

Historical theatre not only permits the voicing orally of alternative- and counter-narratives to official, Western, mainstream histories, it also resuscitates the speakers of those histories. Dracius's play uses multiple Caribbean performance forms to allow the reintroduction of local women's histories within the French and French Caribbean public spheres. Each performance style is adapted to convey female experiences and concerns. Showing the female community on stage evokes the possibility of the revisioning of history and the status of women in society off stage.

Transgenerational Embodied Remembrance

Addressing history and memory on stage is a means of both expressing and asserting marginalized voices. In Caribbean societies, this remembrance is both oral and physical, and can be found in historical plays such as *Lumina Sophie dite Surprise*. But how can Caribbean artforms used in plays set in more contemporary settings create a transgenerational connection between women of different ages and experiences? The manuscript and production history of Ina Césaire's *Mémoires d'île* are of particular use in exploring these questions.[26] First performed in 1983 in a production directed by Jean-Claude Penchenat and featuring Myrrha Donzenac and Mariann Mathéus, the play is a dialogue between two ageing women inspired by Césaire's maternal and paternal grandmothers. They exchange anecdotes and memories of their lives in early to mid-twentieth-century Martinique. The first production team of *Mémoires*

26 First performance directed by Jean-Claude Penchenat, at Théâtre du Campagnol, Bagneux, as *Mémoires d'isles: Maman N. et Maman F.* (April 1983).

First edition: Ina Césaire, *Mémoires d'isles: Maman N. et Maman F.* (Paris: Caribéennes, 1985).

Second edition: Mémoires d'île, Maman N. et Maman F. in Makward, ed., *Rosanie Soleil et autres textes dramatiques*, 199–228.

d'île employed multiple devices to convey efficiently the lives of the play's two elderly female characters, including non-verbal performance techniques such as movement, dance and mime.

The play foregrounds the subversive potential of representations of the female Caribbean body. In the Prologue, this is achieved through Caribbean carnival dances. Both actresses are dressed as *diablesse* figures from Caribbean myth, 'dangerous and maleficent creatures from the oral tradition who seduce men to lead them to their deaths'.[27] They perform the traditional *vidé* dance defined by Gilbert and Tompkins as demonstrative of the liberating potential of Carnival dance, 'displaying at the same time a delight in transgressive sexuality and excessive corporeal states'.[28] As Stéphanie Bérard points out, it also liberates women's agency by announcing 'the coming of the reign of women: it presages Aure and Hermance's seizing power in the second half of the play: indeed, these two strong French Caribbean female personalities symbolize emancipation and independence'.[29] Césaire thus uses the controversial *diablesse* figure to empower the female protagonists, and, on another level, to empower the actresses who perform them.

As Richard Gough and Nanako Nakajima write, 'the female dancing body is a space where past, present and, it is hoped, future meet and empowers women to love their own historical bodies and dance for themselves'.[30] This meeting of 'past, future and present' is ushered in by the *diablesses*' enigmatic dialogue in the Prologue. One *diablesse* utters: 'je serai jeune [I shall be young]', and the other: 'j'ai été vieille [I was old]' (203). This abolishing of temporal linearity ushers the actresses and characters into a space in which past and present cohabit. This permits the actresses, particularly those who are younger than the characters they perform, to transition into the characters of the elderly protagonists. The *diablesses*' dance was instrumental for the actresses Myrrha Donzenac and Mariann

27 Stéphanie Bérard, *Théâtres des Antilles: Traditions et scènes contemporaines* (Paris: L'Harmattan, 2009), 159.

28 Gilbert and Tompkins, 86.

29 Bérard, *Théâtres des Antilles,* 159.

30 Richard Gough, and Nanako Nakajima 'On Ageing (& Beyond)', *Performance Research* 24/3 (2019), 1–8, 5.

Mathéus, who performed in the first production of the play. The dance allowed them to inhabit the roles of Aure and Hermance. Césaire explains:

> I thought that it would be helpful for them to use this *diablesse* symbol from carnival, a symbol of the negation of death and old age. I also wanted to bring out the inner youth of old French Caribbean women. They have such vitality and such remarkable freshness of mind.[31]

Having the same actresses play both the roles of the carnivalesque *diablesses* and the elderly ladies is another subversive element to the characters of Aure and Hermance. The older woman is a key figure in Caribbean narratives, and 'ensures family continuity and the group's cultural coherence'.[32] The *diablesse* is a timeless figure who represents 'toutes les angoisses et tous les poncifs liés à la féminité' [all the anxieties and stereotypes about femininity].[33] Césaire emphasizes the key roles played by both real and mythical female figures in the collective imaginaries of the Caribbean people, showing that 'a *Diablesse* always hides beneath the surface'.[34] Behind each stereotyped woman hides a subversive figure. Indeed, throughout the rest of the play, after the *diablesses's* transformation into Aure and Hermance, the audience knows that behind them hides a *diablesse* and that the transgressive nature of the Carnival may resurface at any time. Nothing is safe from the disturbance of the norm that is the Carnival, not even gendered stereotypes.

Donzenac and Mathéus's immersion into the characters of Aure and Hermance was also achieved through the actresses' own improvisations in the rehearsal process. A process of 'embodied remembrance' redolent of Chamoiseau's vision of dance as a means of retrieving ancestral modes of performance and expression, which entails 'unknotting the body through

31 Suzanne Houyoux, 'Un entretien avec Ina Césaire, Fort-de-France, Martinique, 5 juin 1990' in *Elles écrivent des Antilles (Haïti, Guadeloupe, Martinique)* (Paris: L'Harmattan, 1997), 349–60, 355–6.

32 Kathleen Gyssels, *Filles de solitude. Essai sur l'identité antillaise dans les (auto-) biographies fictives de Simone et André Schwarz-Bart* (Paris: L'Harmattan 1996), 65.

33 Césaire, in Makward, ed., *Rosanie Soleil et autres textes dramatiques*, 23.

34 De Souza, 'Discours carnavalesque chez Ina Césaire', 130.

improvisations'.[35] This embodied memory is at work in the Carnival *vidé* the two *diablesses* perform in the Prologue, which has been preserved in published editions of the play as a guide for future performers. But Donzenac and Mathéus were also inspired by other local performance forms to develop their characters. Sahakian recounts that Mathéus drew on her training as a singer and her memories of 'balls she attended as a young woman' to embody 'Hermance's fierce spirit, coupled with the daily physical pains near the end of a long, laborious life, by dancing an immobile dance from her chair, with her aching leg up on a stool'.[36] In addition, it is said that 'to substantiate her role as Hermance Mathéus drew inspiration from multiple testimonies of French Caribbean women she herself had collected, which included an interview with Césaire's paternal grandmother.[37] This whole process suggests a proximity that goes beyond an awareness of the characters' stories and histories. The actresses had had similar experiences of local artistic and cultural practices as the women of Aure and Hermance's generation, which drew the different generations together.

The inspiration of Caribbean performance forms allowed the production team of *Mémoires d'île* to create characters that could communicate to local audiences through a shared knowledge of cultural practices. The process was instrumental in facilitating the younger actresses to establish a link to the older generations they were expected to embody. It established a connection between Caribbean women of different ages and generations, visible on stage but also physically palpable in the persons of the actresses themselves.

35 Chamoiseau, *Écrire en pays dominé,* 171.

36 Sahakian, *Staging Creolization,* 74.

37 Sahakian, *Staging Creolization,* 75.

See also Mariann Mathéus, 'De l'oralité au théâtre: l'exemple de Berthilia pour le personnage d'Hermance dans Mémoires d'Isles d'Ina Césaire', *Africultures*, <http://africultures.com/de-loralite-au-theatre-lexemple-de-berthilia-pour-le-personnage-dhermance-dans-memoires-disles-dina-cesaire-12419/?utm_source=newsletter&utm_medium=email&utm_campaign=466>, accessed 24 April 2020.

Conclusion

In their plays, Césaire and Dracius exploit the many different ways in which the female Caribbean body can become a site of contestation, debate, and dialogue on stage: from transitions between personas and characters, to the expression and embodiment of marginalized voices, to the crossing of gendered spatial boundaries problematized by the ephemeral space of theatre. In each play, the body is a site which questions the status quo, be it stereotypes of Caribbean femininity or established histories from which women and persons of colour have been marginalized. Through embodiment, the actors of these plays can question bodily norms and binaries by changing shape on stage, giving life to a forgotten historical female figure, and establishing a dialogue between different generations of Caribbean women. The questioning of stereotypes and bodily norms can be found in many areas of postcolonial and feminist theatres. Therefore, while this chapter primarily explores these issues from the perspective of French Caribbean women playwrights, its analysis may also have relevance to other cultural, artistic, postcolonial or regional contexts.

Bibliography

Artheron, Axel, 'Propos liminaire' in Suzanne Dracius, ed., *Lumina Sophie dite Surprise* (Paris: Idem, 2014), 11–40.

—— 'Suzanne Dracius: le "carrefour" du théâtre pour se hisser au- dessus du magma de l'humaine marchandise', *Africultures* 80–81/1 (2010), 224–30.

Bérard, Stéphanie, *Théâtres des Antilles: traditions et scènes contemporaines* (Paris: L'Harmattan, 2009).

Césaire, Ina, *La Diablesse du Morne-Rouge: Pièce en trois tableaux*, in Christiane P. Makward, ed., *Rosanie Soleil et autres textes dramatiques* (Paris: Karthala, 2011), 23–42.

—— *Mémoires d'isles: Maman N. et Maman F.* (Paris: Caribéennes, 1985).

—— *Mémoires d'île, Maman N. et Maman F.* in Christiane P. Makward, ed., *Rosanie Soleil et autres textes dramatiques* (Paris: Karthala, 2011), 199–228.

—— *La Poupée ashanti*, in Christiane P. Makward, ed., *Rosanie Soleil et autres textes dramatiques* (Paris: Karthala, 2011), 347–69.

Chamoiseau, Patrick, *Écrire en pays dominé* (Paris: Flammarion, 2002).

De Souza, Pascale, 'Discours carnavalesque chez Ina Césaire: déferler les Mémoires d'Iles', *Œuvres et critiques* 26/1 (2001), 122–33.

Dracius, Suzanne, *Lumina Sophie dite Surprise* (Paris: Idem, 2014).

Gilbert, Helen, and Joanne Tompkins, *Post-colonial Drama: Theory, Practice, Politics* (London and New York: Routledge, 1996).

Glissant, Édouard, *Le Discours antillais* (Paris: Seuil, 1981).

Gough, Richard and Nanako Nakajima, 'On Ageing (& Beyond)', *Performance Research* 24/3 (2019), 1–8.

Gyssels, Kathleen, *Filles de Solitude. Essai sur l'identité antillaise dans les (auto-) biographies fictives de Simone et André Schwarz-Bart* (Paris: L'Harmattan 1996).

Houyoux, Suzanne, 'Un entretien avec Ina Césaire, Fort-de-France, Martinique, 5 juin 1990', in Susanne Rinne and Joëlle Vitiello, eds, *Elles écrivent des Antilles (Haïti, Guadeloupe, Martinique)* (Paris: L'Harmattan, 1997), 349–60.

Lee, Vanessa, Personal Interview with Suzanne Dracius (La Closerie des Lilas, Paris, 27 December 2015).

Mathéus, Mariann. 'De l'oralité au théâtre: l'exemple de Berthilia pour le personnage d'Hermance dans Mémoires d'Isles d'Ina Césaire', *Africultures*, <http://africultures.com/de-loralite-au-theatre-lexemple-de-berthilia-pour-le-personnage-dhermance-dans-memoires-disles-dina-cesaire-12419/?utm_source=newsletter&utm_medium=email&utm_campaign=466>, accessed 24 April 2020.

Mortimer, Mildred, *Writing from the Hearth: Public, Domestic, and Imaginative Space in Francophone Women's Fiction of Africa and the Caribbean* (Lanham and Plymouth: Lexington Books, 2007).

Pago, Gilbert, *Lumina Sophie dite 'Surprise' (1848–1879): insurgée et bagnarde* (Matoury, French Guyana: Ibis Rouge, 2008).

Pavis, Patrice, *Dictionary of the Theatre: Terms, Concepts, Analysis*, tr. Christine Shantz (Toronto and Buffalo: University of Toronto Press, 1996).

Price, Richard, and Sally Price, 'Shadow-boxing in the Mangrove', *Cultural Anthropology* 12/1 (1997), 3–36.

Sahakian, Emily, *Staging Creolization: Women's Theatre and Performance from the French Caribbean* (Charlottesville: University of Virginia Press, 2017).

Solomon, Alisa, *Re-dressing the Canon: Essays on Theater and Gender* (London and New York: Routledge, 2005).

SETH COMPAORÉ

6 Male Bodily Poetics in André Téchiné *Quand on a 17 ans* (2016): Physical Violence and Teenage Passion

The depiction of beautiful nude bodies has become a recurring rhetoric in André Téchiné's works. In his feature film *Quand on a 17 ans* [*Being 17*] (2016), the male body is, in the violent natural setting of the Pyrenean mountains during a harsh blizzardly winter, first barbarized and then eroticized.[1] In this film, physical violence goes hand in hand with the natural Pyrenean cinematography which rehabilitates the male body to lead it to sexual maturity. With this aim in mind, the director chooses to foreground an aesthetic strategy that highlights the two teen protagonists' constant fighting by poetizing their male bodies as they evolve towards adulthood. Throughout the film, Thomas and Damien seem to have nurtured a natural hatred for one another to the point that their physical combats become, from the first part of the film, the principle language at the disposal of the viewers. Quite unexpectedly, their obvious aversion seems to hide a latent attachment. The diacritical expression of their teenage bodies recalls Roland Barthes, when he states in his *Mythologies* (1957) that 'the physique of the Wrestlers therefore constitutes a basic sign, which like a seed contains the whole fight'.[2] Impulsive body language is necessary to compensate for the incommunicability that prevails in the film's opening trimester. In fact, bodily interactions and long pauses constitute the important features by which Téchiné's aesthetics evoke the notion of 'queerying'. They progressively

1 Téchiné, André, dir. *Quand on a 17 ans,* Fidélité Films, Wild Bunch, 2016.

2 Roland Barthes, *Mythologies*, trans. and ed. Annette Lavers (New York: Hills and Wang, 1972), 18.

work in the film's time and space to evoke the homosexual orientation of the teen protagonists.

In addition to the portrayal of beautiful nude male bodies as a major characteristic of his cinema, Téchiné uses numerous autobiographical features when he refers to the south-western part of France (the Pyrenees region) where he was born. Indeed, he grew up in a similar rural environment as the one depicted in this film. As a matter of fact, Téchiné's family owned a shop selling agricultural tools in Valence d'Agen in the Midi-Pyrénées region. Moreover, *Quand on a 17 ans* evokes a series of historical and philosophical references such as the famous battle of Roncevaux in *La Chanson de Roland* [*The Song of Roland*], which could be traced back to the same region; Hegelian reciprocal recognition through the social interactions of the two teens; and in particular, Mercierian philosophy in connection to their atypical interracial relationship. In the chapter 'Abus de la société' ['Abuses of Society'] from his work *Tableau de Paris* [*Panorama of Paris*], Louis Sébastien Mercier argues that '[...] beat what you love, give it a few bellows, this is the secret of the heart deeply enamoured, and the evidence of a great Love'.[3] Mercier somehow praises domestic violence and denounces the flattening of romantic relationships in Parisian society due to the excess of civility between partners. Along the same lines as Mercier, any physical emotive and cognitive battles in Thomas and Damien's relationship allow their teen bodies to evolve from a collective body to individual bodies, from forbidden bodies to permitted bodies, from bodies as objects to bodies as subjects. Through their barbaric fights, they discover and accept their homosexuality.

What I propose here is to move beyond the unacceptable image of the outright brutality of teenagers and explore the latent aspect of the teen protagonists' passionate manifestations. Indeed, the film progresses through a violent but emancipating coming-of-age narrative to present the male body's poetic through a raging nature, physical fights and philosophical war. First, this chapter will draw connections between the representation of male bodies in this film and others by Téchiné. Second, it will explore how

3 Louis Sébastien Mercier, *Tableau de Paris*, ed. Jean-Claude Bonnet (Paris: Mercure de France, 1994), 709.

the open form of the *mise-en-scène* highlights the brutality of the Pyrenean natural landscape. Third, it will examine the ways that Téchiné represents the physical combat between the male bodies using a silent, elliptical and almost photographic style. Then, it will also engage with questions of psychosexual development in relation to the two teen protagonists. Finally, this chapter will explore how, towards the end of the third trimester, the film's dynamic transforms physical battles to cognitive combat as the male body gains a sexual autonomy and identity.

Recurring Features of Male Bodies in André Téchiné's Films

Although there are many French feature films that implicitly, or explicitly, incorporate the theme of homosexuality in their narratives, there are, on the other hand, very few books in France that deal with the issue of homosexuality in French cinema. Téchiné, however, who is himself a gay filmmaker, has received critical attention within journal articles and other non-academic critical media due to his abundant depictions of male homosexual characters. While Alain Brassart identifies significant features such as unhappy gay love affairs, coming-of-age, sensory sexuality and melancholia within the filmic world of Téchiné,[4] Bill Marshall perceives positive female representations and evolving male gay protagonists as defining features in Téchiné's numerous films.[5] His feature film *Quand on a 17 ans*, which places at centre stage the coming-out of two teen characters living in a small Pyrenean town of south-western France, follows the same tradition as his previous successful films such as *J'embrasse pas* [*I Don't Kiss]* (1991) and *Les Roseaux sauvages* [*The Wild Reeds*] (1994). Damien and Thomas are teenagers from two very different upbringings who attend the same high school but cannot tolerate each other. When difficult circumstances bring Damien's mother, Marianne, to invite

4 Alain Brassart, *L'Homosexualité dans le cinéma français* (Paris: Nouveau Monde, 2007).

5 Bill Marshall, *André Téchiné* (Manchester: Manchester University Press, 2007).

Thomas to live with them, the young men are forced to coexist and work through their emerging attraction and complicated desires.

Just as in Téchiné's previous films and his last two feature films, *Quand on a 17 ans* recurrently depicts beautiful young bodies, and male bodies, in particular. Téchiné's relentless focus on male bodies in this film leads to a certain poetic of the male body which manifests as filmic and aesthetic strategies aimed at creating a harmonious representation of the male body as it evolves towards a state of autonomy in the hostile Pyrenean setting. This poetic shines through the cinematography of the Pyrenean nature, the bodies of the two teen protagonists, and their thoughts which are filled with philosophical and historical references.

In his attempts to encapsulate Téchiné's film productions in the late 1980s, Alain Philippon lists a series of recurrent thematic and stylistic traits within his films.[6] These traits may reveal Téchiné's aesthetic approach to filmmaking, which ultimately makes him an *auteur*, similar to the filmmakers of the French New Wave, François Truffaut and Jean-Luc Godard. Unfortunately, the French New Wave is often reduced to its critical, aesthetical, technical and economic elements. One of its important features that film historians tend to overlook is the vibrant portrayal of young protagonists. Michel Marie, for instance, discusses characters and thematic recurrences of New Wave cinema towards the end of his book.[7] To illustrate this point, one could evoke Michel Poiccard in Godard's *À bout de souffle* [*Breathless*] (1960) and Antoine Doinel in Truffaut's *Les Quatre Cents Coups* [*The 400 Blows*] (1959) as young, rebellious and often fractured protagonists with uncertain futures. In *Quand on a 17 ans*, Téchiné seemingly follows this tradition with his vibrant portrayals of young, mobile and impulsive protagonists. His professional career as a director resonates with the careers of the founding members of the New Wave from whom he learned various techniques of writing and filmmaking. Emulating his mentors, Téchiné was a critic in the *Cahiers du Cinéma* and assistant director under Jacques Rivette in his feature film *L'Amour fou* [*Mad Love*] (1969). Thus, the unconventional techniques such as irrational cuts, a non-linear

6 Alain Philippon, *André Téchiné* (Paris: Cahiers du cinéma, 1988).

7 Michel Marie, *La Nouvelle Vague: une école artistique* (Paris: Nathan, 1997).

narrative, the multiplicity of narrative instances and the juxtaposition between reality and dream in his films are testimony to Téchiné's embodiment of the French New Wave spirit. Following in the footsteps of Godard and Truffaut's earlier characters, Téchiné's young and elegant male protagonists find issue with parental authority, social norms and institutions. As Thomas and Damien constantly fight and attempt to run away from societal constraints in *Quand on a 17 ans*, the virile manifestations of their emerging attraction recall once again Godard's Michel Poiccard in *À bout de souffle* and Ferdinand Griffon in *Pierrot le fou* [*Pierrot the Madman*] (1965), both of whom undergo a sexualization of their bodies.

Furthermore, in Téchiné's numerous films, traditional family always seems to be a major obstacle to total freedom. A common malaise that affects the protagonists in his films is the notion of 'dépaysement' [change of scenery] which Marshall argues constitutes the trademark of Téchiné's cinema.[8] 'Dépaysement' refers to the need to change scenery or a mental state of being disoriented due to a new environment. Thomas and Damien in *Quand on a 17 ans* seem to be suffering from both forms of 'dépaysement'. While their homosexual relationship later in the film breaks away from the traditional constraints of their families, they appear disoriented at times as they discover their complicated desires. This need for change leads Téchiné's protagonists to deterritorialize societal norms in the Deleuzian sense. Gilles Deleuze and Félix Guattari propose the term 'deterritorialization' as a process of moving beyond the territorial borders of where one is born and raised to somewhere else. They add that 'the process of deterritorialization (…) goes from the centre to the periphery'.[9] This displacement from the centre to the periphery is caused by alienation in a place once called home. In fact, 'dépaysement' manifests itself through the oscillating identity and the fluctuating sexuality of Téchiné's constantly evolving protagonists. Pierre in *J'embrasse pas*, Lucien in *Ma saison préférée* [*My Favourite Season*] (1993), François and Serge in *Les Roseaux sauvages*, Yvan in *Les Égarés* [*Strayed*]

8 Marshall, *André Téchiné*, 93.

9 Gilles Deleuze and Félix Guattari, *Anti-Oedipus: Capitalism and Schizophrenia* (University of Minnesota Press, 1983), 231.

(2003), and Natan and Sami in *Les Temps qui changent* [*Changing Times*] (2004), are prime examples of fluctuating male characters.

In the above films, all beautiful male bodies, erotized and illustrated through patterns of close-ups, are engaged in heterosexual adventures or homosexual intercourse. *Les Roseaux sauvages* and *Quand on a 17 ans* indicate some similarities in the representations of male protagonists, their beautiful bodies and their emerging homosexual desires. In *Les Roseaux sauvages*, the socio-historical context depicts an environment dominated by the Algerian war in which François and Serge, two teen candidates for the baccalaureate, discover their homosexuality. In *Quand on a 17 ans*, Téchiné includes a contemporary portrait of the harsh winter in the Pyrenean mountains with an evocation of a war in Africa. In this regard, he also tells the story of this war which remains in the background of the ongoing battle between Thomas and Damien. Damien's father, who is an officer of the Legion of Honour, often calls his family via videoconference from the battlefield. François is sexually attracted to Serge, just as Damien is violently and passionately attracted to Thomas. The poetic nature of the close-ups showing the beautiful bodies of Thomas and Damien is evident in their body language, first barbarized, then eroticized as the sequences progress. It is a double language which is paradoxically tender and violent at the same time. In short, the following repertoire of elegant actors mentioned by Marshall validates Téchiné's poetic trend in the representations of the male body:

> The bodies of Wadeck Stanczak in *Rendez-vous* and especially *Le Lieu du crime*, Simon de la Brosse and Abdel Kechiche in *Les Innocents*, Manuel Blanc in *J'embrasse pas*, Anthony Prada in *Ma Saison préférée*, Stéphane Rideau in *Les Roseaux sauvages* and *Loin*, Benoît Magimel in *Les Voleurs*, Alexis Loret in *Alice et Martin*, Gaspard Ulliel in *Les Égarés*, are all put on display, and are invariably objects of desire – and recipients of point of view shots – of other protagonists.[10]

Indeed, Corentin Fila (Thomas) and Kacey Mottet Klein (Damien) in *Quand on a 17 ans* fit perfectly in this iconic list of beautiful young male actors. Their mutual desire is informed not only by the camera's constant

10 Marshall, *André Téchiné*, 83.

focus on their attractive male body but also by the successions of shots and reverse shots as they frequently gaze at once another.

The Brutality of Pyrenean Nature

Quand on a 17 ans is aesthetically and fundamentally a physical and brutal film. Indeed, a vibrant onscreen portrayal of rural France and the Pyrenean nature characterizes the vast majority of Téchiné's films. Significant natural frames are omnipresent, for instance, in *Ma saison préférée, Les Égarés* and *La Fille du RER* [*The Girl on the Train*] (2009), and this natural setting is often paired with a certain violence. To ensure an artistic and authentic depiction of the violence of the teenagers in *Quand on a 17 ans*, Téchiné collaborated with Céline Sciamma, the director of *Bande de filles* [*Girlhood*] (2014), who co-wrote this film. Instead of an urban setting, considered as the space *par excellence* for representing precariousness and delinquency among adolescents in contemporary French films, Téchiné chose a rural setting. With the contribution of Sciamma, the end result is a very physical film in which the male bodies speak more often for the main characters than they do for themselves. The severe winter season adds yet another layer of physical and mental pain through its relentless snowstorms, harsh blizzards and inaccessible mountains.

Moreover, *Quand on a 17 ans* opens with moving shots, interspersed throughout the opening credits, among which one of the shots includes a tunnel crossing by a car that leads to an open, dazzling and imposing space: the high Pyrenean mountains. As this tracking shot abruptly ends on a dazzling whiteness of the snowy mountains in Bagnères-de-Luchon (in the Pyrenees), a temporal splice replaces the greenery of nature from late autumn to the beginning of the Pyrenean winter. This brief passage from darkness to light is metaphorical of the two main characters' struggle in their quest for sexual identity. This also offers an incursion into the world of this local community, through a tunnel to an open space, which invites the viewer to consider the events of the film in relation to the history and geography of this place. The sequence then progresses to a different camera perspective presenting an overview of the snowy Pyrenees and the surroundings of Bagnères-de-Luchon from a birds-eye view. Several close-ups portray Thomas's arduous descent from the mountain on his way to school. The overwhelming whiteness of the snow and the vast mountainous space overpower the only greyish path that constitutes sole access to the top of the mountain.

Through this hostile Pyrenean environment, Téchiné's camera essentially suggests two things. First, this naturalist frame evokes the difficulty the peasants face in winter in this region of the Pyrenees. Then, the focus on the harshness of the Pyrenean nature elaborates the space in which Thomas's body is going to be tormented by the cold weather, altitude and reciprocal hostilities between the two teenagers. Thomas's daily commute is from the top of the mountain to the bottom. He makes the difficult descent from his home with his parents and climbs back up every evening after school. Then, he must carefully clean the barn and replenish fresh hay to feed the family's cows. To end his daily chores, he cares for his bedridden mother.

In the film, the male body's poetics are evoked through the representation of Pyrenean nature as well as in the violent body language of Thomas and Damien. In 'The Archetypes of Literature', Northrop Frye creates a series of representations of the myth and archetype at stake in the narrative structure of literary work, and he then associates their meanings with the solar cycle of the day, the seasonal cycle of the year and the organic cycle of human life.[11] According to Frye's representation of the daily or seasonal cycle, autumn is identified with twilight and death. This season is associated with the myth of something falling and isolation which corresponds to the archetype of tragedy. Winter is tantamount to darkness and dissolution and is associated with the myth of chaos and violence which correspond to the archetype of satire. Spring refers to the dawn and birth. It indicates the myth of creation and resurrection and corresponds to the archetype of romance. Lastly, summer is identified with zenith and triumph. It represents the myth of apotheosis and unity and corresponds to the archetype

11 Northrop Frye, 'The Archetypes of Literature', in Vincent B. Leitch, ed., *The Norton Anthology of Theory and Criticism* (New York: W. W. Norton and Company, 2018), 1250–62, 1258.

of the idyll. Following this configuration, Frye's series of representations of seasons in literature resonates with the three trimesters that structure the narratives in *Quand on a 17 ans*: autumn, winter and spring.

To ensure a realistic representation of space and time, Téchiné evenly attributes thirty-eight minutes to each trimester. The film begins with a sequence set during a late snowy autumn in the Pyrenees. Frye's configuration of autumn as the myth of fall and isolation literally and metaphorically resounds with the film's inaugural sequence. Of particular interest is a series of bird's-eye shots in which the Pyrenean mountains are portrayed as completely covered with snow making them impenetrable. Thomas is then seen, at numerous moments, in this bad weather as he makes the difficult descent from the snowy mountain to school. To build on the impending danger of an avalanche, Téchiné vividly captures with tracking pan shots the element of suspense in Thomas's descent from the mountain top. Thomas later appears isolated, silenced and misunderstood at school. Similarly, this notion of isolation also seems to affect Thomas's well-off counterpart, Damien, who seems to be suffering from his father's absence, as he isolates himself despite the comfort of his mother's home. In harmony with Frye's configuration of winter as the myth of chaos and pain, moreover, Téchiné stages the Pyrenean winter as a freezing era of snowstorms and despair in which the two teenagers are lost. An enduring, snowy and stormy atmosphere dominates most of the scenes in the first part of the film. Téchiné's camera carefully follows each of the main characters' movements, especially those of Thomas, as he attempts to domesticate the impenetrable flanks of the Pyrenees. The camera takes its time, freezes and lingers on every stride that an out-of-breath Thomas takes into the thick snow during his difficult descent to, and ascent from, school. His body movements are filmed in a manner closer to photography than cinema. That is an elliptical, mute and documentary style. The use of close-ups on Thomas's body onscreen during his difficult trek not only illustrates the severity of the winter weather, but also gives the viewer a sense of what he is enduring. The Pyrenean weather is afflicting him with its most powerful weapons: glacial wind, ice and snow.

The montage in the first sequence depicts Thomas's descent, thereby allowing the viewer to feel the intensity and coldness of his difficult commute. The sound of dead leaves or ice sheets being crunched under the snow with each stride echoes with the frigid wind. The freezing temperature causes a constant smoky stream of condensation from his nose and mouth as he exhales. The trails from where Thomas lives on the mountain are inaccessible to vehicles. His daily commute takes him more than an hour and a half in the snow. Even Damien's mother's truck sinks into the snow when she visits Thomas's sick mother.

Exposure of Physical Violence and Pain

The narrative structure of *Quand on a 17 ans* is three-fold. This triad, composed of three trimesters, covers, on the one hand, the period during which the adolescent male body will reach sexual maturity; and thus, becomes a 'subject body'. In other words, it develops into an autonomous adult body that can support itself. This maturity evokes a certain rebirth of the two teenagers, Thomas and Damien who, in a way which is characteristic of many of Téchiné's characters, are suffering from 'dépaysement'. Brassart adds that all of Téchiné's films question the masculine identity of the male characters and follow the same narrative pattern.[12] A male character must leave the maternal bosom to become a man and, generally, faces setback because of the negative influence of the father. In *Quand on a 17 ans*, if the fathers are the exception to this rule, the maternal figure remains a refuge and a solace for Thomas and Damien. The two teenagers maintain a strong relationship with their respective mothers. Thomas loves his sick mother for whom he cares every day. As for Damien, his mother is his best friend. It is unsurprising that the maternal figure plays a major role in their physical and mental maturity. In fact, the symbolic notion of birth occupies the entire film. It begins with the announcement of the pregnancy of Thomas's mother in the first trimester and it ends with the birth of a sister in the third trimester. The three trimesters that

12 Alain Brassart, 'Une critique du modèle masculin: à propos des films d'André Téchiné', in D.Wezler-Lang, ed., *Nouvelles Approches des hommes et du masculin* (Toulouse: Presse universitaire du Mirail, 2000), 313–19, 314.

structure the film refer to maternity as well as mother nature which is caring and unpredictable at the same time.

Additionally, the tumultuous relationship of the two protagonists in the film leads to physical (adult body), sexual (choice of homosexuality) and intellectual (baccalaureate) maturity. Sigmund Freud states that parents play the greatest role in their children's mental development.[13] To build his male identity, the little boy must separate from the mother and kill in him everything that appears feminine. This separation from the mother can be particularly violent. In the same vein, the separation from the mother in Téchiné's film leads to violent behaviours towards the object of affection. Thomas and Damien constantly fight against one another to suppress their emerging affection for fear of losing their mother and for fear of recognizing their sexual orientation.

By using Thomas Hobbes's notion of state of nature,[14] the three trimesters, forming the three key parts of the film's narrative framework, could be subtitled as follows: encounter and hostilities (the state of nature), the constant fighting and the discovery of one's homosexuality (the manifestation of the state of nature), and the recognition of one's own condition and that of others (the social contract or the state of culture, i.e., the acceptance of one's homosexuality). In other words, the two teenagers' relationship goes through a stage of hostility, then evolves to a state of discovering one another, in order to reach a full recognition stage, which resonates with Hegelian philosophy of reciprocal recognition. Hegel sums up the importance of recognition for human beings in these terms: 'The desire for recognition is of such importance to human beings that they are willing to risk death in order to gain recognition from others.'[15] According to Hegel, this recognition begins with the struggle between two minds who, in order to assert themselves, reject each other. To get out of the distorted representation of the world that one's consciousness makes, the presence

13 Sigmund Freud, 'The Interpretation of Dreams, Uncanny, Fetishism', in Vincent B. Leitch, ed., *The Norton Anthology of Theory and Criticism* (New York: W.W. Norton and Company, 2010), 807–44, 814–15.

14 R. E. Bunce, *Thomas Hobbes* (London: Continuum, 2009), 35–7.

15 Glenn A Magee., *The Hegel Dictionary* (London: Continuum, 2010), 195.

of the other consciousness is necessary since it grants the former access to an externality which allows it to have a relationship with the world.

Since Thomas and Damien express themselves through violence and brutality, the poetic of the male body emerges from their repetitive fights. Three essential concepts particularly help establish its aesthetic strategies: the spectacle, the gaze and the reciprocal recognition. The notion of spectacle finds its most eloquent expression in the chapter 'The world of wrestling' of Barthes's *Mythologies* in which wrestling is defined as 'excessive portrayal of suffering'.[16] Just like ancient theatre, the significance of wrestling combat lies in the spectacular representation of pain. In the same manner, the *mise-en-scène* of Thomas and Damien's constant fights resonates with the excessive suffering with which the viewer is immediately accustomed from the second sequence of the film. While Thomas is introduced to the viewer through his harsh descent, Damien intervenes in the second sequence during the gymnastics class.

For Barthes, since wrestling is meant to be seen, its key function lies in an exaggeration through excessive gestures exploited to the climax for the pleasure of the spectators.[17] Similarly, this spectacular function characterizes the fights in *Quand on a 17 ans* since significant important features highlight each battle as part of a long brutal show. The more Thomas and Damien fight against each other, the better they discover their respective interests socially, and later, intimately. As a result, the violent visual and vocal mix in these scenes – posture of gladiators, bloody noses, hateful growling – transforms the act of spectatorship from just watching to experiencing the fights. The audience senses what the two teens are privately condemning in themselves. Barthes defines such type of physical brutality as 'great solar shows' or 'epic combat in ancient arena'.[18] As a matter of fact, Thomas and Damien seem to have a predilection for open-air fights. Throughout the first trimester, they only attack one another when they occupy the same public space: the gym, the classroom, the courtyard of the high school, in the street, and in the open air at the foot of the Pyrenees. Each time they

16 Barthes, *Mythologies*, 19.
17 Barthes, *Mythologies*, 19.
18 Barthes, *Mythologies*, 18.

bully one another, the viewer is given, through the men's body language, significant cues of their emerging affection.

A particular duel scene at the feet of the Pyrenees is of interest in the second part of the film as it echoes the epic tradition of *La Chanson de Roland*. A savvy viewer could not help but notice the parallel between the 'Battle of Roncevaux' and the final battle between Thomas and Damien at the foot of the mountain. Téchiné celebrates the region of the Pyrenees by juxtaposing the teenagers' final battle with the famous battle of Roncevaux. As they position to fight in their attempt to reach a final resolution about their mutual affection in this scene, an establishing shot depicts them head-to-head, in a duel position, fists clenched, ready to engage in battle. Then, a series of longshots show the two teenagers, as well as the majestic background of the Pyrenean mountain. During this ultimate fight, the cinematography captures not only what is occurring on screen, but also what the protagonists are feeling: tracking shots capture precise punches and kicks, medium-shots show the teenage bodies rolling on the ground and close-ups reveal the extent of their injuries.

The second important element to consider in the poetic of the male body is the gaze. Laura Mulvey argues that cinema offers several possibilities of pleasure, including the pleasure that one feels through the eye. Looking can be a source of pleasure, just as the reverse action, being the object of gaze, can also give pleasure. She observes that the 'voyeuristic' gaze in cinema can be broken down as follows:

> There are three different looks associated with cinema: that of the camera as it records the pro-filmic event, that of the audience as it watches the final product, and that of the characters at each other within the screen illusion. The conventions of narrative film deny the first two and subordinate them to the third, the conscious aim being always to eliminate intrusive camera presence and prevent a distancing awareness in the audience.[19]

In *Quand on a 17 ans*, these three types of gazes are reflected in the poetic of the male body. Mulvey's first level of the gaze echoes the initial look

19 Laura Mulvey, 'Visual Pleasure and Narrative Cinema', in Vincent B. Leitch, ed., *The Norton Anthology of Theory and Criticism* (New York: W. W. Norton and Company, 2018), 1954–65, 1965.

of Téchiné's camera as it gazes at the Pyrenean decor to reveal its every detail. This gaze manipulates the other two types of gazes (the viewer's gaze on the screen, and the protagonists' gazes at themselves). The camera introduces Téchiné's male bodies as objects of curiosity for the viewer since the only form of communication the audience sees is the constant fights between the two teenagers. In this way, to use a term from Mulvey, Téchiné creates a circumstance of scopophilia.

A tone of incommunicability dominates the first part of the film since Thomas and Damien fight but do not speak. Téchiné's silent style forces the viewer to rely on body language to make up for the lack of verbal communication. The viewer then fixes their gaze on the bodies of Thomas and Damien as they evolve in the naturally hostile environment. Pascale-Anne Brault observes that desire and jealousy can often hide behind gaze. In its attempt to capture the aggressive look on the two main characters' faces, the camera identifies 'unilateral glances, exchanged glances and face-to-face glances'.[20] For instance, unilateral glance occurs in the first classroom scene. Thomas, from his seat, glances with disdain at Damien who is reading a poem from Arthur Rimbaud's *L'Indésirable*. When Damien finishes reading the passage and is walking back to his seat, Thomas trips him purposefully. This first unspoken action indicates Thomas's supposed hatred for Damien. The most significant feature about this scene is the exchange of angry glances between Thomas and Damien, which continue in later scenes during math and Spanish classes and at the entrance of the school at the end of the day. In this end-of-day school sequence, Thomas and Damien stare at one another for a long while and the persistent static shot seems to suspend time and space. The scenes in which their eyes meet are usually followed by their violent fights. The clues that precede their physical hostilities hide behind sequences that feature one-sided glances, exchanged gazes and tense face-to-faces as the two opponents gauge each other. When the duel of glances reaches its climax, merciless confrontations ensue. These three types of gazes are successively encoded in close-ups (one-sided gazes),

20 Pascale-Anne Brault, 'Claire Denis et le corps à corps masculin dans *Beau Travail*', *The French Review* 78/2 (2004), 288–99, 290.

medium-shots (exchanged gazes) and longshots (face-to-face gazes), and this creates the sense that the viewer is right alongside the teen fighters.

According to Mulvey, one of the major properties of mainstream cinema is its close relationship to the human form. She reminds us:

> Scale, space, stories are all anthropomorphic. Here, curiosity and the wish to look intermingle with a fascination with likeness and recognition: the human face, the human body, the relationship between the human form and its surroundings, the visible presence of the person in the world.[21]

Thus, it is the reciprocal gaze directed on their respective bodies that reveals Damien and Thomas' similarities, as well as their close relationship to the Pyrenean surrounding.

A consideration of their similarities leads us to take a Hegelian perspective again on the teenagers' relationship. Neither consciousness wants to be the object of the other consciousness. The reciprocal recognition of the two minds as self-aware leads to 'intersubjectivity', which means that each of the two minds recognizes itself as a subject. This Hegelian philosophy can be applied to the behaviour of our two protagonists during the third trimester of the film. Only by recognizing Damien's humanity and attraction to him does Thomas become aware of his own humanity and homosexual inclination. Just as the viewer's gaze seeks to unveil the motives in the teenagers' fights over the course of the film, Thomas and Damien try to discover themselves by looking at their reflections several times in the film. The questioning gaze, directed on oneself through a mirror (in reference to Damien) or through the surface of the water (as for Thomas), evokes the Lacanian theory of the mirror stage developed during early childhood. Indeed, if we consider the incommunicability that dominates the first trimester of the film, this Lacanian reading offers greater insight into the characters' development.

Jacques Lacan places the mirror stage between six and eighteen months of age during which time the child recognizes his own image in the mirror.[22]

21 Mulvey, 'Visual Pleasure and Narrative Cinema', 1957.

22 Jacques Lacan, 'The Mirror Stage as Formative of the Function of the I as Revealed in Psychoanalytic Experience', in Vincent B. Leitch, ed., *The Norton Anthology of*

This phase is crucial for the construction of his ego since the child develops his first impressions of himself from the point of view of his appearance and from the point of view of his physical mastery of the world around him. For Lacan, because the child has not yet learned to speak any language, nor has he learned to interpret the images that others have of him, his perception of himself in the mirror is a perfect self-image described by Sigmund Freud as 'ideal-I'. However, this 'ideal-I' is a fantasy, an unreal and incomplete image, constructed in a fantasy to satisfy his desire for rational order, and a perfect self-image. This biased recognition of oneself in the mirror prepares the child to identify and identify others in the future. Assuming that *Quand on a 17 ans* suggests incommunicability throughout the first trimester, and that the beginning of the film evokes the early childhood of the tumultuous relationship between two teenagers, the Lacanian theory cannot be overlooked here. In fact, Thomas and Damien, after fighting, seem to look at their reflections to search for their 'ideal-I'. The pond on the top of the snowy mountain becomes almost a sanctuary for Thomas, who swims there three times across the duration of the film. Before plunging into the cold water, he gazes at his reflection on the surface of the pond as if to find a perfect image of himself. This bath is a penitentiary and purifying ritual since he goes there after he experiences a setback. Every dive into this 'arctic' water is an attempt to reach the perfect reflection of himself that he sees on the surface of the water. Damien, meanwhile, stares in the mirror of his bathroom after each confrontation with Thomas. He gauges his muscles from his torso and arms, analysing their every imperfection.

Cognitive Combat

The brutality of the Pyrenean nature evoked by Téchiné's camera in the first part of the film goes hand in hand with the rigid historical context of the baccalaureate exam which constitutes the intellectual aspect of this

Theory and Criticism (New York: W. W. Norton & Company, 2001), 1285–90, 1285–6.

violent film. Brutality in this film is not only physical and emotional, it is also cognitive. From Thomas's point of view, cognitive combat is threefold: first, how to reconcile his studies with his poverty; then to master his passion and homosexual inclination for Damien; and finally, to prepare for the bachelor's degree. The film reflects on a series of philosophical references, including the Mercierian conception of passionate love. In his *Tableau de Paris*, Mercier argues for a philosophy of excess that values strong passion because it captivates men and becomes a sign of superior energy. Mercier believes that the form of gallantry that has been established in society has weakened true love and rendered lovers passive. For Mercier, true love does not need civilities but rather a certain irrational manifestation of violence.

A scene that best embodies the cognitive aspect of the hostile relationship between Thomas and Damien is the philosophical debate during the preparation of the baccalaureate in the last trimester of the film. Instead of their ordinary hostilities, they use texts of classical authors (Plato and Leibniz) to debate the legitimacy of their homosexual relationship. To testify his love for Thomas, Damien quotes Plato's *Banquet*:

> Si dans l'accomplissement un homme rencontrerait une femme, il y'aurait génération et l'espèce perpétue. En revanche, si un homme tombait sur un homme, les deux êtres, les deux hommes trouveraient de toute façon la satiété dans leur rapport.
>
> [If in an accomplishment a man would meet a woman, there would be generation and the species perpetuate. On the other hand, if a man came across a man, the two human beings, the two men would find satiety in their relationship anyway.]

In response to Damien, Thomas continues by quoting Leibniz:

> Il faut faire une distinction entre le désir et le besoin. Besoins s'inscrivent dans la nature, nécessaires, vitaux. Désirs, ils ne sont pas d'origines naturelles, artificiels, contingents et superflus
>
> [You must distinguish between desire and need. Needs are part of nature, necessary, vital. Desires are not natural; they are artificial, contingent and from superfluous origins.]

At the end of this philosophical debate, the two protagonists reach a consensus that establishes the legitimacy of their love and the acceptance of their sexuality. This debate is followed by the sequence in which they make love for the first time. The interest of this philosophical debate lies in the fact that it reveals the evolution of the two protagonists from 'object body' to the 'subject body'. Surprisingly, a recurring twist in Téchiné's cinema is that the differences between his protagonists very often serve to unite them at the end. Thomas and Damien, who initially hate each other, end up together as they unite in their homosexuality.

At the end of this discussion, it has become clear that violence occupies a prominent place in *Quand on a 17 ans*. While aversion between Thomas and Damien constitutes a diversion, moreover, it establishes a certain poetic of the male body. What started at first as a film dominated by physical violence is challenged by Téchiné's aesthetic strategies as they transform the young protagonists' beautiful bodies into a language. These male bodies are filmed with precision in order to disclose violent or sexual impulses in keeping with Mercier's suggestions for more meaningful romantic relationships. Stylistically, *Quand on a 17 ans* embodies a violent filmic time and space. Confrontations are embodied in the *mise-en-scène* that favours external locations and open settings of the Pyrenees. In addition, the violent young protagonists are involved in philosophical debates. In a peaceful but argumentative war, Thomas and Damien reason and quote Plato and Leibniz to prove the legitimacy of their love for each other. Furthermore, this film draws a vibrant portrait of the pain and grief that foster togetherness and love. If the barbarized and eroticized male body becomes a common formula in cinema, the value of such discussion of the adolescent body resides in its historical and philosophical references. The poetic of the male body appears through the details in the montage of the hand-to-hand combat between Thomas and Damien, which resonate with Brault's statement: 'The male body, eroticized and stylized to the extreme, its corporality, expressed by a camera to which no detail escapes, is staged; a voice is given to the male body and it becomes more expressive than any speech.'[23] Téchiné succeeds in a double challenge by defying cinematic norms and traditional societal constraints. It is the Pyrenean landscape that imposes its violent nature and barbaric body language to the protagonists

23 Brault, 'Claire Denis et le corps à corps masculin dans *Beau Travail*', 292.

rather than the opposite. While incommunicability defies conventional film norms and the experience of the viewer, the male body blossoms in queering bodily norms. It frees itself from heteronormativity and becomes a permitted body with homosexual tendencies.

Bibliography

Barthes, Roland, *Mythologies*, trans. and ed. Annette Lavers (New York: Hills and Wang, 1972).

Brassart, Alain, 'Une critique du modèle masculin: à propos des films d'André Téchiné', in D. Wezler Lang, ed., *Nouvelles Approches des hommes et du masculin* (Toulouse: Presse universitaire du Mirail, 2000), 313–19.

—— *L'Homosexualité dans le cinéma français* (Paris: Nouveau Monde, 2007).

Brault, Pascale-Anne, 'Claire Denis et le corps à corps masculin dans *Beau Travail*', *The French Review* 78/2 (2004), 288–99.

Bunce, Robin, *Thomas Hobbes* (London: Continuum, 2009).

La Chanson de Roland, trans. and ed. Ian Short, 2nd edn. (Paris: Librairie Générale Française, 1990).

Deleuze, Gilles, and Félix Guattari, *Anti-Oedipus: Capitalism and Schizophrenia* (Minneapolis: University of Minnesota Press, 1983).

—— 'A Thousand Plateaus', in Vincent B. Leitch, ed., *The Norton Anthology of Theory and Criticism* (W. W. Norton and Company, 2010), 1446–63.

Freud, Sigmund, 'The Interpretation of Dreams, Uncanny, Fetishism', in Vincent B. Leitch, ed., *The Norton Anthology of Theory and Criticism* (New York: W. W. Norton and Company, 2010), 807–44.

Frye, Northrop. 'The Archetypes of Literature', in Vincent B. Leitch, ed., *The Norton Anthology of Theory and Criticism* (New York: W. W. Norton and Company, 2018), 1250–62.

Godard, Jean-Luc, dir. *Breathless*, SNC, 1960.

Lacan, Jacques, 'The Mirror Stage as Formative of the Function of the I as Revealed in Psychoanalytic Experience', in Vincent B. Leitch, ed., *The Norton Anthology of Theory and Criticism* (New York: W. W. Norton & Company, 2001), 1285–90.

Magee, Glenn A., *The Hegel Dictionary* (London: Continuum, 2010).

Marie, Michel, *La Nouvelle Vague: une école artistique* (Paris: Nathan, 1997).

Marshall, Bill, *André Téchiné* (Manchester: Manchester University Press, 2007).

Mercier, Louis Sébastien, *Tableau de Paris*, ed. Jean-Claude Bonnet (Paris: Mercure de France, 1994).

Mulvey, Laura, 'Visual Pleasure and Narrative Cinema', in Vincent B. Leitch, ed., *The Norton Anthology of Theory and Criticism* (New York: W. W. Norton and Company, 2018), 1954–65.

Philippon, Alain, *André Téchiné* (Paris: Cahiers du cinéma, 1988).

Platon, *Le Banquet*, tr. Luc Brisson (Paris: Flammarion, 1998).

Rivette, Jacques, dir. *L'Amour fou*, Cocinor, 1969.

Sciamma, Céline, dir. *Bande de filles*, Hold-Up films, Lilies films, and Arte France Cinéma, 2014.

Téchiné, André, dir. *Les Égarés*, FIT Productions, 2003.

—— *La Fille du RER*, UGC, 2009.

—— *J'embrasse pas*, Bac Films, Ciné Cinq, 1991.

—— *Ma saison préférée*, D.A. Films, 1993.

—— *Quand on a 17 ans*, Fidélité Films, Wild Bunch, 2016.

—— *Les Roseaux sauvages*, Ima Films, 1994.

—— *Les Temps qui changent*, Gemini Films, 2004.

Truffaut, François, dir. *Les Quatre Cents Coups*, Les Films du Carrosse, 1959.

PART III

Hybrid and Dysfunctional Bodies

CRISTINA ONESTA

7 Dysfunctional Bodies, Dysfunctional Gazes: Artistic Creation and Death in *Manger l'autre* by Ananda Devi and *Le Génie d'Abou* by Isabelle Boni-Claverie

Representations of bodies are abound in contemporary culture. Many of these representations perpetuate gendered and cultured conceptions of the bodies. In addition to informing our perceptions of the body itself, these constructed bodies have the power to shape how we receive and conceptualise sexuality and pleasure. However, contemporary art and literature depict bodies as a site of resistance against normative ideas about corporeality. This chapter focuses on the representation of female dysfunctional bodies and its visual pleasure in Ananda Devi's most recent novel, *Manger l'autre* [*Eating the Other*] (2018), and Isabelle Boni-Claverie's short film, *Le Génie d'Abou* [*Abou's Genius*] (1998). These two works, set twenty years apart, share many common problematics, which appear in several works throughout Devi and Boni-Claverie's artistic careers. Their common themes include sexuality, dynamics of gender and power, identity, hybridity and racism. Through representing the bodies, sexuality, and social attitudes of two obese women, *Manger l'autre* and *Le Génie d'Abou* question the concept of power and normativity. Their representations of a female dysfunctional body carry criticism of the gaze and voyeurism, while also addressing the place of viewers. The notion of being seen and being desired is subverted to denounce norms and deconstruct identities which can no longer bear the burden of a judgmental gaze. Interestingly, in both works, the dysfunctional body becomes a metaphor for a piece of art. This artwork questions the role of artists and their responsibility in 'our' society, where the 'our' is presumably the Western world. Through a comparative analysis, my study investigates how Devi and Boni-Claverie explore dysfunctional female bodies. Whilst locating themselves as artists within the contemporary artistic scene, Devi and Boni-Claverie denounce the excesses of our society, challenge norms and gender relations, and, ultimately, dismantle historical structures and hierarchies. This chapter poses the following questions: how do these dysfunctional bodies speak within the narratives? How do their representations undo historical and social hierarchies? How do they challenge and renew the space of artistic creation? To answer these questions, this work aims to create a dialogue among different theories. The framework of this chapter is informed by postcolonial theory as well as theories pertaining to gender and disability. This study also makes minor references to food studies and ecocriticism.

The Dysfunctional Body and Its Significance

Manger l'autre tells the story of a teenager who is condemned to a life of exclusion and segregation because of her abnormal body dimension. The protagonist, whose name is unknown, defines herself at birth as a pink elephant weighing ten kilos and carrying the burden of her presumed twin sister's death. Her mother, described as a successful beautiful woman wearing high heel shoes and attractive skirts, left her with her father, who sees his daughter as a royal piece of art and himself as its creator. The girl and the father develop an unhealthy relationship. The father convinces his daughter that she had devoured her twin sister, who is an 'ombre essentielle, parfois consolatrice, parfois tourmenteuse' [an essential shadow, which is sometimes consoling, other times tormenting.][1] Her only objective in life is to feed herself and her sister. She grows rapidly

1 Ananda Devi, *Manger l'autre* (Paris: Grasset, 2018), 25. All translations are my own unless otherwise noted.

until she comes to a point of utter rebellion: by devouring her own flesh in front of a webcam, she takes revenge on her secluded life. *Le Génie d'Abou* is also built around the representation of a female body and her death. Abou, a black sculptor, with his muse, a black femme fatale (a genie granting his wishes), leads towards a 'perverted' creation act, that is, the murder of an obese white woman. After sexual intercourse involving the three characters at the same time, the sculptor and his genie kill the white woman and make a statue from her dead body. At the end, Abou rejects his genie who magically disappears thus losing her powers, and he seems to regret its creation, that is, the statue of the dead white woman.

The two works portray what I refer to in this chapter as a 'dysfunctional' female body. This body is 'dysfunctional' because it does not correspond to societal norms and standards. The Oxford dictionary defines the adjective 'dysfunctional' as: 'not operating normally or properly' or 'unable to deal adequately with normal social relations'.[2] Devi and Boni-Claverie aim to provoke the spectators and the readers by portraying an obese female body that challenges the traditional representation of the body, female sexuality and erotic desire. This chapter uses the term 'dysfunctional' in order to shed light on the efforts the artists make to subvert normative gender and race roles as well as power-based relations and social structures. Devi and Boni-Claverie subvert norms in two ways. Firstly, they encourage their audience to recognize what society marks as 'abnormal' bodies. Secondly, they help their audience to identify the dysfunctional social practices these bodies must adopt in order to be seen. In this study, I will clarify how the dysfunctional body and gaze are a product of a dysfunctional society that leads its members to perform extreme actions in order to demonstrate their existence. Death is in fact the final destination for both of their characters, urging us to ponder on the following questions: what does it mean to carry a 'dysfunctional' body in terms of identity and social relations? What does it mean for female artists to portray a dysfunctional female body? How can we deconstruct, and go beyond, these representations?

2 Oxford Learner's Dictionary, <https://www.oxfordlearnersdictionaries.com/definition/english/dysfunctional>, accessed 26 April 2020.

Devi's character sees herself as a 'representation psychique de notre époque' [the psychological representation of our times] (28). Trapped by her own desires and fears, the teenager is the mirror of her selfish generation who embodies a 'demultipliée image' [multiple image] made of 'leur hypnose, leur ivresse, leurs obsessions égocentriques' [their hypnoses, drunkenness, egocentric obsessions] (29). One of the dominant stylistic and narrative aspects that occur in Devi's novels is the symbioses of characters and setting. In 'Poétique de la ville dans l'œuvre d'Ananda Devi', Abada Medjo describes Devi's city as a dysphoric space [which suffuses the leitmotifs of seclusion, rupture and destruction][3] thus recalling an image of Mauritius portrayed both as a prison and a paradise. Readers are reminded of characters of *Eve de ses décombres* [*Eve Out of Her Ruins*] (2005), *Soupir* [*Sigh*] (2002), *Les jours vivants* [*The Living Days*] (2013), among others, and they also recall the writer herself in her autobiographical novel *Les hommes qui me parlent* [*The Men who Speak to Me*] (2011). All the characters have a strong connection to the environment in which they live, which is either the island or a Western city (or a hotel room in *Les hommes qui me parlent*). This environment is seen as a physical manifestation of their contrasting feelings, traumas and subjectivity. In *Manger l'autre*, the teenager is trapped in her expanding body which simultaneously clashes with the borders of the city and matches its degradation. She states:

> La ville, comme le monde, s'était fracturée en deux. De l'autre côté des barbelés, des yeux immenses et sombres où l'on devinait des désirs de violence nés de l'impuissance, le reflet d'une pierre serrée dans une main. Et à l'intérieur des murs, les retranchés, aussi captivées que moi par un gavage d'une autre sorte, celui du superflu qui leur donnait l'illusion d'être vivants. [...] J'étais le miroir de la ville. Je grossissais, elle se dégradait.
>
> [The city, like the world, was fractured into two parts. On the side with barbwires, big and dark eyes expressed desires of violence due to despair, which become the reflection of a stone held tight in one hand. And on the other side of the walls, the marginalized population, feeling imprisoned like me in another kind of lust that gave them the illusion of being alive. [...] I was the mirror of the city. The more weight I was putting, the more it deteriorated.] (75)

3 Jean-Claude Abada Medjo, 'Poétique de la ville dans l'œuvre d'Ananda Devi', *Loxias* 37 (2012), 3.

The city becomes a figurative site that functions as a locus of violence, illusion, despair and marginalization. Within this space, the obese body is a materialization of the paradoxes of the postmodern society. As I have already outlined, the juxtaposition of city and female subject is not new in Devi's oeuvre. However, an imposing thematic aspect in her recent works is her provocative attempt to challenge the literary *lieux communs* where women are associated with the idea of urban decline and loss of innocence. In *Manger l'autre*, she thus problematizes the social and visual representation of the female body that is no longer the body of a young oppressed girl, but the body of an obese teenager carrying agency while devouring all the suffering of her society. The juxtaposition of her suffering body and the city's degradation recalls the reconfiguration of the 'city-world' that Marc Augé displays within his theory on modernity and mobility.[4] The teenager's body is a mirror of the city, as Devi's character herself states, but it is also a window to the world and its pleas affecting mostly unfranchised people. In *Manger l'autre*, Devi's city also revokes Jean Baudrillard's a-symbolic society, that is, the product of an excessive exchange of commodities.[5] The presence of this ghostly and degraded city calls into question the representation of borders and walls of our contemporary world, which re-shapes our geographical and mental space, and redefines our physical desires as well. The teenager sees in our bodily pleasures the only consolation, and Devi affirms:

> Prisonniers de nos envies pléthoriques, nous nous sommes enfermés au point qu'il est devenu impossible de nous libérer sans éprouver une panique irrationnelle. Ne reste plus que l'assouvissement des envies du corps- gloutonnerie et pornographie, nos deux mamelles.
>
> Notre ville en est l'exemple parfait: les murs et fortifications rehaussées d'année en année lui donnent des allures de forteresse médiévale comme pour mieux signifier son retrait des conflits, des luttes et des peines du monde. Des murs dont la construction a été obtenue par référendum (*dites oui au barricadement urbain*) et qui sont faits pour empêcher l'irruption des invisibles dont les ombres se profilent sur le versant de nos vies.

4 Marc Augé, 'Retour sur les non-lieux. Les transformations du paysage urbain', *Communications* 87 (2010/12), 171–8.

5 Jean Baudrillard, *The Consumer Society. Myths and Structures* (London: Sage, 1999).

> [The prisoners of our plethoric desires, we have been confined for such a long time that it is impossible to find freedom without feeling an irrational panic. The satisfaction of our bodily desires is what we have left- gluttony and pornography are our breast.
>
> Our city is a perfect example: walls and fortifications that rise every year give the city the look of a medieval fortress, which means its pause from conflicts, fights and suffering of the world. The walls have been built upon referendum (say yes to urban isolation) and they are made to prevent invisible people from bursting into our lives where their shadows already stand out] (28)

The use of the personal pronoun 'nous' shows a universal condition of isolation and desolation, which contrasts with the lustful image of the body's needs and desires. The body is our unique source of nourishment (hence the image of breast-feeding), the privileged site of our confinement, which helps us to survive the indifference of the city. The city, similarly the body, is both our prison and shelter blurring the boundaries between visibility and invisibility, freedom and coercion. Through this colourful juxtaposition of the body and the city Devi undoes certain social and historical structured images. She blends social realism with an eerily dramatic literary space in order to powerfully evoke all the hidden aspects of sexuality, femininity, as well as that of the whole society.

Intertwining discourses on the body, the urban city and eating disorders is part of Devi's narrative strategy to highlight women's sexuality and femininity and its gendered and raced relations across history. The city's degradation is proportional to the girl's bodily increase, decomposition and isolation. In *Manger l'autre*, the teenaged girl is a marginalized member of society because of her obese body, which simultaneously becomes her prison and space of 'freedom', wherein she simultaneously denies and affirms herself: 'je suis dans l'isoloir de mon corps, mon seul espace. [...] J'attends que la terre s'ouvre pour disparaitre, mais je suis, hélas, bien trop visible, bien trop massive pour m'effacer si aisément' [I am alone in my body, my only space. I am waiting for the earth to swallow me up, but, alas, I am too visible, too massive, to disappear that easily] (30). This paradox of her body as both a prison and a vessel for her freedom also reveals the implications of her (in)visibility within society. Her obesity makes her an invisible human being because it marginalizes her. At the same time, her excess of bodily matter makes her too visible to the others' gaze, thus undermining her agency. To borrow Susan Sontag's words, her image suggests that she is 'regarded only as someone to be seen and not someone who also sees' with the power to choose to be herself. Her body is her own living space, from where her identity quest starts and tragically ends. At the beginning of the novel, the girl states: 'Je me dévore dans une exquise absence de souffrance. Autour de moi se fige un lac de sang. Toute ma courte vie, j'ai défié la biologie du corps. Maintenant, je défie la biologie de la mort' [I devour myself in a delightful absence of suffering. A lake of blood surrounds me. All my short life I have challenged the biology of the body. Now, I am challenging the biology of death] (9). She perceives her identity through her body which challenges her own existence and even biological death. In fact, her body undergoes an uncanny process of decomposition, not only because she devours herself in front of a webcam, but also because she has been feeding her own body to deliberately decompose it.

Devi's story recalls Bakhtin's trope of the grotesque body, which he conceived in his study of Rabelais' works. Moreover, Devi's girl is built upon the image of Pantagruel who, since his birth, has to feed himself to the point that his body loses its original proportions. According to Bakhtin, the grotesque body:

> is a body in the act of becoming. It is never finished, never completed; it is continually built, created, and build and creates another body. Moreover, the body swallows the world and is itself swallowed by the world [...]. This is why the essential role belongs to those parts of the grotesque body in which it outgrows its own self, transgressing its own body, in which it conceives a new, second body: the bowels and the phallus. Next to the bowels and the genital organs is the mouth, through which enters the world to be swallowed up. And next is the anus. All these convexities and orifices have a common characteristic; it is within them that confines between bodies and between the body and world are overcome.[6]

In order to underline the function of the body as a metaphor for Rabelais' corrupted society and times, Bakhtin's focuses on the collective dimension. Drawing upon the image of the body as a social product, Devi sheds light on the individualistic dimension of her character's adventures, her

6 Mikhail Bakhtin, *Rabelais and His World* (Bloomington: Indiana University Press, 1984), 317.

isolation, as well as her search for love and acceptance. If we consider Devi's text through the lens of Bakhtin's theory, we can see that the teenager's body is grotesque because she undergoes a process of *becoming*, a constant transformation on both individual and organic levels, pushing her own corporeal boundaries. When her father says that he has two beautiful daughters, the girl questions her existence: 'c'est là que débute le mensonge de ma vie duelle, mon impossible tentative de me résoudre' [now starts the big lie of my dual life, my impossible effort to reconcile with myself] (21). She understands that she will never be seen for what she really is, but for the image she gives back to her beholders. She fights this dichotomy, never fully accepting the excuse of having her sister inside her bowels, while paradoxically continuing to feed both her twin and herself.

Arts, literature and media that focus on female bodies depicts them as being controlled and shaped by social codes and powers. These bodies are encouraged to deny their appetites in order to appear more appealing. In her essay, *A Room of One's Own*, Virginia Woolf confirms the importance of eating for a fictional writer: 'One cannot think well, love well, sleep well, if one has not dined well.'[7] A simple and natural stimulus is portrayed as a primary need by a female writer who casts her feminist voice in the Victorian society, thus liberating women from any social and gendered constraints, specifically from the organic matter, food. In Devi's narrative, food is the indirect medium to carry on this feminist portrayal which dwells on materiality and corporality. Devi's novel links the act of eating to discourses of the body and its sexuality. 'Car tout est une histoire de corps. [...] Commencer, donc, par l'orgasme du vivant' [Since everything is a story of the body. ... So let's start from the orgasm of the living body] (10). Echoing Rabelais, Devi points out the importance of the organic matter, which manifests itself through the body. The body is a lively organic matter composed of dead organic matter which constantly transforms the inner body and connects it to the external world. Although Devi does not focus on the language of eating, but rather on the consumption and decomposition of food. Through

7 Virginia Woolf, *A Room of One's Own* (New York: Harcourt, Brace & World, 1957), 18.

the representation of the girl's pantagruelic body, and her hunger, Devi suggests how food and eating are signs of embodied existence and symbolize the life cycle of the body. Dysfunctional bodies are privileged sites where the perception of the *other* and oneself reveal social injustices and imbalanced power relations. It is not by chance that the female character defines herself through dysfunctional relationships with others, such as her dead twin sister, her father, her mother and her lover. All Devi's characters are constantly searching for the other because they need to be loved and accepted. The title, 'Manger l'autre', figuratively translates her radical gesture of eating the other and illustrates her undeniable desire to be accepted as she truly is. In this novel, Devi wants to resituate agency to her character and power to her body. The teenager is aware of her disability. She turns this disability into an asset in order to showcase her ever-changing identity and awareness of her own body and self.

> Pour une fois que je ne suis pas un objet de mépris et de moquerie, je peux jouir sans réserve de cette fascination déferlante, j'en jubile, je l'absorbe comme un aliment de plus, moi qui n'ai vécu que pour manger, qui n'ai eu d'identité que par ce qui passait par ma bouche avant de se décomposer dans mes boyaux et d'en être expulsé- une identité résolument provisoire, donc-, je veux profiter de cette attention comme d'une revanche sur mes années d'exclusion …
>
> [For once, I am not an object of disdain and ridicule, I can freely enjoy this unfolding fascination, I am jubilant, I am absorbing it like another piece of food, I have only lived to eat, I have had no identity other than the one passing through my mouth before it has been decomposed in my bowels and then rejected- I have had a temporary identity, and now I want to enjoy this attention as if it were a revenge on my years of seclusion …] (9).

Devi confines the flexibility and malleability of identity to orifices, explicitly the mouth. According to Bakhtin's analysis, the grotesque body is the representation of degradation, of a transfer to the material dimension, which is further emphasized in Devi's novel by the extreme act of the teenager. That is, she devours herself, and her flesh passes through her mouth, a passage that connects the *inside* and the *outside*, unifying the two parts of the whole structure. At the same time, her grotesque body, along with her cannibal act, defies the boundary between herself and the other, which recalls Kristeva's theory of the abject. If we view the teenager's body through the lens of Kristeva's theory, the teenaged body is an abject object-subject, breaking boundaries and disturbing order: 'It is thus not lack of cleanliness or health that causes abjection but what disturbs identity, system, order. What does not respect borders, positions, rules. The in-between, the ambiguous, the composite.'[8] Additionally, Kristeva points out that the abject is the 'precondition of narcissism'.[9] Indeed, it is narcissism which pushes Devi's character to commit an abject suicide when she imposes her narcissistic image in front of a webcam. Devi combines the organic needs of eating with the sexual drive of the girl. Devi brings this conversation to the extreme by showing the abject aspect of the female body, recognizing its difference and disruption. The body thus becomes an epistemological tool to connect with others, learn about diversity and express oneself in sexual terms. Thus, the teenager states:

> Le lycée accueille les handicapés, malvoyants, malentendants, syndrome d'Asperger, 'autrement capables' - ce qui ne veut rien dire puisque nous le sommes tous, autrement capables-, mais il ne peut accepter une obèse. Selon leur logique, tous les handicapés n'ont pas le choix. Les obèses, eux, c'est évident, l'ont. Ils sont coupables de gloutonnerie, qui est un péché capital. […] Me voir est une preuve de plus de l'échec de l'humanité contre ses pulsions. Je suis la part de vous que vous ne voulez pas être. Le monstre qui se cache en vous tous. Votre peur la plus intime. La main portant la nourriture à votre bouche tremblante de désir ….
>
> [High School hosts the disabled, the visually impaired, the hard of hearing, those with Aspergers, 'differently abled' people- that doesn't mean anything, since we are all differently abled- but the school can't accept an obese person. In their opinion, the disabled don't have a choice. The obese do. They are guilty of gluttony, which is a fundamental sin. […] Seeing me is a further testament to the failure of humanity against its impulses. I am the part of you that you don't want to be. The monster that is hidden in all of you. Your most intimate fear. The hand bringing food to your mouth shaking with desire] (99).

Besides deconstructing the social stereotypes of disabled bodies, the female obese body is a clear means to explore the subject's desire and drives. Her desire of eating resonates with her sexual desire when she meets René,

8 Julia Kristeva, *Powers of Horror. An Essay on Abjection* (New York: Columbia University Press, 1982), 4.

9 Kristeva, *Powers of Horror. An Essay on Abjection,* 13.

the carpenter, who saves her. Because of her body size, she becomes stuck in a door. René rescues her by manipulating her body and the wood with the same precision as a surgeon. Their love affair starts from this moment. Her obese body is both her prison and liberation. Her erotic desire delineates a new map which directs her to explore the most hidden and internal corners of her body. Devi proposes a new geography of female bodies and sexuality, which values diversity and disability as distinctive identity vectors and deconstructs both ideal and abject social bodies. Ultimately, the teenager's grotesque final act is a confirmation of an atavistic desire to go back to the flesh, the organic matter and common material of which we are all made. The importance given to organic matters and fluids is also pertinent to the representation of the body and sexuality in *Le Génie d'Abou*.

Boni-Claverie's *Le Génie d'Abou* resonates with *Manger l'autre* through its challenge to the concept of desire and sexuality. In this short film, the obese woman is mature with blond hair and blue eyes. Her body has typical Arian racial features. Her Fellini-like body is opposed to the two black people's bodies, their plastic beauty and classic geometry. The haptic and visual dimension of the film highlights the sensorial experience and plunges the spectator into an erotic and, almost atavistic, atmosphere that revisits an ancestral rite. Before sexual intercourse with the white obese woman, the sculptor and his genie prepare themselves for the final sacrifice. The woman spreads a white dye on Abou's body and then she cuts a piece of his skin to collect his blood that she will pour onto her body during the sexual act and the murder. Before starting the rite, they spread an oil throughout the body of the white model who dies before reaching her orgasm.[10] The genie also has signs and decorations on her face recalling African masks and rituals. Blood, liquids, erotic screams and sighing frame the sexual act (as well as death and the funeral ritual) redefining the barriers between pleasure, sexuality and power. Blood is the distinctive trait of each human being and a physical manifestation of a transition phase, a process of decomposition of the matter.

Blood is also a symbolic element across Devi's oeuvre. Imagery of blood, and the blood of women in particular, is weaved throughout Devi's novels.

10 Isabelle Boni-Claverie, dir. *Le Génie d'Abou*. Ivory Coast, 1998.

For example, in *Pagli* (2001), *Eve de ses décombres* (2006) and *L'Arbre Fouet* [*The Whipping Tree*] (1997), menstrual blood is emblematic of the oppression faced by women as well as their rebellion against societal norms. In *Manger l'autre*, Devi's character describes her mother at the time of delivery as a 'vache abattue par l'énormité de son œuvre. Sa cicatrice s'était rouverte. Le sang s'épanchait en même temps que son lait. L'intérieur de son corps était rempli d'acide. Elle pleura, elle qui ne pleurait jamais' [a cow destroyed by the heaviness of its work. Her scar reopened. Blood flowed at the same time as her milk. The inside of her body was full of acid. She cried, she who never cries] (14). The blood of the delivery of the obese girl is contrasted to the blood of her death, a cannibal act, anticipating her bloody death. Blood is thus the metaphor for life and death in both Devi and Boni-Claverie's works. The metaphor of blood is nurtured by the image of the grotesque body and the violence carried within it.

In *Le Génie d'Abou*, the excessive flesh of the woman walking into the art studio metaphorically probes the representation of both the decay and consumerism that is encouraged by the Western world. The depicted erotic dance of bodies represents both the excess and lack of proportion through which power generates and creates submissive and subversive subjects. In an interview conducted in February 2017, Boni-Claverie explained to me that the film aims to question the audience's norms and boundaries of what can be perceived as acceptable and desirable in a relationship. Furthermore, she stresses, 'il est évident que le génie (la femme noire) manipule Abou, et en même temps à la fin quand il part, elle perd sa puissance, car pour exister le dominant a besoin du dominé, sans il n'est rien. Se pose alors la question de qui domine réellement?' [it is evident that the genie (the black woman) manipulates Abou, and at the same time when she leaves, she loses her power, since in order to exist the dominant person needs the dominated one, without the latter the dominant person is nothing. Here, we can ask the question: who is the real dominator?].[11] Abou and his genie share the same object of desire and phantasm of power, which are both displayed on the white woman's body through sex and violence. When Abou does not need his genie anymore, and she slowly vanishes, he

11 Interview conducted via Skype on 17 February 2017.

regains awareness of his act: in fact, the last scene of the film shows Abou in a close-up, regretting both his murder and his artwork. The representation of the white and black bodies and their sexual intercourse displays heterogeneous power relations which can occur in various situations and can be reshaped by individual subjects and their dramatic choices. The final piece of art, the anonymous silhouette of an obese woman, is the artistic inscription of the complex and interchangeable power relations, as well as of a fluid conception of sexuality, desire and death, thus calling out the spectators to position themselves within this surreal dance. The erotic dance performed by the three characters is especially unsettling, because of its state of surrealism and lack of normativity. The atmosphere is surreal to the extent that spectators, as well as characters themselves, do not have a clear understanding of the dynamics involved in the relationship between the sculptor, his genie and the model. The genie goes back to the magic bottle immediately after the murder, suggesting that she has never really existed before, and confirming her ephemerality. The white woman is desired by both Abou and his genie, despite her body size that does not correspond to normative parameters of beauty and femininity.

The concept of power and desire must also be read in the light of a new codification of racial roles that the artist proposes: the encounter between the black couple and the white woman retraces the historical power relation between the two races. Yet, this encounter offers a new perspective since, this time, the 'victim' is the white woman. In this short film, as well as in *Manger l'autre*, power and desire are displayed through the representation of an obese body, also defined above as a grotesque or abject body. Achille Mbembe borrows Bakthin's concept of the grotesque body to highlight the peculiarities of a postcolonial state. Specifically, as he clarifies in his article, 'Provisional notes on the Postcolony', the grotesque body becomes the theatrical spectacle on the postcolonial stage, defined as a 'tendency to excess and a lack of proportion as well as by distinctive ways in which identities are multiplied, transformed and put into circulation'.[12] While Mbembe refers to the political relations between rulers and people

12 Achille Mbembe, 'Provisional Notes on the Postcolony', *Africa: Journal of the International African Institute* 62/1 (1992), 3–37, 3.

in a postcolonial state, in *Le Génie d'Abou* the grotesque body of the white woman provocatively embodies the disproportions and inequalities that power-based relations generate within society, characterized also by a colonial past. Black bodies have always been the site of violence, prejudices and tortures. However, in Boni-Claverie's film, the white woman with her grotesque body is the 'violated' victim and the black couple are the executioners. At this point, the following questions arise: what does it mean for Abou to create a sculpture of a white model who he (or his genie) then murders? Is this act voluntary? Can a piece of art be the product of death? These questions lead to a discussion of the role of the artists and the artistic space, as well as the position of the viewers.

The Power of the Gaze: Where Does Art Stand?

Both Devi and Boni-Claverie's works subvert the power of the gaze. The gaze evokes a certain idea of voyeurism with which the two artists play in order to denounce the consequences of excessive consumerism on both social and individual levels. The notion of being seen and desired is foregrounded through the criticism not only of normative rules, but also of a dysfunctional society's need to be amused and entertained. In *Manger l'autre*, the issue of voyeurism takes on a tragic and sacrificial end. Echoing the almost sacrificial act of Abou, Devi's character devours herself on a virtual altar, in front of a webcam that displays the image of her death to the entire world. The presence of the webcam, along with the lens of the camera, is intrusive from the very beginning of Devi's novel: 'l'oeil braqué sur moi, qui me relie à des millions- peut-être des milliards- d'autres yeux, ne fait que renforcer ma determination à aller jusqu'au bout de mon sacrifice' [The eye pointed at me, which connects me to millions – perhaps billions – of other eyes, only reinforces my determination to accomplish my sacrifice] (9). She turns her body-object to a body-subject through the lens of the webcam which allows her to transform her disability and bodily monstrosity into a piece of art and form of entertainment. 'Big Brother' is watching her while she accomplishes her sacrifice, which will paradoxically unite her to the rest of the world and make her feel part of a community from which she had previously been excluded. The 'eye' imposed on her has a twofold function: it represents the others' judgment and failure of society, but it is also the tool that enables her to free herself from her body, thus empowering her identity and femininity. Sacrificing herself in front of a webcam means to restitute to viewers their own image: eating her body is eating the other. Her body is the subject and object of her own virtual piece of art, and the gaze of the spectator is part of the spectacle, thus becoming a mode of interaction between the two. Her image changes according to the photographic tool and the relation she holds with the photographer, whether being René or herself. René, whose name recalls the main character of Nancy Huston's novel, *Infrarouge*, Rena, takes pictures of the girl while having sex. She describes him as a filmmaker, like a *deus in machina*, who prepares his creation:

> Il a apporté un appareil argentique, un trépied, des objectifs, des lumières. [...] il me met en scène, dirige sur moi des lumières douces mais précises qui longent mon corps de tendresse. ... Il oublie parfois ses photos. D'autres fois, juste après avoir fait l'amour, [...] il saisit son appareil et prend des photos de moi après l'orgasme.
>
> [He brought a silver object, a tripod, lenses, lights. ... he displays me, directs soft lights towards me thus filling my body with tenderness. ... He sometimes forgets his pictures. Other times, after making love, ... he gets his camera and takes pictures of me after my orgasm] (182).

The camera captures the sensuality of the act, reconstructing a new image of the girl and her obese body, which speaks of her sexuality and sensuality. Yet, when the novel seems to reach a happy ending, there is a twist in the story. The girl gets trapped into her own image. Her own gaze is the other's gaze: 'ce n'est pas le regard des autres, non: c'est moi qui suis monstrueuse' [it is not the others' gaze, not: it is me who is a monster] (189). When she sees herself, she sees society, thus challenging its dynamics and the implications of the excessive need of being seen. Through her character, Devi explores once again the inner realm of subjectivities within the collectivity. The teenager challenges the viewers and their concept of both acceptance and entertainment. Devi's novel raises the same question Boni-Claverie asks in her film, that is: what makes a body desirable? And who has the right to judge?

In *Le Génie d'Abou*, the statue resulting from the murder of the white model calls to its beholders and provokes their critical eye. The viewers of the short film participate in the ritual from the preparation to the final act. The statue, as a potential piece of art, hides the crime, but clearly portrays the excesses of the body. The statue represents a living body which is deprived of any organic matter, but which will live forever, being a piece of art. The statue holds a double function in the short film: referential, because it is the representation of a real body, and also narrative, because it contributes to defining the power relations among characters (since the creative process of the statue is both sexual intercourse and death) and unpacks the history of black and white people. The short film focuses its attention on the statue and its future, which both the sculptor and the spectators might prospect. Abou 'creates' it in order to respond to his creative inspiration (and sexual drive). However, he regrets this creation at the end of the film, which captures his feelings of resentment and horror towards his own deed. The statue interacts with both Abou's conscience and that of the spectators. The film's audience are encouraged to unconsciously reimagine history, power and gender relations, as well as sexuality and normativity. It is noteworthy how both artists subvert the 'dysfunctional' body, as it has been defined in this chapter, in order to shed light on the dysfunctionalities of today's society on multiple levels. These levels include individual, social and historical conceptualizations of the body. In both works, the body becomes a piece of art that is a materialization of a renewed ethics and responsibility: Devi and Boni-Claverie turn the female obese body into a powerful lens through which rethinking concepts of pleasure, female sexuality and power relations, thus stressing the importance of subjectivity and diversity within the realm of the contemporary Ultimately, the extreme consequences faced by the two bodies suggest a universal question: what are we willing to part with to be entertained? The last word goes to the public at large in both works.

Conclusion

Devi and Boni-Claverie depict anew the female body and its sexuality. Natural processes of eating, representations of obesity and sex, stretched to the extreme, are turned into metaphors for satirizing excessive consumerism, entertainment and propensity for wastefulness. The body is the metaphorical site that shows the complexities of our society. The body thus becomes an aesthetic and narrative tool to establish new discourses on the representation of women, identity and power relations. Displaying a body expressively conceived as a disabled body, Devi's novel challenges the structured classification of woman and the primacy of gender as monolithic categories, while also disrupting the conception of power and voyeurism in a society marked by the digital revolution and an excessive need of being seen and entertained. This chapter has sought to illustrate the distinctive ways in which the two female artists continuously renew the representation of women, body and creation itself. Through adopting multiple perspectives and rewriting feminist, as well as, postcolonial theories, Devi and Boni-Claverie question societal norms and historical structures. In so doing, they encourage the public to go beyond stereotypes and advocate for diversity, acceptance and inclusivity, core values which allow us to understand what it means to be fully human.

Bibliography

Abada Medjo, Jean-Claude, 'Poétique de la ville dans l'œuvre d'Ananda Devi', *Loxias* 37 (2012).

Augé, Marc, 'Retour sur les non-lieux. Les transformations du paysage urbain', *Communications* 87 (2010/12), 171–8.

Bakhtin, Mikhail, *Rabelais and His World* (Bloomington: Indiana University Press, 1984).

Baudrillard, Jean, *The Consumer Society. Myths and Structures* (London: Sage, 1999).

Boni-Claverie, Isabelle, *Le Génie d'Abou*, Ivory Coast, 1988.

Butler, Judith, *Bodies that Matter: On the Discursive Limits of Sex* (New York: Routledge, 1993).

Devi, Ananda, *Manger l'autre* (Paris: Grasset, 2018).

Huston, Nancy, *Infrarouge* (Arles: Actes Sud, 2010).

Kristeva, Julia, *Powers of Horror. An Essay on Abjection* (New York: Columbia University Press, 1982).

Lionnet, Françoise, *Postcolonial Representations: Women, Literature, Identity* (Ithaca, NY: Cornell University Press, 1995).

Mbembe, Achille, 'Provisional Notes on the Postcolony', *Africa: Journal of the International African Institute* 62/1 (1992), 3–37.

Onesta, Cristina, 'Pluralité du corps, corporalité de l'espace: les jours vivants d'Ananda Devi', in Jean Claude Medjo and Kumari R. Issur, eds, *Espace, mémoires et savoirs dans la fiction d'Ananda Devi* (Maroua: Revue Mosaïques, 2017), 11–23.

Sontag, Susan, *Regarding the Pain of Ohers* (New York: Picador, 2003).

Woolf, Virginia, *A Room of One's Own* (New York: Harcourt, Brace & World, 1957).

SARA BÉDARD-GOULET

8 *14* or the Missing Arm: Ontological Instability of the French Contemporary Novel in Jean Echenoz's Work

Introduction

Hybrid proliferation has received considerable attention in recent research, where it has been named differently depending on perspectives and scholars. Notions such as 'hybrid',[1] 'cyborg',[2] 'quasi-object quasi-subject',[3] 'stuff',[4] 'queer critter',[5] 'vibrant matter'[6] account for the current need to think the world in the light of its destruction. Cultural representations such as French contemporary novels also display this significant interest in a renewed conception of the human-nonhuman relationship. Although nature writing is not a significant genre in the French literary tradition,[7] French novels presumably address the nature-culture divide in

1 Bruno Latour, *Nous n'avons jamais été modernes* (Paris: La Découverte, 1991).

2 Donna Haraway, *Simians, Cyborgs, and Women: The Reinvention of Nature* (New York: Routledge, 1991).

3 Michel Serres, *Le Parasite* (Paris: Grasset, 1980).

4 Maurizia Boscagli, *Stuff Theory. Everyday Objects, Radical Materialism* (London: Bloomsbury, 2014).

5 Karen Barad, *Meeting the Universe Halfway. Quantum Physics and the Entanglement of Matter and Meaning* (Durham, NC: Duke University Press, 2007).

6 Jane Bennett, *Vibrant Matter. A Political Ecology of Things* (Durham, NC: Duke University Press, 2010).

7 Hannes De Vriese, 'On the Meaning of Being Alone with Nature: Sylvain Tesson's Ecocritical Sincerity and Ecopoetic Sensuality in *Dans les forêts de Sibérie*', in Daniel A. Finch-Race and Stephanie Posthumus, eds, *French Ecocriticism. From the Early Modern Period to the Twenty-First Century* (Frankfurt: Peter Lang, 2017), 231–49, 232.

a similar way as French eco-thought does, 'by *reciprocally problematizing* "nature" and "humanity"'.[8] Correspondingly, ecologically informed studies of literature in France often adopt a more aesthetically oriented approach to texts, paying attention to form and structure, which are central to the French literary institution.[9]

Despite a growing reflection on the dissolution of boundaries between human and nonhuman, several scholars have pointed out the problems posed by 'anthropocentric mind talk'.[10] Hybrids may question the ontological norms formed during the sixteenth century but studies that 'conflate representation and human language [...] perpetuate Cartesian dualism because the atomic elements remain either human mind or unfeeling matter'.[11] Strikingly, a 'hybrid postnature' would still imply 'a refusal to deal with real alterities' where nonhumans are homogenized with humans without attention to their irreducible alterity.[12] Hence, Karen Barad has argued for a renewed consideration of ontological indeterminacy in order to 'queer the nature of identity, calling into question the [...] binary'.[13] She invites us to trouble the presumption of the *anthropos* by paying attention to the 'materializing practices of differentiation' without assuming any relevance of the distinctions between humans and nonhumans.[14]

The challenges raised by hybrids thus require further investigation based on the instability of matter and the boundary making practices, such as bodily norms, that constitute the 'human' and the 'nonhuman'. The

8 Kerry H. Whiteside, *Divided Natures: French Contributions to Political Ecology* (Cambridge: MIT Press, 2002), 3.

9 Nathalie Blanc, Denis Chartier and Thomas Pughe, 'Littérature & écologie: vers une écopoétique', *Écologie & Politique* 36 (2008), 17–28; Pierre Schoentjes, *Ce qui a lieu: essai d'écopoétique* (Marseille: Wildproject, 2015).

10 Eduardo Kohn, *How Forests Think. Toward an Anthropology beyond the Human* (Berkeley: University of California Press, 2013), 40.

11 Kohn, *How Forests Think. Toward an Anthropology beyond the Human*, 40.

12 Baptiste Morizot, 'Nouvelles alliances avec la terre. Une cohabitation diplomatique avec le vivant', *Tracés* 33 (2017), 73–96 (74). All translations are my own unless otherwise noted.

13 Karen Barad, 'Nature's Queer Performativity', *Women, Gender & Research* 1/2 (2012), 25–53, 26.

14 Barad, 'Nature's Queer Performativity', 32.

purpose here is to analyse representations of human and nonhuman and their interactions in the contemporary French novel *14* by Jean Echenoz, published in 2012 (translated as *1914* by Linda Coverdale in 2014), in which five characters from Vendée are mobilized to fight in the First World War. This text, echoing all of this author's work, neither relates to nature writing nor does it take an ecological stance, 'away from any pacifist or ecological activism' according to Pierre Schoentjes.[15] Yet, its close attention to material details, revealing matter's strangeness as well as companionship,[16] makes it 'an open mesh of possibilities, gaps, overlaps, dissonances and resonances'.[17] Its 'queer textual form'[18] suggests that it can contribute to an ecocritical theory related to the queer ecology advocated by Timothy Morton as it presents valuable features regarding nonhuman agency and its aestheticization. Indeed, as its title suggests, *14* is a war novel that insists on the material implications of the Great War, providing a strong narrative agency[19] to the numerous nonhumans involved (insects, gear, trenches, etc.). Like many war novels, it also focuses on human bodies, interacting with their environment and, more specifically, assuming a singular position, between human and nonhuman, thus queering and querying bodily norms. Considering matters of body and body matter in *14* within the framework of 'agential separability'[20] provides an insight into normative identity not limited to the human and on deconstructive ways of being, or becoming, if we consider it as ongoing phenomenal, transformative process.[21] As such,

15 Pierre Schoentjes, '*14* de Jean Echenoz. Un dernier compte à régler avec la Grande Guerre', *Critique* 11/786 (2012), 978.

16 Donna Haraway, *When Species Meet* (Minneapolis: University of Minnesota Press, 2007).

17 Eve Kosofsky Sedgwick, 'Queer and now', *Tendencies* (Durham, NC: Duke University Press, 1993), 8.

18 Timothy Morton, 'Guest Column: Queer Ecology', *PMLA* 125/2 (2010), 276.

19 Serpil Oppermann, 'From Ecological Postmodernism to Material Ecocriticism: Creative Materiality and Narrative Agency', in Serenella Iovino and Serpil Oppermann, eds, *Material Ecocriticism* (Indianapolis: Indiana University Press, 2014), 21–36.

20 Barad, 'Nature's Queer Performativity', 32.

21 See Gilbert Simondon, *L'Individuation à la lumière des notions de formes et d'information* (Paris: Jérôme Millon, 2017).

it also offers a favourable avenue to reflect on vibrant matter, including bodies, as non-binary.

This chapter is structured as follows. First, it explores the specificities of the war novel regarding the interaction between humans and nonhumans on the battlefield and puts them in dialogue with the narrative characteristics of *14*. Examples of characters' and objects' plasticity are presented to underline the ontological instability at work in Echenoz's novel. Second, proliferation of nonhumans, often presented as lists in Echenoz's work, is analysed from the angle of identity as a phenomenal process. Third, the analysis focuses on individuation, or the construction and transformation of the individual, in close connection with the body, as a specific place of indeterminacy and fragmentation, highlighted by the main character's severed arm.

Indeterminacy and Uncertainty

If 'ecological literature is an end-of-the-world literature',[22] end-of-the-world literature can be considered an ecological literature widely speaking, as it gives attention to the interaction of living beings in their failing milieu. Indeed, end times, collapse, catastrophe are necessarily concerned with how destruction affects the world and its inhabitants, and literature featuring this kind of situation examines its process in greater or lesser detail. By presenting characters that are both witnesses and actors of the environment's degradation, war novels may draw parallels between the trauma made to/by humans and the violence that equally disturbs the environment.[23]

22 Alain Suberchicot, *Littérature et environnement: pour une écocritique comparée* (Paris: Champion, 2012), 13.

23 Donia Boubaker, 'Représentation littéraire de la grande guerre et éco-critique au XXIe siècle dans l'œuvre de Laurent Gaudé', *French Studies Bulletin* 36/137 (2015), 77–80 (77–8).

The First World War narratives insist on the close and constant presence of the earth in the trenches, seen as representative of the '"involution process" suffered by soldiers on the way of [sic] dehumanization'.[24] Alternatively, we can argue that this presence questions humanization and redistributes the places that are usually attributed to humans and nonhumans. While sometimes 'the earth, ultimate symbol of the voiceless, becomes a fully fledged character-entity',[25] its anthropomorphizing quality can be an opportunity to 'shak[e] loose the crusty toxic scales of anthropocentricism, where the human in its exceptional way of being gets to hold all the "goodies" like agency, intentionality, rationality, feeling, pain, empathy, language, consciousness, imagination, and much more'.[26] In *14*, dead soldiers provide the earth with arms (echoing, as we will see further, the protagonist's severed arm), which, rather than sketching an imploring gesture of the scarified ground, are ironically turned into useful props by the sappers: 'les sapeurs transpirent de fatigue et de peur, ôtent leur capote pour travailler plus aisément, la suspendent à un bras qui, saillant du sol retourné, leur tient lieu de portemanteau.'[27] [[sappers] sweat from fatigue and fear, take off their greatcoats to work more freely, and might hang them on an arm sticking out of the tumbled soil, using it as a coat tree.][28] Here, limbs no longer provide an anthropocentric advantage to humans as they lose vitality and agency in death and are treated as any other objects, thus interrogating together the humane and the human.

It is common knowledge that war disrupts normality and the rules applied in peaceful times, hence revealing the artificiality of norms, such as ones that rule identities and define individuals, objects and so on. In *14*, the presence of numerous nonhuman entities pairs with a definite indeterminacy, affecting characters and things, and goes together with a narrative uncertainty. Kris Peeters has convincingly insisted on the significant

24 Boubaker, 'Représentation littéraire de la grande guerre et éco-critique au XXIe siècle dans l'œuvre de Laurent Gaudé', 78.

25 Boubaker, 'Représentation littéraire de la grande guerre et éco-critique au XXIe siècle dans l'œuvre de Laurent Gaudé', 77.

26 Barad, 'Nature's Queer Performativity', 27.

27 Jean Echenoz, *14* (Paris: Minuit, 2012), 79.

28 Jean Echenoz (trans. Linda Coverdale), *1914* (New York: New Press, 2014), 68.

meta-discourse at work in Echenoz's novel, which questions how to narrate the war, showing how the epistemological and ethical issues become aesthetic ones.[29] As fictional reconstruction of a historical event is uncertain, novelists' 'mode of storytelling is not the affirmation of a fictional experience but its interrogation'.[30] This interrogative mode not only allows for a critique of the horror of a mechanized war as well as the 'sensational realism that dominates much of the writing [...] on the Great War',[31] it also destabilizes the determinate definition of humans and nonhumans. Where fiction is believed to provide a human individual experience of war, as opposed to documents and historical objectivity, which dehumanize and de-personalize it,[32] I argue that it can also reveal the trajectories of all kinds of entities.[33] War novels, and the individual reality of armed conflicts they display, would thus lead to a literal 'subjective truth of others'.[34] This subjective truth includes nonhuman others, where 'individual entities are not separate determinately bounded and propertied objects, but rather are (entangled "parts of") phenomena (material-discursive intra-actions)'.[35]

29 Kris Peeters, '*14/1914*: Jean Echenoz's Great War, Meta-Discourse and the English Reception', in C. Declercq and J. Walker, eds, *Languages and the First World War: Representation and Memory* (London: Palgrave Macmillan, 2016), 140–63, 144.

30 Peeters, '*14/1914*: Jean Echenoz's Great War, Meta-Discourse and the English Reception', 144.

31 Peeters, '*14/1914*: Jean Echenoz's Great War, Meta-Discourse and the English Reception', 151.

32 Peeters, '*14/1914*: Jean Echenoz's Great War, Meta-Discourse and the English Reception', 144.

33 Comparable to the 'lived experience' of animal existence described by Florence Burgat in 'The Unexpected Resemblance between Dualism and Continuism, or How to Break a Philosophical Stalemate', in Louisa Mackenzie and Stephanie Posthumus, eds, *French Thinking about Animals* (East Lansing: Michigan State University Press, 2015), 49–59 and *Une autre existence: la condition animale* (Paris: Albin Michel, 2012).

34 Dominique Viart, '"L'exacte syntaxe de votre douleur": la Grande Guerre dans la littérature contemporaine', in C. Milkovitch-Rioux and R. Pickering, eds, *Écrire la guerre* (Clermont-Ferrand: Presses universitaires Blaise Pascal, 2000), 463–74, 474.

35 Barad, 'Nature's Queer Performativity', 32.

In Echenoz's novel, this is made visible through the indeterminacy that affects humans and nonhumans alike. The main character, Anthime Sèze, whose first name and description suggest the opposite of an intimate perspective on the action,[36] interestingly placing him between the individual and the de-personalized experience of the war, is identified by Blanche, the woman who is waiting for him to come back from the war,[37] as someone who accommodates to any situation: 'vous savez comme il est, il s'adapte toujours.' (70) [You know how he is: he always adapts. [60)]. In addition to this inherent plasticity, he shows signs of contradictory efforts towards other characters, which enhances his unsettled position. First, when encountering his brother during mobilization, 'Anthime a dû se forcer à se raidir et se détendre en même temps, tâche antinomique mais nécessaire pour vaincre l'espèce d'embarras intimidé que la présence de Charles, quoiqu'il advînt, faisait naître en lui.' (13) [Anthime had to steel and calm himself at the same time, a paradoxical yet necessary procedure he followed to master the intimidating uneasiness he felt in the presence of Charles, no matter what the occasion. (6)] A few days later, during a parade, he adopts a similar technique to respond to Blanche's smile: 'Anthime, n'y a réagi que par un regard, le plus court et le plus long possible, se forçant à le charger du moins d'expression disponible tout en en suggérant le maximum – nouvel exercice cette fois doublement antinomique' (20) [Anthime, had responded only with a look, the shortest and longest one possible, forcing himself to invest it with the least amount of expression while at the same time suggesting the maximum: a novel approach, doubly paradoxical this time (14)]. In a way, Anthime occupies a position between the individual and the generic character, as the novel retells the well-known tale of the Great War by focusing on one character's experience. Fiction, then, would provide a decentred historical view through one human character among other entities. The character's expression further blurs the human-nonhuman binary, placing his rigid body between the animate and the inanimate, and aestheticizing his double-binding effort.

36 Peeters, '*14/1914*: Jean Echenoz's Great War, Meta-Discourse and the English Reception', 147.

37 She is also waiting for Anthime's brother's return, who, as we will see, dies on his first mission.

More generally, the character's liability and the incompatible strains that disturb his unity and pull his body in opposite directions go together with the undecided identification of other characters and objects. For example, when Anthime sees Blanche in the parade's crowd, he fails to identify her at first glance: 'Anthime a cru distinguer Blanche sur le trottoir gauche de l'avenue. Il a d'abord pensé que c'était une resemblance et puis non, c'était elle' (19) [he thought he noticed Blanche on the left sidewalk of the avenue. At first, he took her for a lookalike but then, no, it was she, Blanche (13)]. This kind of misidentification is obviously more common on the battlefield, where soldiers wear the same uniform and are made to conform to certain standards. For example, as their attire evolves following technical improvements, they acquire at some point a shiny blue helmet: 'quand on les a coiffés, on s'est d'abord bien amusés de ne plus se reconnaître tant ils étaient couvrants.' (74) [Putting them on, the men found it funny not to recognize one another, for the helmets obscured much of their faces. (63)] The covering helmets point the status of soldiers as undefined, unknown individuals that contribute, in this novel, to deconstructing the personalized privilege of humans. This is the case even for Charles Sèze, Anthime's brother, who is portrayed as a snob, very particular about his appearance, and quickly moved to the air force where, nevertheless, he is undistinguishable from the pilot on the plane with him:

> Sous leur casque et leurs grosses lunettes de protection, mêmement vêtus de combinaisons de toile noire caoutchoutée, doublées de lapin et renforcées de chèvre, vestes et pantalons en cuir, gants et chaussons fourrés, les deux hommes se ressemblent d'autant plus que rien n'est visible de leur corps sauf leurs joues, leurs mâchoires et leur bouche par laquelle ils essaient de se parler – mais sans pouvoir guère échanger mieux que des exclamations qu'ils articulent mal et n'entendent qu'à peine, assourdis par les quatre-vingts chevaux du moteur, leur parole coupée par l'air vif. (52)
>
> [Underneath their helmets and big protective goggles, dressed alike in leather jackets and trousers, overalls of black rubberized cloth lined with rabbit fur and reinforced with goatskin, plus fur-lined boots and gloves, the two men look all the more identical because their bodies are invisible, aside from their cheeks, jaws and mouths, as they try to talk to each other but prove unable to exchange more than poorly articulated exclamations they can hardly hear, deafened as they are by the eighty-horsepower engine, while the brisk air sweeps away their words. (44)]

Importantly, the indeterminacy that affects characters is shared by objects, which are also confused with others, blurring boundaries between them, and causing a general sense of uncertainty. In the war zone, this misidentification can be prompted by the horror and its denial, which is the case for Anthime during his first battle, as he is forced to watch what is happening:

> Tout de suite quelques hommes, pas loin d'Anthime, se sont mis à tomber, il a cru voir jaillir deux ou trois gerbes de sang mais les a rejetées avec vigueur de son esprit – n'étant pas même certain, n'ayant pas le temps d'être certain que ce fût du sang sous pression, ni d'ailleurs d'en avoir jamais vu à ce jour, du moins pas de cette façon ni sous cette forme. (61)
>
> [Right away a few men not far from Anthime set about falling. He thought he saw two or three great spurts of blood but shoved them vigorously out of his mind, not being even certain, not having had time to be certain, that it was blood under arterial pressure–or even that he'd ever really seen blood until then, at least not in that way or that form. (51)]

Beside these extreme conditions, nonhuman entities are confused with one another, as deceptive appearances are common in Echenoz's work.[38] A striking example of this is the opening of *14*'s seventh chapter:

> Ce moustique, à treize heures, apparaît dans l'air normalement bleu d'une fin d'été, sur le département de la Marne. Propulsons-nous vers cet insecte : à mesure qu'on l'approche, il grossit peu à peu jusqu'à se transformer en petit avion, biplan biplace de modèle Farman F 37 (51)
>
> [This mosquito, at one o'clock, appears in air of a normal end-of-summer blue over the département of the Marne in northeastern France. Let's propel ourselves up toward this insect: as we draw closer, it gradually grows into a small plane, a Farman F37, a two-seater biplane (43)]

This metamorphosis of an insect into a plane not only insists on the general contrast between appearance and reality, as mentioned by Pierre Schoentjes,[39] it also confuses the ontological status of nonhuman entities

38 Schoentjes, '*14* de Jean Echenoz. Un dernier compte à régler avec la Grande Guerre', 979.

39 Schoentjes, '*14* de Jean Echenoz. Un dernier compte à régler avec la Grande Guerre', 979.

by mixing the semantic fields of common ('moustique', 'air bleu', 'fin d'été', 'Marne') and military ('à treize heures', 'département', 'propulsons-nous', 'biplan biplace') discourses. By playing with identification, Echenoz's work explores the contemporary concern with the instability prompted by the current situation through a historical event that, retrospectively retold, provides a renewed perspective on a world that is being destroyed and on human bodily identity that is fragmented.

Multiplicity and Performativity

The presence of abundant nonhumans contributes to the instability of matter in Echenoz's novel, as they unsettle the 'order of things'. Blanche's bedroom, described as discordant, is a significant example of the mix created by multiplying objects:

> Il règne une drôle d'ambiance disharmonieuse dans cette chambre, pourtant si calme et bien rangée. Sur son papier peint fleuri légèrement décentré, des cadres enserrent des scènes locales […] et les meubles témoignent d'un effort de diversité forestière tel un arboretum: bonnetière à miroir en noyer, bureau en chêne, commode en acajou et placages de bois fruitier, le lit est en merisier et l'armoire en pitchpin. Drôle d'atmosphère, donc, dont on ne sait si elle tient à la disjonction […] des lais de ce papier peint passé […] ou à cette surprenante variété mobilière de bois : on se demande d'abord comment des essences si diverses peuvent s'entendre entre elles. Et puis on le sent très vite, elles ne s'entendent pas bien du tout, elles ne peuvent même pas s'encaisser (22–3)
>
> [A strangely discordant atmosphere reigns in this albeit [sic] peaceful and orderly room. Framed local scenes […] adorn the slightly off-centered flowered wallpaper, and the furniture bespeaks an effort toward woodlands diversity worthy of an arboretum: a mirrored walnut *bonnetière*, a writing desk of oak, a mahogany chest of drawers with fruitwood veneer, while the bed is of wild cherry, the armoire of yellow pine. So, an unusual ambiance, and one ponders whether it arises from the mismatched edges […] of this faded wallpaper […] or from the astonishing variety of furniture woods: one wonders at first how so many different materials can get along together. And then one quickly senses that they do not get along at all, they cannot even stand one another (17–18)].

In this passage, the dissonant atmosphere joins with a slight decentring of the wallpaper ('légèrement décentré'), as if testifying to a displaced interest in objects, while the different pieces of furniture are treated as individuals, dissatisfied with each other's presence. An anthropomorphized inventory such as this one gives a voice to the voiceless, who nevertheless participate in the world and in fiction. In this respect, it is not only factual, as Pierre Schoentjes argues,[40] but it also shows an overflow of hybrids and questions the privileged agency of humans. Interestingly, the wood provided by different tree species only becomes disharmonious indoors, when transformed into furniture material and forced to coinhabit, whereas this diversity is presented as prized in an arboretum, thus pointing to the double standard that applies to 'nature' and 'culture' or to what happens when nonhumans integrate with the human realm.

This kind of enumeration is common in Echenoz's works,[41] as it accounts for the multiple objects that share the characters' lives and provides an insight into the contemporary reality of the mass production of commodities.[42] In *14*, such lists would provide an indirect insight on the war while avoiding repetition of the direct witnesses' discourses.[43] Additionally, I suggest that these lists offer a relative autonomy to the items they contain, while proposing interpretative space to the readers, as shared, 'open, flexible structures'[44] that, as is the case in Georges Perec's work,[45] involve recognition and gathering but also 'keep a space open for the unknown and unclassifiable'.[46] For Perec, enumeration constitutes an attempt to 'send thought back to the unthought that establishes it, the classified to the unclassifiable (the unquantifiable, the inexpressible) that

40 Schoentjes, '*14* de Jean Echenoz. Un dernier compte à régler avec la Grande Guerre', 970.

41 Florence Bouchy, 'Démystification et invention du quotidien: les objets des romans de Jean Echenoz', *Recherches & Travaux* 77 (2010), 77–89.

42 Dominique Carlat, 'De la vertu critique de l'humour à l'ère industrielle de la reproduction: *Les Grandes blondes* de Jean Echenoz', *Roman 20–50* 38 (2004), 71–6.

43 Schoentjes, '*14* de Jean Echenoz. Un dernier compte à régler avec la Grande Guerre', 968.

44 Anna Kemp, 'Playing and Being in Georges Perec', *French Studies* 72/4 (2018), 564.

45 Echenoz is greatly inspired by Georges Perec.

46 Kemp, 'Playing and Being in Georges Perec', 566.

it insists on concealing'.[47] Thus, 'preceding thought and denying the false order of taxonomic structures, such loose groupings eschew the mania for closure and completion'.[48] As such, lists suspend binary identification of nonhumans (and humans) while preserving particularity.

Indeed, indeterminacy queers identity but it does not exclude an 'agential cut', a differentiation between agents in the mesh of matter, not relying on 'human practices of differentiating, that is, as cultural distinctions'[49] but rather on 'the world's performativity – its iterative intra-activity'.[50] For Karen Barad, performativity is not iterative citationality, a citation of all previous performances, as it is the case for Judith Butler,[51] but intra-actions that separate entities together-apart, simultaneously distinguishing and connecting them in a given time and space, as a 'condition of exteriority-within-phenomena'.[52] Because 'the agential cut enacts a "local" resolution within the phenomenon of the inherent ontological indeterminacy', 'identity is a phenomenal matter; it is not an individual affair'.[53] Such an understanding of identity steers away from a classical ontology that postulates discrete entities that interact within a determinate causality and a linear time flow. In that respect, *14* attempts to queer traditional time flow with an assertive post hoc narration, where hindsight is recalled, sometimes to justify considerable ellipses: 'on connaît la suite.' (115) [We all know the rest. (101)] It also uses the uncommon *passé composé* tense, which 'sets the narration at the very intersection of the past and the present',[54] to narrate the past action while reinforcing the present position adopted towards it and suspending the modern kind of temporality.[55] Twisting time conception and its associated ontology necessarily influences individuation, which

47 Georges Perec, *Penser/Classer* (Paris: Hachette, 1985), 153.

48 Kemp, 'Playing and Being in Georges Perec', 566.

49 Barad, 'Nature's Queer Performativity', 31.

50 Barad, 'Nature's Queer Performativity', 32.

51 Judith Butler, *Bodies That Matter: On the Discursive Limits of "Sex"* (New York: Routledge, 1993).

52 Barad, 'Nature's Queer Performativity', 32.

53 Barad, 'Nature's Queer Performativity', 32.

54 Peeters, '*14/1914*: Jean Echenoz's Great War, Meta-Discourse and the English Reception', 155.

55 Lionel Ruffel, *Brouhaha. Les mondes du contemporain* (Lagrasse: Verdier, 2016).

then becomes a process. Gilbert Simondon has observed this phenomenon in humans, which he compares to the genesis of crystals in a metastable milieu; in other words, possessing a potential for transformation.[56] The individual is the process rather than the product: 'The true individual only exists for an instant during the operation of crystallization: it exists as long as the shaping occurs.'[57] I will now relate these considerations with the current stakes of the French novel concerning respectively the 'return to/of the subject'[58] and its deletion.[59] Both trends are present in Echenoz's works and made particularly visible in the 'fragments de chair militaire' (82) [bits of military flesh (71)] scattered on the battlefield.

Body and Identity

Contemporary French novels are moved by two apparently contradictory tendencies. On the one hand, they tend to represent characters engaged in a deletion, withdrawal, disappearance process[60] echoing a certain trend in the contemporary period.[61] On the other hand, following on from the postmodern novel, they present a return *to* the subject,[62] a return *of* the subject[63] visible in the topics that they address and in their characters' presentation. This second trend is made particularly noticeable in genres

56 Simondon, *L'Individuation à la lumière des notions de formes et d'information.*

57 Simondon, *L'Individuation à la lumière des notions de formes et d'information*, 61.

58 Dominique Viart and Bruno Vercier, *La Littérature française au présent* (Paris: Bordas, 2008), 19; Áron Kibédi Varga, 'Le Récit postmoderne', *Littérature* 77 (1990), 3–22, 16.

59 Dominique Rabaté, *Désirs de disparaître. Une traversée du roman français contemporain* (Rimouski: Tangence, 2015), 23.

60 Rabaté, *Désirs de disparaître. Une traversée du roman français contemporain.*

61 David Le Breton, *Disparaître de soi. Une tentation contemporaine* (Paris: Métaillé, 2015); Alain Ehrenberg, *La Fatigue d'être soi. Dépression et société* (Paris: Odile Jacob, 2008).

62 Viart and Vercier, *La Littérature française au présent*, 19.

63 Kibédi Varga, 'Le Récit postmoderne', 16.

such as autofiction but also in experience narratives that equally insist on the banal and the extraordinary through the embodiment of a character, which allows a strong identification from the readers. As already discussed, this is the case for war novels such as *14*, which attempts to provide an individual perspective on a historical event. This novel also presents a deletion process of the subject, not only, and as expected from a war novel, because it involves innumerable deaths, but also because it pursues an 'experience of the impersonal',[64] a desire to disappear, with characters who wish to abstract themselves from the tyranny of the situation in a form of negative resistance to control and assignment devices. As such, it mentions three ways to get out of the battlefield, besides being killed by the enemy: (1) 'la bonne blessure' (94) [that 'good wound' (81)], (2) suicide or (3) desertion. This third solution is adopted by Anthime's friend, Arcenel, as a passive form of resistance 'sans qu'il l'eût d'ailleurs vraiment choisie, sans préméditation mais sous l'effet d'une impulsion: juste un état d'âme, produisant en chaîne un moment d'humeur puis un mouvement.' (95) [without truly choosing it, actually; there was no premeditation, just an impulse, a mood, producing in turn a moment of pique, and then–motion. (83)] Unfortunately, Arcenel's unplanned walk gets him quickly caught by the gendarmes, summarily court-martialled and executed by the firing squad, before 'un défilé devant son corps [ait] été ordonné de sorte que ce verdict fît méditer la troupe.' (104) [the men were ordered to march past his body so they would reflect upon his fate. (90)] The character's body then joins the millions of others who fell during the war, while his identity changes drastically. Before his stroll, Arcenel was an ordinary soldier fighting for his country, whose body endured the harsh conditions, until the military police identify him as a deserter, 'catégorie dans laquelle Arcenel venait sans le savoir ni le vouloir de s'inscrire.' (101) [into which [...] category Arcenel had just unknowingly and unwillingly placed himself (88–9)]. This evolution efficiently shows how differentiation processes concerning the body are culturally inflected on an otherwise undetermined reality and how Echenoz's novel attempts to emphasize these mechanisms.

64 Rabaté, *Désirs de disparaître. Une traversée du roman français contemporain*, 71.

This is already highlighted in *14*'s second chapter, where Anthime's three friends are introduced according to the correlation between their appearance and profession:

> Padioleau, sujet frêle, un peu timide, visage maigre et cireux, affichait tout le contraire d'une prestance de garçon boucher quand c'était, justement, son métier. Bossis, non content de détenir quant à lui un physique d'équarrisseur, l'était authentiquement, Arcenel exerçant pour sa part la profession de bourrelier qui ne suppose pas d'habitus particulier. (15)
>
> [Padioleau, slightly built, a touch timid, thin-faced with a waxy complexion, had nothing of the sturdy presence of a butcher's boy even though that was, in fact, his profession, whereas Bossis, not content with possessing the physique of a knacker, actually was one. As for Arcenel, he was a saddler, a craft that presupposes no particular habitus.] (9)

In France, the term 'habitus' is inevitably associated with Pierre Bourdieu's work,[65] which examines the connection between individual action and socialization. The habitus is constituted by dispositions acquired by individuals through their social experience, which instils social structures into subjectivity and leads to social reproduction. Bourdieu's vision of the social has been criticized as deterministic and Echenoz's novel seems to point out the randomness of the habitus by presenting how bodies do not necessarily match the expected standards for given occupations in the case of Padioleau and Bossis, or how Arcenel's work does not produce any expectations regarding his body. In the above passage, Arcenel's body appears particularly undistinguishable, until it later becomes a 'deserter's body'.

In First World War novels, human bodies are paradoxically largely expendable and singularly suffering, often on the border between subject and object as they are 'consumed' in large numbers thanks to the army's confidence in mass tactics. Fragmented bodies are common and wounded soldiers are numerous, enhancing the body's fragility and instability, and its connection with identity. Echenoz's novel shows this through metonyms that objectify individuals, replacing, for example, military musicians with

65 Pierre Bourdieu, *La Distinction. Critique sociale du jugement* (Paris: Minuit, 1979).

their instruments: 'le bras du baryton s'est vu traversé par une balle et le trombone est tombé, très mauvaisement blessé [...] comme ils reprenaient la mesure où se lève l'étendard sanglant, la flûte et l'alto sont tombés morts.' (62) [the baritone sax was shot in the arm and the trombone fell gravely wounded [...] when they began to reprise the measure in which 'the bloody standard is raised' the flute and tenor sax fell down dead. (52–3)] Not only do those metonyms 'suggest that the ideal of epic warfare they metonymically represent was soon shattered',[66] they also connect intimately, through their bodies, humans and nonhumans. This situation is enhanced by the literal illustration of the French anthem's line, as a kind of self-fulfilling prophecy, and feeds the uncertainty towards each entities' definition.

Bodily identity becomes even more elusive when, after a year and a half in the trenches, the principal character loses his right arm, severed by a piece of shrapnel, and is sent home. At first, Anthime does not realize that he has lost his arm, 'ne revenant à la réalité de son absence que lorsque son regard s'appesantissait' (118) [returning to the truth of its absence only when his gaze lingered too long (103)], but quickly gets used to being left handed and gives up activities and postures that require both hands. A few months later though, 'il a senti renaître [...] un bras droit imaginaire mais d'allure tout aussi réelle que le gauche.' (118) [he felt the return of a right arm that was? felt? imaginary but seemed just as real as the left one. (104)] On the one hand, this missing yet present arm insists, as a 'témoin muet' (120) [silent witness (105)], on the testimony of 'a non-existent element of war reality', underlining the importance of 'an imaginary witness such as Anthime being as important as the real ones'.[67] On the other hand, 'le vieux coup du membre fantôme' (120) [the old story of the phantom limb (106)] pinpoints the body's paradoxical state through what is presented as a cliché, as if to insist on this usual condition of presence/absence. Through Anthime's arm, the body is present and absent at the same time, in a quantum indeterminacy that embodies its possibilities of differentiation. The missing arm also reminds us of the complexity of matter's agency as,

66 Peeters, '*14/1914*: Jean Echenoz's Great War, Meta-Discourse and the English Reception', 150.

67 Peeters, '*14/1914*: Jean Echenoz's Great War, Meta-Discourse and the English Reception', 147.

even as it is absent, it still has a clear role in the continuous meaning-making process of the world. This is revealed less than a year before the end of the war, when the character has to travel to Paris with Blanche for business reasons and encounters men on leave who sing the 'The Internationale', as insubordination becomes more common after high casualties are attributed to the suicidal attacks planned by the army's command. Anthime observes the crowd: 'son visage est demeuré inexpressive, tout son corps immobile, cependant qu'il a levé le poing droit par solidarité, mais personne ne l'a vu faire ce geste.' (123) [Anthime stood perfectly still and his face showed no expression as he raised his right fist in solidarity, but no one saw him do it.] (108) This gesture recalls matter's invisible agency and suggests, through the possibilities of fiction, a different apprehension of bodily existence and identification.

Conclusion

To conclude, through their representation of humans and nonhumans, contemporary French novels such as *14* can inform the conception of hybrids. Their narrative devices, such as anthropomorphism, question the privileged agency of humans over nonhumans and the metonyms highlight the shared characteristics of all entities. By representing destruction, war novels like this one show an unstable state of things that questions matter and its apparent determinacy in 'peaceful times'. In *14*, an interrogative mode of storytelling reflects on historical narratives, while the multiplication of nonhumans, enumerated in various contexts, and deceptive appearances that create ambiguous characters, contribute to destabilize identity and its normative definition. Irony is used to underline the randomness of differentiation and oppose a certain social determinism while post hoc fiction, playing on its awareness of the event outcomes, works against previous discourses on the Great War. As the main character is particularly indeterminate, although he offers an individual perspective on the war, his lost arm highlights the body's presence/absence state, its quantum indeterminacy that opens its potential for phenomenal differentiation, outside usual bodily norms. In a way, this conception of the body connects two opposite tendencies of the contemporary French novel, the return of/to the subject and its disappearance, by insisting, through fictional means, on the ontological instability that marks the contemporary period. As such, Echenoz's novel proposes a different model for identifying entities and their bodies, more sustainable in considering and maintaining their potentials,[68] rather than reducing and simplifying them. Through a significant implication of nonhumans, it deconstructs the anthropocentric vision of the body and queers the usual human subject, pointing to its inherent indeterminacy and continuous individuation process.

Bibliography

Barad, Karen, *Meeting the Universe Halfway. Quantum Physics and the Entanglement of Matter and Meaning* (Durham, NC: Duke University Press, 2007).

—— 'Nature's Queer Performativity', *Women, Gender & Research* 1/2 (2012), 25–53.

Bennett, Jane, *Vibrant Matter. A Political Ecology of Things* (Durham, NC: Duke University Press, 2010).

Blanc, Nathalie, Chartier, Denis and Pughe, Thomas, 'Littérature & écologie: vers une écopoétique', *Écologie & Politique* 36 (2008), 17–28.

Boscagli, Maurizia, *Stuff Theory. Everyday Objects, Radical Materialism* (London: Bloomsbury, 2014).

Boubaker, Donia, 'Représentation littéraire de la grande guerre et éco-critique au XXIe siècle dans l'œuvre de Laurent Gaudé', *French Studies Bulletin* 36/137 (2015), 77–80.

Bouchy, Florence, 'Démystification et invention du quotidien: les objets des romans de Jean Echenoz', *Recherches & Travaux* 77 (2010), 77–89.

Bourdieu, Pierre, *La Distinction. Critique sociale du jugement* (Paris: Minuit, 1979).

Burgat, Florence, 'The Unexpected Resemblance between Dualism and Continuism, or How to Break a Philosophical Stalemate', in Louisa Mackenzie and Stephanie

68 Yves Citton, *Renverser l'insoutenable* (Paris: Seuil, 2012).

Posthumus, eds, *French Thinking about Animals* (East Lansing: Michigan State University Press, 2015), 49–59.

Burgat, Florence, *Une autre existence: la condition animale* (Paris: Albin Michel, 2012).

Butler, Judith, *Bodies That Matter: On the Discursive Limits of "Sex"* (New York: Routledge, 1993).

Carlat, Dominique, 'De la vertu critique de l'humour à l'ère industrielle de la reproduction: *Les Grandes blondes* de Jean Echenoz', *Roman 20-50* 38 (2004), 71–6.

Citton, Yves, *Renverser l'insoutenable* (Paris: Seuil, 2012).

Echenoz, Jean, *14* (Paris: Minuit, 2012).

—— *1914*, trans. Linda Coverdale (New York: New Press, 2014).

Ehrenberg, Alain, *La Fatigue d'être soi. Dépression et société* (Paris: Odile Jacob, 2008).

Haraway, Donna, *Simians, Cyborgs, and Women: The Reinvention of Nature* (New York: Routledge, 1991).

—— *When Species Meet* (Minneapolis: University of Minnesota Press, 2007).

Iovino, Serenella and Oppermann, Serpil, 'Introduction. Stories Come to Matter', in Serenella Iovino and Serpil Oppermann, eds, *Material Ecocriticism* (Indianapolis: Indiana University Press, 2014), 1–17.

Kemp, Anna, 'Playing and Being in Georges Perec', *French Studies* 72/4 (2018), 557–71.

Kibédi Varga, Áron, 'Le Récit postmoderne', *Littérature* 77 (1990), 3–22.

Kohn, Eduardo, *How Forests Think. Toward an Anthropology beyond the Human* (Berkeley: University of California Press, 2013).

Latour, Bruno, *Nous n'avons jamais été modernes* (Paris: La Découverte, 1991).

Le Breton, David, *Disparaître de soi. Une tentation contemporaine* (Paris: Métaillé, 2015).

Morizot, Baptiste, 'Nouvelles alliances avec la terre. Une cohabitation diplomatique avec le vivant', *Tracés* 33 (2017), 73–96.

Morton, Timothy, 'Guest Column: Queer Ecology', *PMLA* 125/2 (2010), 273–82.

Oppermann, Serpil, 'From Ecological Postmodernism to Material Ecocriticism: Creative Materiality and Narrative Agency', in Serenella Iovino and Serpil Oppermann, eds, *Material Ecocriticism* (Indianapolis: Indiana University Press, 2014), 21–36.

Peeters, Kris, '*14/1914*: Jean Echenoz's Great War, Meta-discourse and the English Reception', in C. Declercq and J. Walker, eds, *Languages and the First World War: Representation and Memory* (London: Palgrave Macmillan, 2016), 140–63.

Perec, Georges, *Penser/Classer* (Paris: Hachette, 1985).

Rabaté, Dominique, *Désirs de disparaître. Une traversée du roman français contemporain* (Rimouski: Tangence, 2015).

Ruffel, Lionel, *Brouhaha. Les mondes du contemporain* (Lagrasse: Verdier, 2016).

Schoentjes, Pierre, *Ce qui a lieu: essai d'écopoétique* (Marseille: Wildproject, 2015).

—— '*14* de Jean Echenoz. Un dernier compte à régler avec la Grande Guerre', *Critique* 11/786 (2012), 964–81.

Sedgwick, Eve Kosofsky, 'Queer and now', *Tendencies* (Durham, NC: Duke University Press, 1993), 1–22.

Serres, Michel, *Le Parasite* (Paris: Grasset, 1980).

Simondon, Gilbert, *L'Individuation à la lumière des notions de formes et d'information* (Paris: Jérôme Millon, 2017).

Suberchicot, Alain, *Littérature et environnement: pour une écocritique comparée* (Paris: Champion, 2012).

Viart, Dominique, '"L'exacte syntaxe de votre douleur": la Grande Guerre dans la littérature contemporaine', in Catherine Milkovitch-Rioux and Robert Pickering, eds, *Écrire la guerre* (Clermont-Ferrand: Presses universitaires Blaise Pascal, 2000), 463–74.

Viart, Dominique, and Vercier, Bruno, *La Littérature française au présent* (Paris: Bordas, 2008).

De Vriese, Hannes, 'On the Meaning of Being Alone with Nature: Sylvain Tesson's Ecocritical Sincerity and Ecopoetic Sensuality in *Dans les forêts de Sibérie*', in Daniel A. Finch-Race and Stephanie Posthumus, eds, *French Ecocriticism. From the Early Modern Period to the Twenty-First Century* (Frankfurt: Peter Lang, 2017), 231–49.

Whiteside, Kerry H., *Divided Natures: French Contributions to Political Ecology* (Cambridge: MIT Press, 2002).

KATE FOSTER

9 The Cyborg's Undecidable Body: A Game of 'Who am I?' in Gaston Leroux's *La Poupée sanglante*

In Ridley Scott's *Blade Runner* (1982), bounty hunter Rick Deckard administers the Voight-Kampff empathy test in order to differentiate cyborg replicants from humans. In a world where 'skin jobs', as they are known in the film, so closely approximate human beings, a test which functions through the external imposition of normative categories or identities onto another being is the only way to flush out the artificial copies. Later that decade, Donna Haraway celebrated the innate hybridity of the cyborg's human-machine body and its attendant boundary-dissolving potential. The cyborg's combination of organic and technological elements renders its categorization uncertain while also allowing it to undermine the bodily norms of the human. Sixty years earlier, Gaston Leroux's diptych *La Poupée sanglante [The Kiss that Killed]* and *La Machine à assassiner [The Machine to Kill]* (1924) had already deployed the cyborg in order to trouble identities. Gabriel, Leroux's cyborg *avant la lettre*, comprises a clockwork body and the brain of a serial killer, an incongruous coupling of artisanal craft and cutting-edge science which anticipates the anachronistic nature of the late twentieth-century cyborg. Gabriel is defined differently by each of his three creators as, variously, a surrogate child/potential lover, the physical proof of scientific genius and an automaton which contains the secret of perpetual motion. If others' definitions are what constitute bodily norms, Leroux's text implicitly asks whether such varying definitions suggest that bodily norms are perhaps not as stable as we might assume. While Haraway argued that her hybrid did not entail disembodiment, as N. Katherine Hayles has noted, embodiment has frequently been marginalized in cybernetic posthumanist discourses.[1] Although Leroux's text predates these alternative conceptions of the posthuman – a disembodied uploading of consciousness versus embodiment as the bedrock of human existence – it nonetheless provides an interesting lens through which to consider such questions.

In this chapter, I suggest that Gabriel's cyborg body works constantly to disrupt and subvert fixed definitions and relationships, because his origins in miscegenation (he is a hybrid of man and machine) equip him to resist identities inflicted on him by others. This man-machine figure foreshadows the word 'cyborg', coined by Norbert Wiener in 1960, as well as Haraway's boundary-breaking version. Haraway's posthumanist manifesto imagines a utopia made possible by her 'argument for *pleasure* in the confusion of boundaries.'[2] She claims that the cyborg allows us to 'embrac[e] the possibilities inherent in the breakdown of […] distinctions structuring the Western self'.[3] Haraway's cyborg upends the traditional dichotomy between natural and mechanical because, like Gabriel, it is simultaneously both and neither. Yet Gabriel does not contain the same utopian potential as Haraway's metaphorical cyborg: his technologized body is a prison devoid of physical sensations, a deprivation which leads to his suicide, suggesting the insufficiency of a disembodied (or only partially embodied) human mind, thus questioning the bodily norm of Cartesian dualism which clearly separates it from the body. The text's engagement with contemporary scientific debates around energy and organ transplants underscores the cyborg's propensity to breach the traditional limits of the human body and reinforces its talent for unsettling fixed identities.

The journalistic career of Gaston Leroux (1868–1927) began in 1894 with *L'Écho de Paris*, followed by employment at *Le Matin*, where he reported the trials of several anarchists who were executed by guillotine, a

1 Donna Haraway, *Simians, Cyborgs and Women: The Reinvention of Nature* (London: Free Association, 1991), 180; and N. Katherine Hayles, *How We Became Posthuman: Virtual Bodies in Cybernetics, Literature, and Informatics* (Chicago: University of Chicago Press, 1999), 4.

2 Haraway, *Simians, Cyborgs and Women: The Reinvention of Nature*, 150.

3 Haraway, *Simians, Cyborgs and Women: The Reinvention of Nature*, 174.

method of dispatch which would be key to the plot of *La Poupée*.[4] In 1907, he became a full-time novelist, publishing over thirty books.[5] There is a dearth of criticism on *La Poupée*, and little more on its author. Alfu's quasi-biography of Leroux highlights the latter's propensity for using historical figures and scientific debate in his literary output, while Emma Bielecki's analysis of Leroux's *Chéri-Bibi* [*Cheri-Bibi*] stories stresses the importance of Alexis Carrel's work in those texts, particularly the hybrid bodies which it appeared to make possible through transplantation.[6] The creation of the cyborg in *La Poupée* is frequently compared within the text to Carrel's discoveries, and the links between the real-life scientist's organ transplants and contemporary discourses of energy and fatigue form a significant part of my reading. The lived experience of a man-machine hybrid is hypothesized by Leroux as chaotic, isolating and, ultimately, doomed to failure.

In *La Poupée*, the clockmaker Norbert lives with his daughter Christine, an artist, and prosecutor nephew Jacques. Christine and Jacques are engaged to be married. Their bookbinder neighbour Bénédict obsessively spies on Christine, the object of his unrequited love, and learns that she keeps a 'man' called Gabriel locked in a wardrobe, who is in reality a clockwork automaton built by Norbert and Jacques. Both Norbert and Jacques have been pursuing perpetual motion, the older man in clockwork machines, the younger in living organisms. Bénédict is accused of murdering his housemaids, all of whom have mysteriously disappeared. He is convicted and, after his execution by guillotine, Jacques obtains Bénédict's head from the executioner's basket, and transplants the brain into the clockwork body, a pre-posthuman fusion of man and machine which I term 'cyborg'.[7] Newly autonomous and in possession of Bénédict's memories, Gabriel (after the human brain

4 I will refer to the story comprised in the two texts as *La Poupée*.

5 Alfu, *Gaston Leroux: parcours d'une œuvre* (Encrage: Amiens, 1996), 13, 20, 115, 124.

6 Emma Bielecki, '"Fatalitas!" The Criminal Body in Belle Epoque Crime Serials: The Strange Case of *Chéri-Bibi*', *Journal of European Popular Culture* 4/2 (2013), 195–209.

7 Although the word 'cyborg' did not exist at the time, Gabriel is more than simple automaton. The addition of Bénédict's brain to Gabriel's clockwork body marks a critical shift in behaviour and, crucially, identity, which requires a different nomenclature.

is added, the cyborg is always referred to thus) kidnaps Christine and flees, pursued by Jacques. Gradually, Bénédict's innocence becomes apparent (the real murderer was the Norberts' landlord, the vampiric marquis) but, depressed that his mechanical body denies him so much of life's physical experience and sensations, Gabriel throws himself off a cliff, smashing his body to pieces. The constant querying of Gabriel's bodily identity by various characters propels the narrative forwards. Bénédict, for example, obsesses over Christine's strange companion, unable to decide if he is a relative, a secret lover or an invalid, a preoccupation which drives him to flee in a jealous rage. Eventually of course, Bénédict's brain and the body of the 'strange companion' become one, and so Bénédict's interrogation of Gabriel's identity inadvertently foreshadows the querying of normative limits of the human body which the cyborg's creation will engender. After Bénédict's execution, the assumption that Gabriel is a murderous man-machine running amok causes a frenzied chase across France, and a media-fuelled panic amongst the public. Gabriel's subversion of normative categories is such that other characters are driven to emotional, unreasoned behaviour in response.

Keeping It in the Family

While Gabriel's body has been built by Norbert and Jacques, and Jacques's medical skills allow him to incorporate Bénédict's brain into the clockwork shell, it was Christine who sculpted his face, rendered as beautiful as his archangel namesake. Gabriel, then, is the product of three parthenogenetic 'parents'. Christine frequently codes her relationship with Gabriel as parental, insisting that she expresses her love to him 'comme une mère le dit à son enfant' [as a mother to her child].[8] This assumed identity of mother is also detected by others, as the proprietors of the hotel to which

8 Gaston Leroux, *La Machine à assassiner: roman d'aventures et de mystère* (Paris: Tallandier, 1924), 183. All emphases original. All translations are my own unless otherwise noted.

Gabriel and Christine flee describe her 'soins quasi maternels pour son compagnon' [almost maternal attention towards her companion]. Yet, the hoteliers had originally assumed a different connection: 'c'est plaisir de les voir [...] la main dans la main [...] C'est beau, l'amour!' [it is a pleasure to watch them [...] hand in hand [...] Love is beautiful!] (172–3). This same ambiguity is present from the text's beginning, uncovered by Bénédict as he tries to convince himself that Gabriel is a family member, while acknowledging that Christine 'ne l'embrasse pas comme un parent' [does not kiss him like a relative].[9]

While viewing one's life's work as a child already represents a queering of heterosexual reproduction, a second level of queering is at work in the quasi-incestuous overlap of the assumed parent-child relationship and Christine's sexual feelings for Gabriel. This 'incest' has already been vaguely foreshadowed by the fact that Jacques and Christine are cousins. Such an interplay of different types of near-transgression speaks to *La Poupée's* most obvious intertext, Mary Shelley's *Frankenstein* (1818): already cousins, Victor and Elizabeth are brought up in the same household as siblings and, like Jacques and Christine, will go on to marry.[10] Much like Victor, Christine and Jacques have a 'child' together in Gabriel, although Christine insists more strongly on the existence of this relationship. Just as Victor does, Jacques will soon come to hate his hybrid 'offspring' and will set out to destroy it. Originally seeing his creation as evidence of his own genius, Jacques nevertheless maintains a level of secrecy around Gabriel's creation which continues after Gabriel escapes with Christine as his captive. The transgressive nature of their work, like Christine's relationship with Gabriel, prevents them from revealing the truth for as long as possible.

Christine, consciously or not, betrays a nebulosity in her feelings for Gabriel. Yet in a key passage from the first novel, the child metaphor is

9 Gaston Leroux, *La Poupée sanglante: roman d'aventures et de mystère* (Paris: Tallandier, 1924), 75. All emphases original. All translations my own unless otherwise noted.

10 A second intertext is Bram Stoker's *Dracula* (1897), which relates to the vampire side-plot in Leroux. While the vampires in *La Poupée* might invite a queer reading, they remain tangential to the question of the cyborg Gabriel's identity, and as a result I have not developed that discussion here.

absent in her description of him: 'oui, j'ai embrassé sa beauté!… Hélas! […] je ne peux plus l'aimer! […] C'est une tête vide' [yes, I embraced his beauty! Alas! […] I can no longer love him […] He is just an empty head] (*La Poupée sanglante*, 142). Gabriel will always be wanting as a potential lover because he is nothing more than a beautiful image. Even after the brain transplant when Gabriel is no longer empty-headed, any possible romantic relationship between Christine and Gabriel is displaced by the assumption of Bénédict's guilt. Yet, it is significant that this potential relationship remains unrealized, because it allows Christine to maintain the two imagined identities of mother and lover. The tension between the two positions is never resolved because the sexual relationship is only ever a fantasy. Gabriel, for his part, does not refer to any mother–child relationship, instead acknowledging briefly (for there is very little mention of Gabriel's conception of his own identity) that being unable to feel Christine's touch is too difficult to bear: Gabriel would rather die than live a disembodied love affair with Christine. While he has successfully repudiated the categorizations ascribed to him by others, his own failure to incarnate a normative bodily identity – a thinking mind in a feeling body – leads him to suicide.

Energy

Predictably, the identities ascribed to Gabriel by his male creators relate more to their own professional activities than the personal relationships and emotions which influence Christine's categorization of the cyborg. At the beginning of *La Poupée*, the narrator recounts that Norbert has a project which consists of 'une sorte "d'échappement" contraire à toutes les lois connues de la mécanique', equipped with '[un] "mouvement" [qui] durait depuis des années et qu'il ne […] remontait jamais' [a sort of 'escapement' which breaks all known laws of mechanics equipped with a 'movement' which functioned for years and which he never needed to wind] (*La Poupée sanglante*, 8). Norbert, then, seems to have found the key to perpetual motion, and which he will incorporate into Gabriel's body. Yet, unable to monetize it, Norbert 'ne semblait plus travailler que pour l'art, à la poursuite d'une chimère où d'autres, avant lui, avaient laissé leur raison' [only seemed to work for work's sake, chasing a pipe dream, where others before him had lost their minds] (8). For Norbert, Gabriel's clockwork mechanism is the embodiment of an obsession, an old riddle solved to no obvious purpose. This masculine 'birth' of a hybrid almost-man – here carried out by two men instead of one – queers the usual process of human reproduction by almost completely erasing woman's role in the process of creation. It also serves as a further reference to *Frankenstein* and, like Shelley's text, is an attempt to overcome death, or rather, to redefine the meaning of death. While he does not explicitly link his musing to Gabriel's creation, Jacques asks rhetorically, 'où commence la vie?… où commence la mort?… Partout! nulle part! […] *Une chose que l'on croit morte n'est que de la vie en sommeil*' [where does life begin? Where does death begin? Everywhere! Nowhere! *Something which we believed to be dead is but life sleeping*] (101).[11] Jacques is working on a variant of perpetual motion in living tissue, as Bénédict exclaims, 'avec ses études sur les pulsations du cœur!' [with his research on the beating of the heart!] (103). Of course, the suggestion that mechanical or bodily energy could continue ad infinitum is pure conceit on Leroux's part, a myth which allows him to create such a body, albeit one with something of a scientific basis.

La Poupée's engagement with the scientific debates of its time mark out its author as 'un homme attaché au progrès scientifique' [a man with an interest in scientific progress].[12] As the science of energy was altered by nineteenth-century discoveries, energy was newly relevant in the worlds of both work and literature. Modernity seemed to demand ever more energy, and many were concerned that the human body would be left behind. As these concepts crept into the public consciousness in the late nineteenth and early twentieth centuries, the idea emerged that movement was an inherent property of living bodies. Energy seemed to coalesce around political issues concerning workers and social decline. Anson Rabinbach has outlined how

11 Victor Frankenstein admits that he had thought that 'if I could bestow animation upon lifeless matter, I might in process of time […] renew life where death had apparently devoted the body to corruption'. Mary Shelley, *Frankenstein, or the Modern Prometheus* (London: Penguin, 2012), 47.

12 Alfu, *Gaston Leroux: parcours d'une œuvre*, 45, 80.

the reprinting of Julien Offray de La Mettrie's *L'Homme machine* [*Man a Machine*] in 1865 gave renewed impetus to the idea of man as machine and made the machine metaphor more relevant. Accompanying that was the hope that fatigue – from which machines were blissfully free – could be eradicated from the human worker. For the first time, the machine was the model for man to emulate, rather than the reverse, yet such discourses were troubled by the discovery of entropy, which subjected both man and machine to the dissipation of energy.[13] The bodily norm which the human represents is questioned through the pursuit of superhuman strength and everlasting energy, a force in itself which drives Jacques and Norbert to create Gabriel. Their quest examines whether such a restrictive norm (as they see it) actually constitutes a limit, as they seek to discover whether it might be transgressed or surpassed. Yet the attempt to harness energy within their creation comes undone as Gabriel's excessive energy searches desperately for an outlet, moving beyond the control of either body or maker, resulting in destruction and chaos. The science of thermodynamics, then, acts as a lens through which to view ideas of energy and force. Excessive energy can only mean destruction because thermodynamics dictates that energy cannot be created, and that energy in a given system tends always towards disorder. In *La Poupée*, Gabriel's death puts right the breach which his creation engendered, and peace and order are restored.[14]

Jacques' quest for perpetual motion in living beings is linked to contemporary advances in organ transplants, particularly those developed by Alexis Carrel. The work of French-born physician Carrel (1873–1944) at the Rockefeller Institute in New York on transplantation made him internationally famous, earning him a Nobel Prize in 1912.[15] His ground-breaking

13 Anson Rabinbach, *The Human Motor: Energy, Fatigue, and the Origins of Modernity* (New York: Basic Books, 1990), 1, 48, 63, 65.

14 Bernard Brunhes, the author of a text on perpetual motion from which Bénédict inaccurately quotes, believed that the inherent appeal of energy conservation, despite evidence to the contrary, explained the continued search for *le mouvement perpétuel*. Bernard Brunhes, *La Dégradation de l'énergie* (Paris: Flammarion, 1908), 376–84.

15 Andrés Horacio Reggiani, *God's Eugenicist: Alexis Carrel and the Sociobiology of Decline* (New York: Berghahn, 2007), 2–3, 32.

discoveries were frequently reported. *Le Matin* – Leroux's former employer and publisher of *La Poupée* in *feuilleton* – published over twenty articles on Carrel between 1908 and 1923. These were not lengthy scientific features, but interesting titbits, and an attempt by his homeland to reclaim one of their own.[16] One of Carrel's most famous experiments was known as 'the immortal chicken heart'.[17] The reality was that tiny fibroblasts (a type of connective tissue cell) were removed from the heart, and that the fibroblasts – not the heart – pulsated for over 100 days. After the fragments stopped 'beating', technicians extracted cells which continued to 'live' until 1942 when an assistant forgot to add fresh nutrients to the artificial environment.[18] All of which is to say that while Carrel was well-known to the French public, his work was neither accurately reported nor perhaps widely understood.

Taking up this theme, Birouste, the Norberts' neighbour, claims in *La Machine à assassiner* that 'on a vu faire revivre un cœur mort!' […] c'est-à-dire qu'il a ressuscité le mort!' [they reanimated a dead heart! […] in other words, he brought a dead man back to life!]. He tells his neighbours that 'Carel' [sic] was the scientist responsible, 'l'un de ceux pour qui les Américains ont créé l'Institut Rockefeller' [one of those scientists for whom the Americans built the Rockefeller Institute] (19).[19] Birouste's poor grasp of Carrel's research was likely not unusual among a non-specialist audience, given the way the press reported it. Birouste also insists that Carrel had preserved a brain in serum, claiming that Jacques is pursuing similar work and 'qu'il laissera un jour derrière lui tous les Carel [sic] et tous les Rockefeller!' [that one day he will surpass all the Carels and Rockefellers!] (20). Birouste's erroneous suggestion that Rockefeller was a scientist like Carrel aside, more interesting is the *mise-en-abyme* through which other characters present Jacques's work as ground-breaking despite lacking a

16 'L'animal ne meurt pas tout entier tout de suite', *Le Matin* (23 November 1912).

17 'Un Cœur retiré de l'organisme et qui bat pendant plus de trois mois', *Le Matin* (19 June 1912).

18 Reggiani, *God's Eugenicist: Alexis Carrel and the Sociobiology of Decline*, 41–2.

19 This is one of many untruths concerning Carrel put forward in Leroux's text: the Institute was created in 1901, and Carrel commenced his employment there in 1906. Reggiani, *God's Eugenicist: Alexis Carrel and the Sociobiology of Decline*, 21.

complete understanding of it, just as the public did not understand Carrel's. Gabriel is the evidence of Jacques's genius (and to a lesser extent Norbert's), but he is consistently the least understood character of the story, even by his creators.

One reason that Carrel's research attracted such interest was because it suggested an imminent prospect of immortality.[20] Indeed, one article on his work alleged that 'le phénomène mystérieux de la vie pourra dorénavant être étudié dans les laboratoires' [the mysterious phenomenon which is life can now be studied in laboratories].[21] Birouste makes a comparable claim when he suggests that 'nous pouvons envisager le moment où *nous supprimerons la mort!*' [we can envisage the moment when we will overcome death!] (18). Jacques has previously spoken in such terms and is driven by ambition and a belief in his own brilliance: '[l]a science n'a point d'aboutissement si elle n'arrive pas à faire d'une créature une créatrice! [...] Nous passons notre temps à recevoir la vie et à la donner!' [science will never be complete if it does not succeed in making a creature into a (female) creator! [...] We spend our time giving and receiving [eternal] life!] (77). Jacques is presented as the most intelligent and reasoned character, and as such is the first to consider that Bénédict might be innocent, correctly suspecting the marquis instead. Yet he remains convinced that Gabriel has kidnapped Christine and determines to liberate her from the 'tyran [...] son œuvre ... son enfant' because 'il ne s'agissait plus d'amour-propre d'auteur!' [tyrant [...] his life's work ... his child because it was no longer a question of a creator's love for his creation!] (169). Despite his openness to extending the boundaries of scientific knowledge, Jacques clings to the fixed idea that he holds of Gabriel's character.

In another allusion to *Frankenstein*, Jacques follows the pair to a snow-covered mountain village, but after learning that Christine now believes in Bénédict's/Gabriel's innocence and is no longer his captive, but his willing companion, Jacques's vehemence is newly motivated by jealousy.[22]

20 Reggiani, *God's Eugenicist: Alexis Carrel and the Sociobiology of Decline*, 32.

21 'On pourra cultiver des cellules vivantes comme on cultive des microbes', *Le Matin* (7 May 1913).

22 At the end of Shelley's novel, Victor follows the monster to 'the everlasting ices of the north', whose cold does not affect the creature. See Shelley, *Frankenstein*, 211 *et passim*.

Perversely pleased that his automaton cannot get up from the floor unassisted, he smiles as he imagines Gabriel falling over. Jacques's characterization of Gabriel, then, is mediated through Christine's own interpretation of their cyborg creation, and changes in line with hers. Jacques's genius and his status as a man of science are challenged by his petulance, which Christine highlights: 'toi, Jacques, la sagesse même, tu es jaloux d'une poupée!' [Jacques, you are wisdom itself, and you are jealous of a doll!] (188). Christine knows that Gabriel is much more than a doll, yet here she chooses to define him as such in order to make her point. Signalling the return to the status quo ushered in by the text's ending, in using the word 'poupée', she reduces him to his corporeality, thus disregarding the inherent querying of bodily norms which his existence makes possible. Gabriel, it seems, is simultaneously the proof of Jacques's prodigy and the very thing which undermines it. Gabriel's changing status in the eyes of his makers not only affects the identity/ies which they ascribe to him, but also influences the performances of their own identities and personalities, suggesting that even normative bodies do not possess fixed and unchanging identities. After Gabriel's death, Christine retrieves his broken body, and in a reference to the cyborg's beginnings, keeps it in her wardrobe. She keeps the brain separately in a jar, but when she goes to find it, she learns that Jacques has removed it in order to thwart any attempt to reconstruct Gabriel. Jacques's jealousy of Gabriel, motivated by the potential romantic relationship with Christine – that is, Gabriel's potential to love and be loved by a human woman – is the reason why Gabriel's body can never be reconstructed. The threat is not the cyborg itself, but that the cyborg might usurp Jacques's place in Christine's affections, that she might prefer the man-machine to the supposedly perfect man of humanist imaginings. This danger is too real for Jacques, and so he eliminates it.

A Duel with Dualisms

Gabriel's clockwork body needs winding up to prevent him running out of energy, a task which Gabriel performs himself, as Christine explains: 'il sait se servir de ses clefs […] j'ai entendu hier certain bruit d'engrenage suivi d'un effrayant tintinnabulement de clefs' [he knows how to use his keys […] Yesterday, I heard a strange noise of moving gears followed by a dreadful grating of keys] (*La Machine à assassiner*, 90–1). Christine fears this noise before she comes to believe in Gabriel's innocence, because it precedes a renewal of his energy and strength. The winding of the keys also underscores the reality of Gabriel's unusual body:

> J'ai parlé de la danse des clefs', says Christine, 'mais c'est de leur rire […] qu'il faut avoir peur! Elles remplacent le rire effroyable qu'il ne peut pas avoir, mais qu'il aurait sûrement s'il pouvait rire après être descendu, d'un coup d'œil […] au fond de son gouffre intérieur!
>
> [I have told you about the dance of the keys, but it is their laughter which we should be afraid of! They have replaced the horrifying laugh that is denied him, but which would surely be his if he could speak, after he peers into the depths of his [own] inner void!] (93)

Gabriel frequently stares into the inner void behind the flap in his chest, an obvious metaphor for a more philosophical notion of emptiness. Christine knows that what he is really scrutinizing in his chest is what he lacks, what it is that makes him not human (although, paradoxically, his insight into what he lacks is a very human quality). When Christine believes that Gabriel is running out of energy, moreover, she realizes in horror that 'il ne se ralentissait que pour mieux bondir! […] L'effroyable machine s'est réveillée!' [he slowed down only to spring up more forcefully […] The dreadful machine is awake!] (94). Indeed, Christine's fear of Gabriel's cranking mechanism may not be misplaced. Earlier in the text, Birouste watches Gabriel wind himself up, following which the cyborg 'se heurtait à la glace, dans ses gestes désordonnées! […] C'est cette fois qu'il avait les yeux d'assassin!' [threw himself at the mirror, with wild movements! […] This time he had the eyes of a murderer!] (46–7). Gabriel appears to have less control over his body in the moments after his mechanism is wound. His body struggles to contain its energy, which bursts out erratically and destructively. His dreadful eyes suggest that his state of mind is also affected by this excess energy, as if the chaos let loose by his mechanical body is linked to his emotions.

Gabriel has a particular gift for inspiring jealousy in the men around him. Very early on, Bénédict fantasizes about 'le monsieur de l'armoire' [the man from the wardrobe] who he would like to 'tu[er] comme un chien' [kill like a dog], such is his envy for the man who receives Christine's clandestine kisses (*La Poupée sanglante*, 13). But despite himself, Bénédict understands the attraction, describing Gabriel as 'ce magnifique morceau d'humanité' [this magnificent specimen of humanity] (21), an aesthetic beauty which will later give him pause when he contemplates his reflection after his brain has been transplanted into Gabriel's clockwork body, 'penché sur cette image comme un jeune dieu se regardant dans une source' [fixated on this image like a young god looking at his reflection in a spring] (*La Machine à assassiner*, 43). Yet from here on, we learn very little about Gabriel's image of himself, as descriptions of Gabriel, and his activities, are based on other's interpretations of him. Gabriel as creation is barely given the textual space to reflect upon and interpret himself, let alone consider the type of self he might want to express to society. He has been created by others, and this originary act of proprietorship seems to relegate his own self-image, and thus his self-hood, out of the text.[23] More important is how others view and define him, for in labelling Gabriel, they are really testing and defining the limits of the human. It is only as the text closes that the reader learns something of Gabriel's self-identity from his letters to Christine, in which Bénédict's voice seems to have been perfectly preserved: 'oui, je suis un pur esprit et je m'en fais gloire!' he writes. 'Et ce sera ta gloire à jamais, ô Christine! d'avoir aimé une pensée mieux peut-être que tu n'eusses aimé mon cœur même s'il avait habité, [...] un corps idéal' [Yes, I am only a mind and I am proud of it! And it will forever be to your credit, Christine, that you have loved a mind more than you would have loved my heart, even if it had been in a perfect body] (*La Machine à assassiner*, 254). Quite why it would be preferable to love Bénédict's disembodied mind rather than a mind in his hypothetically beautiful body is unclear: it lingers as one more unresolved ambiguity in this sensational text. Another element

23 This is clearly an inversion of the Narcissus myth. While others' perceptions of him are important to him as they were to Narcissus – and the physical beauty of both characters is acknowledged within each story – Gabriel himself is not permitted self-contemplation.

which perhaps remains unspoken here is the suggestion that Christine's romantic feelings remain frustrated so long as Gabriel is trapped within his mechanical body, and so she prefers his non-normative body because it insulates her from her own emotions. Gabriel is distressed by his absence of true embodiment, but his body functions nonetheless: it is a question of living a life which is acceptable to him. A purely intellectual existence will not suffice for him, and what had seemed like liberation from a corporeal existence is ultimately experienced as an imprisonment of the mind.

As Gabriel's superhuman and never-ending energy spreads out from his body, it dismantles the boundary between body and world, inside and outside, just as his creation has dismantled that between man and machine. In this way, Gabriel encapsulates both of Hayles' suggested futures for the posthuman. Hayles' dream (like Haraway's) is that the posthuman will allow boundaries to be broken down, but her nightmare is that the posthuman will render human bodies obsolete, 'as posthumans who regard their bodies as fashion accessories rather than the ground of being'.[24] To a degree, Gabriel's existence undoes established dualisms of man/machine, natural/artificial, for which his boundless energy is a metaphor. However, his unnatural strength and energy are no match for his human pursuers. His physical prowess makes the human body pale into insignificance. Indeed, he only 'dies' because he takes matters into his own hands and does the deed himself, and so in this respect he encapsulates the more pessimistic side of posthuman thought.

As Haraway has argued, it is precisely the cyborg's hybrid nature which endows it with such boundary-breaking power. In Leroux's cyborg, this internal hybridity is represented as chaos, a destructive energy which seeps outwards. On the one hand, the text's ending could be read as the reinstatement of norms, as the cyborg is killed off for being an affront to nature. On the other hand, equally possible is a reading in which Gabriel must die because an existence without embodied consciousness – in other words, a mind that both emerges out of sensory bodily experiences as well as nurturing them – is always incomplete. That is to say, that a peaceful

24 Hayles, *How We Became Posthuman: Virtual Bodies in Cybernetics, Literature, and Informatics*, 5.

mind requires a sensing body. Or perhaps, like the cyborg, the 'truth' of the ending is somewhere in between the two. Leroux's text asks whether embodiment is key to the functioning of a healthy, happy mind, and broadly concludes that it is. It is his hybridity, his half-life, which will induce Gabriel to destroy himself in the closing pages of the text. In a note to Christine, he exclaims: 'j'ai pressé sur mon sein glacé ton corps et ton visage convulsés!... mais je n'ai pas senti la tiédeur de ton sein!... Oh! ta chaleur, ton parfum bénis! qui me les rendra jamais?' [I pressed your sobbing face and body against my frozen breast! But I did not feel your warmth! Oh, your blessed warmth and smell! How will I ever get them back?] (*La Machine à assassiner*, 254–5). While Gabriel can see and hear, he has no sense of touch, smell or taste. Initially, he could remember these sensations: 'tel un opéré à qui l'on vient d'ôter le bras et qui croit toujours sentir sa main blessée', but 'peu à peu, cette imagination s'effaça [...] je fus réduit à ma seule mécanique' [like a post-operative patient whose arm has just been amputated and who believes he can still feel his injured hand [...] little by little, this sensation faded [...] I was nothing more than machine] (255). He is now left only with sight and hearing, the more cerebral and philosophical senses, according to Aristotle's hierarchy.[25] In theory, then, Gabriel has attained a sort of spiritual nirvana, in which his mind has been freed from the constraints of the physical, sensing body and the base desires of drives like hunger or thirst. And yet it is the lack of such a body which so tortures his mind. What seems like a rather obvious metaphor actually works in reverse. Gabriel has no 'soul', seemingly no humanity, precisely *because* he has no innards, no sensing body with which to experience the world around him. Gabriel's story, then, gives the lie to Cartesian dualism, because his mind alone can never be enough for him: he needs a physical, sensing body in order to live fully. While Gabriel is not the monster the public assumed – it was someone else who murdered the maids – nevertheless, the hybrid nature of his existence means that he sees himself as little more than a brain imprisoned inside an unfeeling shell. Despite the cyborg's potential for destroying dichotomies, Leroux's machine-man

25 Aristotle, *Metaphysics*, trans. Hugh Tredennick (Cambridge: Harvard University Press, 1933), I, 908a.

cannot escape, to quote Rosi Braidotti, the 'difficulties inherent in trying to overcome Humanism as [...] a normative frame'.[26] Ironically, the thing which makes him seem so human – that is, his grief at not being able to feel the touch of the woman he loves – is caused by his nonhuman state, his inner void. In this way, the dissolving of boundaries – particularly those between human and machine, mind and body – in this text, at least, holds little pleasure. Gabriel's posthuman state struggles for existence because it needs first to overcome the human which, as Braidotti suggests, is a position fraught with contradictions. What arrogance to assume that humans hold the key to expunging humanism from our lived reality.

Embodiment

Leroux's foreshadowing of the posthuman results from an engagement with key questions of posthuman theory, namely Cartesian dualism and embodiment, and in this way his text can be considered pre-posthuman. Embodiment is key to Hayles' and Braidotti's concept of the posthuman: for them, the idea that human consciousness could be separated from its physical body is absurd.[27] While *La Poupée* seems to concur on this point, Leroux's text remains founded on the assumption of a mind-body split in which the mind – in this case, the only human part of the cyborg – is the most important element. Critiques of Cartesian dualism, which incorporate that same binary opposition, can also be found in science-fiction texts such as William Gibson's *Neuromancer* (1984) and Phillip K. Dick's *Do Androids Dream of Electric Sheep?* (1968). Both texts relate the experience of connecting one's consciousness to a virtual reality and leaving the body behind (if only temporarily), suggesting that physical embodiment is less consequential than cognition, thus 'continu[ing]

26 Rosi Braidotti, *The Posthuman* (Cambridge, UK: Polity, 2013), 30.

27 Hayles, *How We Became Posthuman: Virtual Bodies in Cybernetics, Literature, and Informatics*, 1; Braidotti, *The Posthuman*, 36.

the liberal tradition rather than disrupt[ing] it'.[28] *La Poupée* reverse engineers this idea by placing a human brain into a tangible body rather than an information network or virtual reality programme, but this too is predicated on the idea that consciousness is what makes the man. Without the thinking brain, Gabriel is just a *poupée*, stuck in a cycle in which his lack of human innards continually forces him to confront his fleshless state, as his energy becomes depleted and he needs to open the *volet* and wind his mechanism again. He is a thinking mind trapped in an unfeeling body.

Gabriel's hybrid body – part human, part machine, not quite human but not entirely Other – exists on the periphery of humanity. In a sense, this text might represent a reassertion of Western anthropocentrism, as the human brain is what animates Gabriel and gives him subjectivity. Without a human brain, he is a wind-up doll who crudely apes humankind without conscience or individuality. Yet mind-body dualism, so core to the reasoning Cartesian subject, is undone by Gabriel's existence, as he cannot continue to live without embodiment. While for Gabriel his non-normative body is inadequate, it nevertheless shows the way to a posthumanism which understands Cartesian dualism differently, even if that understanding – which is not fully livable by Gabriel – is only available to the reader. Gabriel's relative disembodiment – or rather, being embodied in the wrong sort of body – is the source of his torture. Despite this, the reader continues to recognize Gabriel as human, even if his is an entirely new configuration of that name. For Leroux, humanity is a mode of being rather than a set of specific behaviours like speaking, eating and sensing. Gabriel approaches the human because he is tortured by his missing viscera: he is human because he suffers. Initially, the project to create Gabriel is a proto-transhumanist one, driven by the inventor's desire to create something even more marvellous than the human: a superman who would never tire. As the story progresses, Leroux toys with questions of embodiment which are fundamental to late twentieth- and twenty-first-century posthumanism, while never abandoning completely the dominant position awarded to cognition. This is a pre-posthumanism which has not yet exorcized the demons

28 Hayles, *How We Became Posthuman: Virtual Bodies in Cybernetics, Literature, and Informatics*, 5.

of humanism from its thinking, particularly the uneven weighting on the cerebral side of a mind-body dualism. Ultimately, despite some conceptual inconsistencies, the blame for the death of the cyborg is placed at humanity's feet. In the end, Leroux seems to say, we have little to fear in the man-made 'monster' (the cyborg), except humankind's own monstrous hubris which purports to imprison 'un pur esprit' inside a metal body. By insisting on some of the humanist dualisms which it sets out to undermine, to a degree Leroux's text problematizes humanity's attempt to undo itself, thus querying querying habits themselves. Gabriel's 'death' ensures that any possibility of a romantic relationship between Christine and Gabriel is precluded, thus reinstating her normative bodily and social role as wife and mother and subverting earlier attempts at a queering of heteronormativity.

Bibliography

Alfu, *Gaston Leroux: parcours d'une œuvre* (Encrage: Amiens, 1996).

'L'animal ne meurt pas tout entier tout de suite', *Le Matin* (23 November 1912).

Aristotle, *Metaphysics*, trans. Hugh Tredennick (Cambridge: Harvard University Press, 1933).

Bielecki, Emma, '"Fatalitas!" The Criminal Body in Belle Epoque Crime Serials: The Strange Case of *Chéri-Bibi*', *Journal of European Popular Culture* 4/2 (2013), 195–209.

Braidotti, Rosi, *The Posthuman* (Cambridge, UK: Polity, 2013).

Brunhes, Bernard, *La Dégradation de l'énergie* (Paris: Flammarion, 1908).

'Un Cœur retiré de l'organisme et qui bat pendant plus de trois mois', *Le Matin* (19 June 1912).

Haraway, Donna, *Simians, Cyborgs, and Women: The Reinvention of Nature* (London: Free Association, 1991).

Hayles, N. Katherine, *How We Became Posthuman: Virtual Bodies in Cybernetics, Literature, and Informatics* (Chicago: University of Chicago Press, 1999).

Leroux, Gaston, *La Machine à assassiner: roman d'aventures et de mystère* (Paris: Tallandier, 1924).

—— *La Poupée sanglante: roman d'aventures et de mystère* (Paris: Tallandier, 1924).

'On pourra cultiver des cellules vivantes comme on cultive des microbes', *Le Matin* (7 May 1913).
Rabinbach, Anson, *The Human Motor: Energy, Fatigue, and the Origins of Modernity* (New York: Basic Books, 1990).
Reggiani, Andrés Horacio, God's *Eugenicist: Alexis Carrel and the Sociobiology of Decline* (New York: Berghahn, 2007).
Shelley, Mary, *Frankenstein, or the Modern Prometheus* (London: Penguin, 2012).

PART IV

Bodies in Flux

LOREN K. WOLFE

10 Mediating Eve: Female Protagonists and the Contingent Body in Hervé Guibert's Late Narratives

With over twenty works of varying genres attributed to his name, nearly half written after he tested positive for HIV in 1988, Hervé Guibert, prolific writer, journalist, photographer and filmmaker, did not consider himself a homosexual. He explicitly resists the term in a late interview with Christophe Donner:

> 'Homosexualité, pour moi c'est un mot qui n'a jamais eu vraiment un rapport avec moi, bizarrement, alors qu'il en a évidemment un, mais je ne vois pas les choses comme ça, ce n'est pas la façon dont je vis, c'est pas la façon dont je me sens, j'ai l'impression que je suis ailleurs que dans ces ...'
>
> [Homosexuality doesn't ha[ve] any relationship to me, bizarrely, because obviously it has one, but I don't see things like that, it's not the way I live, it's not the way I feel, I have the impression that I am somewhere other than in these ...][1]

Michael Lucey explains the closing ellipsis as a holding space for an extraverbal form of expression: 'The three dots represent not just a pause [...] but also an effect of intonation, and also, perhaps, a physical gesture [...] as if to ward off an intrusion of the categories of the normative world into the space of his own existence.'[2] According to Lucey, Guibert's 'gestures' point to a spatial configuration in excess or 'elsewhere', beyond the confines delimiting the 'homosexual'.

1 Christophe Donner, 'Pour répondre aux quelques questions qui se posent ... Hervé Guibert. Entretien avec Christophe Donner', *La Règle du jeu* 3/7 (1992), 135–57, 157. All translations are my own unless otherwise noted.

2 Michael Lucey, *Someone: The Pragmatics of Misfit Sexualities, from Colette to Hervé Guibert* (Chicago: University of Chicago Press, 2019), 205.

This chapter queries Guibert's sexuality at the end of his life when, with biting irony, '[il] ne supportai[t] plus les hommes, déjà érotiquement [...] c'était quand même un gros problème pour un pédé'. [[He] could no longer stand men, already erotically [...] it was indeed a big problem for a queer.][3] His libidinal shift towards strong, *feminine* characters displaces the boundaries of heteronormative logic that dictate what constitutes 'straight behaviour'. In *Queer Phenomenology: Orientations, Objects, Others* (2006), Sara Ahmed lays out the heuristic stakes of sexual reorientation: 'Orientations toward sexual objects affect other things that we do, such that different orientations, different ways of directing one's desires, means inhabiting different worlds.'[4] And, I would add, inhabiting familiar worlds differently.

Proposing alternative models of belonging and community, Ahmed co-opts Freud's category of the 'contingent invert' to endow the 'contingent lesbian' with recuperative touch: 'it is useful to recall that the word "contingent" has the same root in Latin as the word "contact" (*contingere: com-*, with, *tangere*, to touch). Contingency is linked in this way to the sociality of being "with" others, to getting close enough to touch'.[5] 'Contingent sexuality' – as opposed to inherent or innate sexuality – requires exposure. It also implies new social forms that exceed closed dyadic structures and escape the patriarchal laws of social (and biological) reproduction.

Ahmed references 'contingent heterosexuality' only in passing, as an instance where contingency, though still in operation, is often overlooked.[6] The Guibertian no-man's land of late-stage AIDS, however, gives life and relevance to the 'contingent heterosexual'. For Guibert, the heterosexual IS queer. In his last texts, he tweaks his narrator's sexual – and textual – object alignment and unexpectedly reaches for a feminine hand. In what follows, using Ahmed as a guide, I will explore how Guibert frames sexuality in terms of repeated actions, concentrating on the effects that two of Guibert's heroines have on his habits.

3 Hervé Guibert, *Le Protocol compassionnel* (Paris: Gallimard, 1991), 260.

4 Sara Ahmed, *Queer Phenomenology: Orientations, Objects, Others* (Durham, NC and London: Duke University Press, 2006), 68.

5 Ahmed, *Queer Phenomenology: Orientations, Objects, Others*, 103.

6 Ahmed, *Queer Phenomenology: Orientations, Objects, Others*, 94–5.

In *Le Protocole compassionnel* [*The Compassionate Protocol*] (1991), the sequel to his bestseller *À l'ami qui ne m'a pas sauvé la vie* [*To the Friend Who Did Not Save My Life*] (1990) that launched his AIDS writing, the narrator switches doctors, having befriended the internist who had been treating him; too much 'humanity' had entered into their relationship. He needs 'd'autres médecins, d'une brutalité et d'une dépersonnification de cette relation' [other doctors, brutality and depersonalization in this relationship] (33). He and Doctor Claudette Dumouchel, 'championne de l'efficacité' [champion of efficiency] (34), establish new routines; they share ephemeral and creative spaces predicated on end-of-life care that call for new mediums of representation.

The awkward innocence of his relationship with Claudette gives way to a no holds barred exposition of heterosexual physicality in *Le Paradis* [*Paradise*] (1992). The text sits somewhere between a diary, travel log and mystery novel, and spans multiple spaces and timeframes that obfuscate a clear chronology; the reader labours to connect the dots revealed in flashbacks and flashforwards. The narrator begins in Zurich, a writer 'qui n'[a] jamais rien publié' [who has never published anything] and son of a rich businessman.[7] He meets Jayne Heinz, who works for one of his father's colleagues. They go to Africa, return to Zurich where the narrator has a cerebral attack, travel to Washington for an MRI, to Bora Bora (Jayne's 'paradise'), and finally to Martinique, where Jayne perishes on a coral reef. The text begins as her body washes up on the Antillean beach. In contrast to Claudette who expands the narrator's field of action, Jayne – and her disappearance(s) – progressively strip him of his bearings, both spatial, psychic and creative.

Claudette and Jayne, whose touch brings out the narrator's sexual contingency, join a contingent of very real, vitally important women in his life. These women take control of his *corpus* and transform the stark certainty underpinning Guibert's late narratives – his death from AIDS – into a tenable afterlife, both artistically and legally. They secure his legacy, not through heteronormative reproduction, but by extending imaginary and concrete lifelines, 'livings-on' otherwise foreclosed to his dis-integrating self.

7 Hervé Guibert, *Le Paradis* (Paris: Gallimard, 1992), 57.

Claudette's Titillating Takes

The Parisian hospital's phlebotomy lab excites the writer as a space for linguistic improvement:

> J'aimerais manier parfaitement le jargon des médecins, c'est comme un truc codé, ça me donne l'illusion vis-à-vis d'eux de ne pas être le gosse devant lequel on parle anglais pour les histoires de cul. J'aime le langage fluide, presque parlé, et j'aime maintenant porter mon sang alors qu'auparavant je serais tombé dans les pommes.
>
> [[I] would like to speak doctor's jargon perfectly, it's like something coded, it gives me the illusion of not being the kid whose parents use English to talk about sex. I like fluid language, almost spoken, and I now like carrying my blood when before I would have fainted.] (*Le Protocole compassionnel*, 123)

His newly acquired skills evoke a scene of original sin: the narrator, rather than *falling into apples* (*tomber dans les pommes*), metaphorically takes a bite, his mouth contaminated by 'naughty', medical words. Contamination – derived from the same Latin root as contingent and contact (*contingere*) – provokes a different kind of fall: *tomber dans les pommes* is replaced by *tomber amoureux*, falling in love, which gets his creative juices flowing.

Claudette is a masculine, surly woman who 'n'a jamais un mot en trop ou en moins' [with never too many nor too few words] (34). Her brusque bedside manner corresponds to the impersonal doctor/patient relationship the narrator seeks. She sparks his writerly interest – 'elle pourrait être une héroïne de roman' [she could be a heroine in a novel] (34) – and is subsequently cast as an object of desire: '[I]l se pourrait que je tombe amoureux de cette jeune femme toujours mal disposée.' [I could fall in love with this young, ill-disposed woman] (34). They enter a ludic, flirtatious exchange in Claudette's basement office, a no-frills setting to match her curt demeanor. He and she 'jou[ent] au médecin' [play doctor] (56) transforming neuropathy tests into games of footsie: 'j'ai les yeux fermés, elle bouge mon doigt de pied et moi je dis: "Vous. Moi. Vous. Vous. Moi. Moi. Vous. Moi. Vous. Vous. Moi"' [my eyes are closed, she moves my toe and I say: 'You. Me. You. You. Me. Me. You. Me'] (56–7). Here, the performative aspect transforms the clinical relationship between a patient and his doctor into an intimate exchange, 'une déclaration forcée et camouflée' [a forced and camouflaged declaration] (57) that leads the narrator to wonder whether she is young and straight, whether he is her favourite: the kind of leitmotivs that traverse all boy-meets-girl love stories.

Ahmed defines 'wonder' in terms of its relationship to cliché: 'To wonder is to remember the forgetting and to see the repetition of form as the "taking form" of the familiar.'[8] The narrator marvels at how *new* these commonplace questions about his crush feel, surrendering to the 'eloquent' fantasy (to borrow a word from Benjamin Gagnon Chainey) activated by the sexual difference between them.[9] His heightened awareness to the process of 'falling in love' pushes him into a space of missed potential, but potential nonetheless. He imagines the doctor as someone that '[il] aurai[t] dû ... marie[r]' [[he] should have married] (125), a fiancée he could call 'mon petit hérisson' [my little hedgehog] (252), a wife to whom he could write hackneyed postcards: 'Moi ou vous? Haut ou bas? Quel jour sommes-nous? Je pense à vous (pour le rime)' [Me or you? High or low? What day is it? I'm thinking of you (for the rhyme)] (151).

His imagination runs wild on these banalities. Claudette's spiky red hair and her hands, for instance, transport the narrator to tales of old: 'les mains d'autrefois d'une gente dame du Moyen Age' [the hands of a fair damsel from the Middle Ages] (254). He associates her hands, which control his movements in the exam room, with his embodied creative practice. He becomes acutely aware of this dependence one night during a bout of insomnia:

> Je fais ma gymnastique et j'écris mon livre, à blanc [...] sans papier ni stylo [...] jusqu'à l'oubli. Je tends les jambes et je refais les mouvements que m'ordonne Claudette Dumouchel et que je fais dans ses mains, j'appuie comme elle dit sur l'accélérateur de son poing, mais il manque sa main.'

8 Ahmed, *Queer Phenomenology: Orientations, Objects, Others*, 82–3.

9 '[I]t is in the relationship between sexualities, in the intersubjective rapport held between them that Guibert's sexual disorientation ... becomes the most subtly eloquent.' Benjamin Gagnon Chainey, 'Du protocole compassionnel à l'anarchie passionnelle,' *Revue Critique de Fixxion Française Contemporaine/Critical Review of Contemporary French Fixxion* 12 (2016), 84–95, 87.

> [I do my gymnastics and I write my book, blank […] with neither paper nor pen […] into forgetting. I stretch out my legs and I do the movements that Claudette Dumouchel told me to do, those I do in her hands, I push like she said on the accelerator of her fist, but her hand is missing.] (174–5)

The corporal and psychic limits between the narrator and Claudette stay intact, but words fail to capture the contingency her touch creates; the narrator seeks a medium to bear witness to these gestures. To capture them, he relinquishes form to the unpredictable eye of the video camera. Smuggling it into the examination room, he initiates a tug-of-war of consent, arguing for his right to film his own body against her reluctance to have her body appear (258). As a solution, the narrator rearranges her desk, displacing some objects, removing others, finding an angle acceptable to them both.

Ahmed (following Edmund Husserl) underscores how the table organizes power by virtue of its orientation. Its directionality determines where, on whom and on what to direct attention, while relegating other objects, people and actions to the background.[10] In our case here, the two tables, face-to-face and organized as they are, give rise to what Judith Butler calls a 'field of heterosexual objects' whereby the renunciation of certain objects not only foregrounds but produces others.[11] The narrator asserts mastery over Claudette's desk, a counterbalance to the power she wields over the examination table. He carves out a space for Othered togetherness through the camera. 'J'ai calé la caméra sur son bureau en direction de la table d'examen, je me déshabille, et j'entre dans l'image. Claudette m'y rejoint'. [I propped the camera on her desk pointing towards the exam table, I get undressed. Claudette joins me there] (259). A contingent 'heterosexual field' results from the framed compromise that captures repetition, giving light and life to new representational forms.

After their brief 'coming together' in the lens, Claudette immediately changes directions, bringing her 'back story' into the room: 'mon copain est en train de lire votre livre, il aime beaucoup, moi je n'ai pas le temps

10 Ahmed, *Queer Phenomenology: Orientations, Objects, Others*, 31.

11 Judith Butler, *The Psychic Life of Power* (Stanford: Stanford University Press, 1997), 21. Quoted in Ahmed, *Queer Phenomenology: Orientations, Objects, Others*, 87.

avec tous les articles que je dois me farcir pour ma thèse …' [my boyfriend is reading your book, he likes it a lot, me, I don't have time with all of the articles that I'm stuck reading for my thesis …] (259). In including this exchange, Guibert, a contingent heterosexual activated by his female doctor's touch, foregrounds the background of heterosexuality, showing the reader what Ahmed calls the 'work' of putting the background in the background. Throughout his 'courtship' with her, the narrator emphasizes their routine, their repetitions that create their makeshift world, where a budding love story disguises the reality of their precarious togetherness in the 'la zone de l'incontrôlable' [uncontrollable zone] (33) of the doctor's office. As Chainey writes: '[Claudette] becomes the vector of a medical practice not only beneficial despite its brutality, but also profoundly reassuring, like reading a children's story, or even more lofty an artistic performance to which the patient would be invited.'[12] In terms of creative medium, the mundane existence of Claudette and her boyfriend is tied to the narrator's words. His 'rival' is reading him, but she is apologetically elsewhere.

To underscore the queer potential of the 'new normal' (a contingent heterosexual smitten with his queerly fair doctor, where the 'back story' has no bearing), he exchanges his pen for a video camera and transforms the reader into a frustrated spectator. He adjusts the angle and surreptitiously films Claudette alone, establishing a new power dynamic between them by cutting himself out of the frame. At the same time, he prolongs the reader's desire by visually depriving her of Claudette's 'longues mains blanches' [long white hands] and 'son visage dans cette lumière sublime' [her face in this sublime light] (260). The 'Fin de bande' [End of the tape] (260) titillates the reader and leaves her wanting more. In *Le Protocol compassionnel*, the parallel presence/absence of a new medium, inspired by the narrator's shift in object desire and made possible by the enchanted 'heterosexual field' between two tables, goes beyond the page, with its ostensibly written end, opening the door to other aesthetic and temporal horizons.

12 Chainey, 'Du protocol compassionnel à l'anarchie passionnelle,' 92.

The Strai(gh)ts of Jayne

With clearly demarcated roles, Claudette and the narrator foster a 'safe zone' of repetition and play where the narrator feels comfortable ceding creative control; these new habits stabilize his sense of self. *Le Paradis* presents the opposite scenario where the narrator's psyche and expressive abilities unravel as he attempts to hold on to Jayne, a woman adverse to all attachment. Andrew Asibong argues that the representation of Guibert in *Le Paradis* – with the three-fold transformation of the narrator into a heterosexual, hexagonal and healthy man – is undermined by the text's inability to maintain boundaries.[13] I agree with Asibong that the narrator's 'integrity has come apart, his body has become unrecognizable to itself'.[14] However, instead of viewing *Le Paradis* as a text meant to keep integrity and background (i.e. identity) intact (what Asibong implies when he evokes Guibert's 'fantasy predicated on a transcendent ability to negotiate movement across the frontier of life and death'), I see it as an exploration of what happens when the 'background' is questioned and then undone, when habits fall away, leaving the body radically exposed to new touches.

Le Paradis starts with a cautionary tale of when habits fail. In a long, sinuous sentence, Guibert places his narrator face-to-face with Jayne, champion swimmer, torn 'du pubis à la poitrine' [from pubis to chest] (11) by a coral reef off the shores of Martinique. The paragraph surfs on the narrator's stream of consciousness, progressively revealing the collateral damage of Jayne's accident that leaves the narrator 'seul au bout du monde' [alone at the end of the world] (11).

Ahmed, discussing the relationship between the body and its surroundings, evokes Merleau-Ponty's notion of the 'habitual body': a body that acts without drawing attention to the action, blending into the background. By extension, anything the body uses to act out a habit becomes

13 Andrew Asibong, 'Travel sickness: Marie NDiaye, Hervé Guibert and the Liquidation of the White Fantasy-Subject', *International Journal of Francophone Studies* 12/1 (2009), 109–25, 113.

14 Asibong, 'Travel Sickness', 116.

one with the body, no longer an object in its own right.[15] The body touches objects, uses them and – over time – integrates them as part of the self, as we saw above in the phlebotomy lab with the contaminated blood and jargon. These prostheses – whether a pen, a computer, a car, a crutch, or even a language – insert the body into contingents: groups of people who share a common feature. They allow the body to take up space; the habitual body inhabits.

Both bodies in *Le Paradis* are non-habitual: Jayne because she leaves places as soon as she starts inhabiting them; and the narrator because he fails to take up space. She is his prosthesis, and she is always on the move. Coded masculine, Jayne wears the pants, makes the decisions, leads the way and lives for three things: having sex, driving fast and giving things up.[16] She abandons something every day (20), a habit that explains, for the narrator, their incessant movement. At no point does Jayne crave familiarity or a feeling of home; she is not interested in developing social habits or settling spaces or inserting herself into social groups. And since she sets the tempo, she prevents the narrator, who sticks to her like glue, from doing any of these things, too.

Unlike Jayne, the narrator craves stillness. Her exaggerated expansiveness is paired with his withdrawal. He does not drive (the car he and Jayne had rented was useless after her death) (11), and he only walks reluctantly. At one point, Jayne criticizes him for his inertia, while marvelling at his able-bodiedness: '[T]u n'es tout de même pas paralysé, tu n'as pas de béquilles, pas de chaise roulante, tu n'a même pas besoin d'une canne'. [[F]or god's sake, you're not paralysed, you don't need crutches, nor a wheelchair, you don't even need a cane] (24). The narrator does not have – nor should he need – implements to help him move; strictly speaking, he is not disabled. And yet, without something to prop him up, the narrator fails

15 Ahmed, *Queer Phenomenology: Orientations, Objects, Others*, 131.

16 Several critics read Jayne as a female version of Guibert's long-time obsession and occasional (mostly heterosexual) lover Vincent, Guibert's travel partner to both Africa and Martinique, according to his journal (*MA* 448; 547). James Agar, in particular, carefully explores the psychic and literary ramifications of transforming Vincent into a woman. See James Agar, 'Self-mourning in Paradise: Writing (about) AIDS through Death-bed Delirium,' *Paragraph* 30/1 (March 2007), 67–84.

to find his footing. Jayne takes him to the beach, dumps him and leaves to frolic in the sea. His feet barely touch; he gets knocked over by a wave and is unable to get out (25). Jayne has to swim to his rescue. In their relationship, traditional gender roles are inverted: Jayne –strong, competent, autonomous – saves the 'fragile' (22), reliant narrator. But like the wave, her whirlwind expansion – her frenetic movement, the ways she uses, abuses and loses objects – drowns the narrator in 'son trou' [his hole] (25).

Jayne disappears even more violently after her physical death: the police, finishing their investigation, announce that she never existed (32). The narrator reels: 'c'est moi qui ai maintenant l'impression [...] de n'avoir été qu'un fantôme aux côtés de Jayne, d'avoir été déjà mort au moment où elle m'a rencontré, et je crois aimé' [now I have the impression [...] to have been a phantom at Jayne's side, to have been dead already at the moment when she met, and I believe loved, me] (38). He betrays his existential dependence. Even the locals, for whom Jayne 'est déjà une légende' [is already a legend] (38), call him 'l'homme sans tête et sans mains, l'homme invisible' [the headless and handless man, the invisible man] (42). Ahmed writes: 'The body extends its reach by taking in that which is "not" it [...] The "not me" is incorporated into the body.'[17] Without hands, the narrator fails to incorporate anything, even losing touch with his own corporality. As Jayne's identity dissolves, he wonders whether *he* ever existed.

Jayne's abstraction – her lack of origins – is paired with her inability to originate anything. Her birth canal leads only to dire straits, as foreshadowed on page one: '[son] corps [...] rose bleuté, comme une vulve tailladée par un sadique sur toute la longueur du tronc' [[her] body [...] bluish pink, like a vulva shredded by a sadist all along her trunk] (11). Dramatic images of failed reproduction proliferate: miscarriages; a trafficked foetus found in an icebox; a stillborn; an abortion due to STDs. As if to underscore Jayne's hostile terrain, the couple's love games – very different from the self-affirming footsie played with Claudette – centre around the one object treasured by both: 'au début c'était une fois comme ça, et puis *c'est devenu une habitude*, nous n'en parlions même plus, mais *il nous fallait ça pour faire l'amour*, et le pistolet lui entrait de plus en plus

17 Ahmed, *Queer Phenomenology: Orientations, Objects, Others*, 115.

facilement dans le con' [in the beginning we did it once, and *then it became a habit*, we no longer even spoke about it, but *we needed it to make love*, and the pistol went more and more easily into her cunt] (18, my emphasis). The gun, metonymically connoting death and metaphorically symbolizing his sex, extends the narrator's body into Jayne, who voraciously swallows it up. She even incorporates it iconically as a shoulder tattoo, making the narrator 'le remplir d'encre' [fill it in with ink] (77). Her body negates his ability to expand; she is another black hole – just as strong as the one that pulled him down at the beach. After her death, he throws the pistol into the ocean, the one object that gave him access to her even as it negated his reach, relinquishing his last figurative 'limb'.

HIV radically opens the body to the other. While the boundaries with Claudette in *Le Protocole compassionnel* remained productively clear – 'You. Me. You. You. Me' – in *Le Paradis*, relationships are messy: we cannot differentiate between the 'you' from the 'me', the 'in' from the 'out', particularly when all traces of the other vanish. Julia Kristeva, theorizing the abject, gives words to this confusion: '*Not me. Not that. But not nothing either*. Something that I don't recognize as a thing [...] At the frontier of inexistence and hallucination, of a reality that, if I recognize it, annihilates me.'[18]

In *A l'ami qui ne m'a pas sauvé la vie*, Guibert uses the metaphor of colonization to describe the virus, charting its 'cartography'.[19] In *Le Paradis*, contagion flows surreptitiously, spreading like the coral in Jayne's insides and settling in the body of a small African boy, stuck in the back of a dingy café on the road to Bamako (the only seropositive character in the text) (87). Indeed, *Le Paradis* is one of his few texts to raise questions of race, explicitly projecting blame and sickness onto the black body. Like compulsory heterosexuality, Ahmed characterizes whiteness as a bad habit, 'an unconscious routine that becomes second nature'.[20] The narrator – a rich, white man in a 'pays de savages dont [il] ignorait la langue' [country of savages whose language he doesn't speak]) (11) – repeatedly reveals his

18 Julia Kristeva, *Pouvoirs de l'horreur* (Paris: Seuil, 1980), 10 (my emphasis).

19 Hervé Guibert, *À l'ami qui ne m'a pas sauvé la vie* (Paris: Gallimard, 1990), 48.

20 Ahmed, *Queer Phenomenology: Orientations, Objects, Others*, 131.

colonial prejudices; Africa becomes an abjected fantasy that he needs to master to reassert control over his own corporal boundaries.

The narrator accuses Jayne of sleeping with Bouba, one of servants at their dilapidated colonial palace and the suspected origin of the chlamydia Jayne and the narrator keep passing back and forth (134). He even explains her decision to impale herself as her way of avenging Bouba 'en [le] privant [le narrateur] de cet amour' [depriving him (the narrator) of this love] (137). As such, Jayne uncomfortably incarnates colonial contagion, and makes it impossible – even in death – for the narrator to separate himself from her and from Africa.

Isabelle Décarie argues that the narrator figuratively 'kills off' AIDS by killing off Jayne: 'Jayne is thus defined by the metaphor of a writing that erases itself [...] of a book whose pages are unreadable.'[21] Even unreadable, though, the pages – reduced to 'un petit carnet vierge' [a small, virgin notebook] (20) – a blunt contrast with Jayne's body that lost its hymen even before penetration (12) – exist. Though any sense of fixed, recognizable, nameable coordinates are abolished, paradoxically (or paradisaically) the text – and the signifier – survive.

L'enfant d'antan [Yesteryear's Child]

Losing his mind from repeated losses has physical ramifications. Three days after his return from Africa, the narrator startles from sleep in a panic, loses consciousness and falls into a coma (59). He awakens with amnesia, remembering nothing from his trip. He travels to Washington D.C. for an MRI scan to explain his memory loss. The scan shows only 'de tout petits points blancs' [tiny white points] (66), uninterpretable signs within the 'matière blanche' [white material] (66). He wonders whether these white points might visually represent his lost memory (129). He fears damage to his motor skills: '[I]l n'est même pas sûr que je puisse *continuer* à tenir ce

21 Isabelle Décarie, 'L'identité posthume dans *le Paradis* d'Hervé Guibert', *L'Esprit Créateur* 40/1 (Spring 2000), 100–10, 104.

stylo […] pour *continuer*, pour me raccrocher à ça' [it's unclear whether I'll be able to continue holding this pen […] to continue to hang onto it] (113). Through Claudette's touch, the narrator formed new bodily memories; the repetition of movement led to new habits and new ways of artistically seizing the world. Here, even the most fundamental bodily habits are jeopardized. He forgets how to dress himself (114), never mind the possibility of innovative gestures: will his body even let him 'continue' – to hang on, hold on, and extend through his pen?

After Jayne's death, he seeks new company, first with the 'grands fous' [great crazies] – Nietzsche, Strindberg and Robert Walser – Jayne's thesis 'companions' (114), then with his literary 'fathers', Rimbaud, Roussel, and their African tales. They all fail to show him the path, and even confuse his words:

> Rimbaud pour effacer son passé […] loin de ses frasques de jeunesse et de son écriture d'antan. Les mots sont de plus en plus doubles, j'ai failli écrire enfant, ça sonne pareil […] à quoi bon tout ce tintouin pour un mot qui n'est pas un contresens de surcroît.
>
> [Rimbaud to erase his past […] far from the escapades of his youth and his writing from before ["d'antan"]. The words are more and more doubled. I almost wrote infant ["enfant"] it sounds the same […] and why all of this hullabaloo anyway about words that are not antonyms.] (112–13)

In contrast to his experience with contaminated blood and medical jargon, where a sense of doubling accompanied skill acquisition, here it indicates lost competency. He shrugs his shoulders, gives up trying to fix meaning, and regresses: 'je suis perdu. Je ne retrouve plus mon chemin. Je me suis perdu. Je suis un enfant.' [I am lost. I can no longer find my path. I lost myself. I am a child.] (125). Rimbaud stopped writing in Africa, moving past his '*écriture d'antan/enfant*' to traffic arms not words. African adventures and guns also threaten Guibert's writing project to the point where both the narrator and the reader have trouble holding on to the text, spatially and temporally: '[O]n ne revient jamais d'Afrique […] Je resterai fou, fou et amnésique […] Rimbaud dit qu'on y vieillit de cinq ans en un an, mais c'est peut-être plus. Je suis déjà si vieux.' [[O]ne never comes back from Africa […] I will stay crazy, crazy and amnesic […] Rimbaud says that one ages five years in one there, but it may be much more. I am already so old] (134).

Childhood writing, in one sense, signals irrevocable loss. And yet, it also flags a point where the world as blank slate emerges, a textual body stripped of stilting habits and open to movement, action and repetition, where new spaces and new contingents can be projected. Perhaps this is the lesson to take from Jayne and her 'virgin' notebook. With Nietzschean flair, Guibert ends *Le Paradis* with his body (and humanity) somewhere between 'nothing', 'no one', and 'everything'.[22] A body on which all has been erased – marking a demise – but where all is also yet to be written as the reader re-pieces scattered pages together to write the Africa – and the Jayne – that are missing, creating infinite combinations contingent upon what storylines are followed.

'I am already married'

It is unclear in *Le Paradis* when the narrator's Great Aunt Suzanne dies. At first, the narrator claims he found out from his father over the phone after returning from Africa. Later, the reader learns that he may have travelled to Africa to grieve (*réaliser un deuil*) (120), implying she passed away before his trip. The inconsistencies point to an increased blurring between the narrator and Monsieur Hervé Guibert, the writer, who pops up by name (the first and only time in text) in a psychiatric report that mentions a 'deuil non fait d'une grande-tante' [unfinished mourning of a Great Aunt] (120). The generic boundaries that fixed *Le Paradis* squarely in the realm of fiction bend as the writer's life fragments increasingly interrupt the action.

22 'A mon retour du Mali, j'avais cru comprendre que l'homme n'était rien ni personne. Et j'aurais pu aussi bien dire qu'il était tout.' [Returning from Mali, I thought I understood that man was nothing and no one. And I could have said, just as well, that he was everything] (137).

Similarly to Jayne, Suzanne has left the narrator bereft and – worse than stranded – disinherited; she donated her body and money to science. The physical end state of both women mirrors the narrator's emptiness: Jayne is 'éventrée' [disemboweled] (11), and Suzanne's insides are sucked out by the medical establishment: 'on l'avait vidé comme un poulet de son cœur, de son foie et de ses poumons'. [She had been emptied of her heart, liver and lungs like a chicken] (108–9). The narrator grabs everything he can from Suzanne's home and rushes out. But the objects turn against him. Suzanne's broken clock reminds him of his 'marche … déréglée' [erratic gait] (122). Even her lamp, with its 'antediluvian', naked cord, short-circuits, 'mettant le feu à [s]on bureau et détruisant tous [s]es papiers avec ce roman en cours' [setting his desk on fire and destroying all of [his] papers, including this novel being written] (124). The narrator's brain and lamp both short-circuit, leaving him to wonder about his contingent state and to what contingents he still belongs. Most pressingly, who is going to re-write the pages that have been lost?

Guibert's Great-Aunt Suzanne recurs as a character in many of his texts and as the muse, with her sister, of the 1980 photo-journal *Suzanne et Louise*. He entertains a complicated emotional relationship with her that spans from deep devotion to aggression.[23] In *Le Protocole compassionnel*, Guibert, speaking about his body in time, makes a surprisingly jubilant declaration:

> Le sida m'a fait accomplir un voyage dans le temps, comme dans les contes que je lisais quand j'étais enfant […] En 1990 j'ai quatre-vingt-quinze ans, alors que je suis né en 1955 […] Ça me rapproche de Suzanne, qui a elle-même quatre-vingt-quinze ans […] Maintenant nous pouvons de nouveau nous comprendre et communiquer. Nous sommes presque pareils dans nos corps et dans nos pensées dans l'expérience du très grand âge. *Nous sommes enfin devenus mari et femme.*
>
> [AIDS made me time travel, like in the stories I read when I was a kid […] In 1990, I'm ninety-five years old, even though I was born in 1955 […] This brings me closer to Suzanne, who also is ninety-five […] Now we can understand each other and communicate again. We are almost the same in our bodies and our thoughts in the

23 In his journal, for example, he mentions working on an unfinished biography of her entitled *Destroy Suzanne* (*MA* 484).

experience of very old age. *We have become husband and wife at last.*] (*Le Protocole compassionnel*, 130, my emphasis)

Guibert's contingent heterosexuality leads him to an unexpected contingent – the elderly. Here, he joins his soul mate, his other half who is 'almost the same' in body and mind, her Adam to his Eve. Lines of kinship blur as sexuality falls away. The relationship between husband and wife – in their difference – most aptly encompasses the complicity Guibert experienced with his beloved friend, inspiration and guide.

The most important hand to turn Guibert queerly hetero, however, belongs to Christine ('Berthe' in the AIDS trilogy). When the narrator was playing doctor with Claudette, speculating about her age and whether to ask her to marry him, he reaches this conclusion: '[J]e suis fou […] Et puis je suis déjà marié.' [I am crazy […] And besides, I'm already wed] (*Le Protocole compassionnel*, 57). On 17 June 1989, Hervé Guibert married Christine, Thierry's lover, mother of Thierry's two children, Thierry who remained Guibert's soulmate until his death. They are 'The Club of Five' ['Le Club de Cinq'],[24] a family and Berthe (birth?), though given relatively little textual space, was 'la personne qu['il] admirai[t] le plus au monde' [the person [he] admired the most] (*À l'ami qui ne m'a pas sauvé la vie*, 163). He married her, ostensibly, to prevent his parents from claiming his royalties, to protect the rights to his work, and to give her financial stability.

Guibert congratulates himself for securing the economic future of Christine and her children. But in fact, it is Christine's intervention that saves Guibert; she tosses him a lifeline, a living-on that, according to Ahmed, escapes the heteronormative, linear thinking according to which inheritance necessarily passes through reproduction.[25] Christine carries Guibert's name for him – she, to this day, goes by Christine Guibert – and judiciously protects his work. More significantly, however, she took control of it after his death, finishing the works in progress. She made sure his last three texts were edited and published. She even manually finished

24 Hervé Guibert, *Le Mausolée des amants* (Paris: Gallimard, 2001), 446.

25 Ahmed, *Queer Phenomenology: Orientations, Objects, Others*, 18.

his journal for publication in 2001, noting her contribution on the copyright page of *Le Mausolée des amants* [*The Lovers' Mausoleum*]: 'j'ai tapé les cinquante-huit dernières pages provenant du dernier carnet avant de tout remettre aux Éditions Gallimard' [I typed the last fifty-eight pages coming from the last notebook before giving everything to Gallimard.]

And Christine was not the only one. Three other women also played pivotal roles in finishing up and promoting Guibert's works: Agathe Gaillard, a long-time friend and gallery owner, curated several exhibits devoted exclusively to his photographic work; Pascale Breugnot, a TV producer and Maureen Mazurek, a film editor, finished *La Pudeur ou l'impudeur*, a documentary film compiling the footage Guibert had taken over the last two years of his life (including the footage with Doctor Dumouchel). The film aired on French TV in Jan 1992, a month after his death.

Guibert laconically declares in his journal: 'il ne faut pas se passer des femmes.' [You shouldn't go without women] (*Le Mausolée des amants*, 490). Claudette's efficient hands played games with the narrator's body. They performed new movements in new spaces, a new version of a worn-out hetero love story, tickling the reader with a new medium: the written film. Jayne both dragged him along and also habitually abandoned him. Her resistance to inscription mediates his impulse to fold in and stop the pen. She keeps the writer writing, showing him that death is not the end: pages, identity, memories get erased, but also rewritten, contingent on which body is writing. Suzanne, Christine, Agathe, Maureen, Pascale and others, accompanied him, supported him, took on his work. They continue to carry it (most recently, Christine and Agathe curated a photographic exhibition in early 2020 at Les Douches la Galerie in Paris entitled '*Hervé Guibert – Les palais des monstres désirables*' [*Hervé Guibert – The Palace of desirable monsters*]). The public knows Guibert and his work largely thanks to them. Finally, Guibert's contingent heterosexual – who escapes normative definitions of heterosexuality and homosexuality – touches the reader: she, herself, becomes a contingent body, integrating Guibert's books as prostheses, working to take sentences apart and string them together otherwise, joining this eclectic contingent of women dedicated to keeping, if not his body, then at least his *corpus* alive.

Bibliography

Agar, James, 'Self-mourning in Paradise: Writing (about) AIDS through Death-bed Delirium,' *Paragraph* 30/1 (March 2007), 67–84.

Ahmed, Sara, *Queer Phenomenology: Orientations, Objects, Others* (Durham, NC and London: Duke University Press, 2006).

Asibong, Andrew, 'Travel Sickness: Marie NDiaye, Hervé Guibert and the Liquidation of the White Fantasy-Subject', *International Journal of Francophone Studies* 12/1 (2009), 109–25.

Chainey, Benjamin Gagnon, 'Du protocole compassionnel à l'anarchie passionnelle', *Revue Critique de Fixxion Française Contemporaine/Critical Review of Contemporary French Fixxion* 12 (2016), 84–95.

Décarie, Isabelle, 'L'identité posthume dans *le Paradis* d'Hervé Guibert', *L'Esprit Créateur* 40/1 (2000), 100–10.

Donner, Christophe, 'Pour répondre aux quelques questions qui se posent … Hervé Guibert. Entretien avec Christophe Donner,' *La Règle du jeu* 3/7 (Mai 1992), 135–57.

Guibert, Hervé. *A l'ami qui ne m'a pas sauvé la vie* (Paris: Gallimard, 1990).

—— *Cytolamégalovirus: Journal d'hospitalisation* (Paris: Seuil, 1992).

—— *L'Image fantôme* (Paris: Minuit, 1981).

—— *Le Mausolée des amants* (Paris: Gallimard, 2001).

—— *Le Paradis* (Paris: Gallimard, 1993).

—— *Le Protocole compassionnel* (Paris: Gallimard, 1991).

Kristeva, Julia, *Pouvoirs de l'horreur* (Paris: Seuil, 1980).

Lucey, Michael, *Someone: The Pragmatics of Misfit Sexualities, from Colette to Hervé Guibert* (Chicago: University of Chicago Press, 2019).

JENNIFER BOUM MAKE

11 Exploring Encounters in *Passages* by Emile Ollivier: The Role of Testimonial Responsibility to Othered Bodies

Introduction: Incorporating Testimonial Voices in *Passages* by Emile Ollivier

In his 1991 novel *Passages* [*Passages*], for which he received the Grand Prix du Livre de Montréal the same year, Emile Ollivier develops insight into the lives of Haitian exiles in the Americas with multiple narrators that speak in the first person.[1] Such a narrative configuration allows a range of voices of exile to intersect in unexpected ways. Normand Malavy and his wife, Leyda, have left Haiti and settled in Montreal years before a group of Haitian exiles has no other choice but to leave a dismal Port-à-L'Écu, a coastal city in the northwest of Haiti, following the overthrow of Jean-Claude Duvalier, also known as Baby Doc, in 1986. When their boat, *La Caminante*, founders a few miles off the coast of Southeast Florida, the few survivors, including one of the narrators Brigitte Kadmon, are immediately met by police forces and taken to the Krome detention centre in Miami where Normand and Brigitte will eventually meet.

This particular event resonates with the flow of so-called 'boat people', or Haitian migrants who, according to official reports, began arriving in Southern Florida in 1972.[2] That first boat from Haiti is ominously called the

1 Emile Ollivier, *Passages* (Montreal: Typo, 2005 [1991]).

2 For a detailed chronology of relations between Haiti and the United States and the evolution of migration policy during the Duvalier years and Jean-Bertrand Aristide's troubled presidency and exile, see Kelly Greenhill, 'An Invasion to Stop the Invasion: The United States and the Haitian Boatpeople Crises' in *Weapons of*

'Mayflower des damnés de la glèbe et du glaive' [Mayflower of the damned from the feudal lands with their gladius swords] in Jean-Claude Charles's work of reportage, *De si jolies petites plages* [*Such So Nice Little Beaches*].[3] Adding to a recalcitrant welcome, if at all, of Haitian 'boat people',[4] journalistic and literary accounts of Haiti and Haitians published in English since the early 1960s, Michael Dash notes, disseminate 'images of obscene visibility, of a deviant physicality', fuelling the Western imagination with 'a discourse of moral fallenness and corrupt carnality'.[5] Such stereotypical and derogatory portrayals corroborate the politics of exclusion and detention of Haitian 'boat people' led by the US in tandem with the Duvalier regime starting in the mid-1970s. Writers such as Charles with *De si jolies petites plages*, Ollivier with *Passages*, and Edwidge Danticat with *Krik? Krak!* (1995), among others, reveal often unknown or disregarded circumstances behind Haitian migration during the Duvalier years (1957–86) and the treatment of Haitian exiles held captive in American detention facilities at the time. In particular, Ollivier insists on the need for the Haitian writer to tell and bring together stories of dispersed populations, claiming for himself the testimonial figure of 'à la fois celui qui observe et atteste' [the one who both observes and reports].[6]

Mass Migration: Forced Displacement, Coercion, and Foreign Policy (Ithaca: Cornell University Press, 2010), 180–226.

3 Jean-Claude Charles, *De si jolies petites plages* (Paris: Stock, 1982), 18.

4 US migration policy in the second half of the twentieth century reveals a differential treatment of refugee populations, in particular between Cubans and Haitians. After Fidel Castro came to power in 1959, Cuban refugees who entered the US were admitted on political and humanitarian grounds in the context of the Cold War, unlike Haitian 'boat people' who were often deemed as economic migrants fleeing poverty and thus refused access to the US. Successive US administrations offered support for the Duvalier regime, who were making clear their fierce anti-communist sentiment. For a more detailed comparison of US refugee policy towards Haitians and Cubans in the 1970–80s, see Gaëlle Cooreman, '"La Mer, la plage, l'épouvante": l'imaginaire des "Boat People" haïtiens dans la littérature caribéenne anglophone et francophone', *L'Esprit Créateur* 51/2 (2011), 34–46.

5 Michael J. Dash, *Haiti and the United States: National Stereotypes and the Literary Imagination* (Basingstoke: Palgrave, 1997), 78.

6 Emile Ollivier, 'L'Enracinement et le déplacement à l'épreuve de l'avenir', *Études Littéraires* 34/3 (2002), 87–97, 93.

The two entangled timelines of Haitian exiles in *Passages* underscore the often difficult and strenuous life itineraries of those migrants and therefore encourage a cautionary tone regarding facile celebrations of exile and transnational flows. Critics of Ollivier's work are in fact careful to point to ways in which the Haitian writer steers clear of a prevailing praise of Caribbeanness in terms of fluidity and fragmented identities.[7] Martin Munro argues, for instance, that with his presentation of an exilic Haitian sensibility, Ollivier '[…] refuses to join the critical chorus that celebrate exile and unrootedness as endlessly creative, positively-experienced situations'. Rather, 'his writing', Munro continues, 'constitutes a persuasive counternarrative to the dominant, celebratory theories of Caribbeanness'.[8] Or, to put it in another way, Ollivier neither hesitates to bear testimony to the degrading living conditions that force Haitians into exile, nor to call into question simple notions of hospitality towards bodies of Haitian migrants being washed up on American coasts or placed in detention.

The testimonial dimension is, I suggest, key to articulating the possibility for interaction and exchange among Othered bodies, in the sense of bodies whose presence is perceived as unsettling and distant. The act of 'bearing testimony' refers here to storytelling and/or story-listening experiences, as narrators in *Passages* respectively serve to explore the possibility for interpersonal connections and participate in changing and evolving intimacies. They not only bear witness to one another's stories, but are also involved in passing on the testimonial function to each other repeatedly. In the broad sense, the role of witness is therefore not limited to the writer lifting the veil of ignorance and misunderstanding regarding Haitian lives in the Americas, or the fictional survivors of the *Caminante* interrogated at the Krome camp, but is rather taken up by successive narrators, including

7 See Max Dominique, 'L'Écriture baroque d'Ollivier et la crise des idéologies' in *Esquisses Critiques* (Port-au-Prince: Mémoires, 1999), 179–208; Martin Munro, 'Theorizing the Haitian Fragment and Fragmenting Caribbeanist Theory in Émile Ollivier's *Passages*', *The Romantic Review* 97/2 (2006), 213–29; Christiane Albert, 'L'Écriture de "L'Entre Deux" dans *Passages* d'Émile Ollivier' in *Intercâmbio* 1/1 (2008), 67–76.

8 Martin Munro, 'Theorizing the Haitian Fragment and Fragmenting Caribbeanist Theory in Émile Ollivier's *Passages*', 215.

Normand and Régis, who are part of a previous generation of Haitian exiles to Canada, and Brigitte Kadmon, held prisoner at Krome after attempting the journey to the US from Port-à-l'Écu.

The character of testimony, as Jean-Philippe Pierron reminds us, is twofold: it not only gestures at the act of telling and what is being said, but also 'involves the self in relation to others, regarding or in front of whom one bears testimony, one bears witness for'.[9] Considering the testimonial dimension as an essential narrative strategy in Ollivier's text, I choose to reflect on successive calls for the circulation of stories structured around encounters with testimonial figures, in order to (i) assess their use in telling, writing, and resisting physical and figurative forms of bodily closure and (ii) provide critical material for the expression of a contemporary ethics and politics of encounter with bodies perceived as Other, thus kept at bay.

In light of those considerations, I ask the following questions: what is the critical potential of portraying elements of immediacy and unexpectedness in encounters with Othered bodies to interrogate notions of openness and attentiveness to human differences? In this context, can we think of testimony, that is, the act of endorsing a testimonial responsibility, as an ethical tool to cultivate habits of openness and attentiveness in the immediacy and unexpectedness of the encounter with seemingly distant others?

Writing Closure: On Suspicion of Others and Unwelcome

As a narrative device in *Passages*, testimony incorporates multiple and shifting voices at different times and places, each of which respectively induces forms of ethical questioning. To avoid endowing the text's ethical perspective with imperatives, Ollivier is careful to raise ethical concerns instead. In this context, ethical concerns refer to a set of events and attitudes that call into question the sustainability of social interactions across personal sensibilities and cultural differences. All entangled narratives

9 Jean-Philippe Pierron, 'De la fondation à l'attestation en morale. Paul Ricœur et l'éthique du témoignage', *Recherches de Science Religieuse* 91 (2003), 435–59, 435.

make direct or indirect mention of the transnational experiences of exiles emphasizing a variety of situations wherein displaced bodies find themselves in foreign parts of the world. In particular, in making the contemporary plight of Haitian populations in exile known in a first layer of testimony, Ollivier, and henceforth the many narrators in *Passages*, tell of closure, that is spaces or, more broadly, forms of exclusion, and point to its immediate consequences.

Critics such as Fernando Lambert identify closed and wasted spaces in Ollivier's descriptions of the Caribbean as a radically uninhabitable place. Ollivier himself, Lambert cites in an interview with the writer, suggests that Haiti is caught in a 'temporal, historical circularity'[10] arguing that 'the history of this country, from independence to today has been an endless series of banditry, corruption and chaos'.[11] These are all driving forces that contributed to the forced exile of Haitian populations most intensively during and following the Duvaliers' repressive rule.[12]

In *Passages*, an induced departure from Haiti is the culmination of an irrevocable land dispossession of Port-à-l'Écu villagers. In a conversation with Normand Malavy in the detention camp in Florida, Brigitte Kadmon reports the self-imposed resolve of her husband Amédée Hosange to leave for America: 'ici, nous sommes claquemurés [...]. Il nous faut abandonner une terre qui ne nous donne plus ni vivres pour apaiser notre faim ni herbes pour nourrir notre bétail' (37) [here, we are trapped [...]. We *must* abandon a land that no longer gives us victuals to appease our hunger nor grass to feed our cattle] (6–7).[13] Subsequent visions of Port-à-l'Écu only reinforce the

10 For more on the circular vision of Haitian history in Ollivier's works, see Dominique, 'L'Écriture baroque d'Ollivier et la crise des idéologies', 179–208.

11 Fernando Lambert, 'Émile Ollivier, écrivain d'Haïti du Québec', *Notre Librairie* 133 (1998), 154–9, 155.

12 Massive arrivals of 'boat people' continued in the 1990s under the effect of former Haitian president Jean-Bertrand Aristide's engineered migration pressuring the US to restore him to power following the 1991 military coup.

13 Emphasis mine. All translations in English of quoted material from the original text in French come from *Passages*, Leonard Sugden, trans. (Victoria, BC: Ekstasis, 2003).

urgency for its inhabitants to leave, calling special attention to a decaying landscape.

Adding to the portrayal of Haiti as an insular wasted land, images of Haitian migrants often denote an extensive imagery of filth and degradation enclosing the Haitian body within a restrictive frame of representation. Dash's study of the literary stereotyping of Haitians points in particular to the image of a 'defiled body' by reference to dominating views of Haitian society in the Western imagination.[14] Used to justify further exclusion, images of the black body, Dash notes, are bound up with 'a discourse of moral fallenness and corrupt carnality'.[15] Often unflattering and distorted received ideas about Haiti and Haitian populations are thus integrated within a popularized cultural unconscious. Such ideas precede the possibility of a direct encounter and induce by extension closure in a physical sense by denying migrants entry, as well as in a figurative sense by systematizing the Othering of migrant bodies.

Early signs of closure are found in representations of suspicion and control of assumed foreigners in border spaces. For example, Normand recounts his arrival at Miami airport and encounter with a civil servant at border control. When asked where he comes from, Normand replies: 'du Canada, mais je suis haïtien' (47) [from Canada, but I'm Haitian] (59), which is apparently sufficiently confusing to mislead the immigration officer into thinking Normand needs a visa to enter the US. Preceding the *Caminante* shipwreck, such an event only heightens a pervasive shielding from others within the socio-political and legal realm.

There are, moreover, certain figurations of death prior to and correlating with the outcome of some of the *Caminante* passengers' journey to the US. Several moments in the narrative make mention of a hecatomb of migratory birds on beaches in Florida, detailing the circumstances of their death: 'des dizaines de milliers d'oiseaux migrateurs viennent agoniser sur les plages, atteints d'un mal mystérieux' (116) [tens of thousands of migratory birds are flying in to die on the beaches, victims of a mysterious illness] (107); a zoologist explains further that, 'les oiseaux de haute mer souffrent

14 Michael J. Dash, *Haiti and the United States*, 124.

15 Michael J. Dash, *Haiti and the United States*, 118.

de malnutrition. Ils ne trouvent plus de quoi se nourrir. Si un mauvais temps se prolonge, [...] les oiseaux maigrissent, s'épuisent à lutter et, finalement, se laissent porter par les vents dominants' (85) [the birds out at sea suffer from malnutrition. They can no longer find any food. If the bad weather continues, [...] the birds grow thinner, become exhausted with the struggle and, finally, are borne away by the prevailing winds] (93). Mentions of this ecological catastrophe constitute intratextual elements that not only prefigure future events, but also identify the beach (and more specifically American shores) as a recurring site of disaster, therefore reflecting a hardly life-sustaining space in the currently represented state of things.

In particular, closure and its effects are mobilized in *Passages* through an extensive use of metaphors of waste and figurations of 'wasted lives', to use Zygmunt Bauman's term.[16] Such a metaphor of waste is not uncommon to conjure visions of displaced bodies. Already in *Cahier d'un retour au pays natal* (1939) *[Notebook of a Return to the Native Land]*, Aimé Césaire refers, in an account of the so-called Middle Passage, to African enslaved bodies as 'vomissure de négrier' [slave trader-vomit].[17] In a more contemporary work on forced movement from Africa to Europe, Fatou Diome uses the metaphor of bodily waste to evoke the indigestibles of migration and displacement.[18] Like those literary accounts deconstructing normative images of the body, Ollivier's text populates the imaginary with disquieting visions of corpses, wastes and decay. A striking example is found in Brigitte Kadmon's recounting of the shipwreck scene to Normand during their encounter at the Krome detention centre, comparing the *Caminante* passengers to 'crabes vomis par les flots' (117) [crabs vomited up by the surf] (146).

16 In his essay *Wasted Lives*, Bauman suggests that the lives of refugees, the displaced, asylum seekers, migrants, and the *sans papiers* are more specifically the human cost of global economic inequalities. Zygmunt Bauman, 'Are there many of them? Or the Waste of Economic Progress' in *Wasted Lives: Modernity and its Outcasts* (Cambridge: Polity, 2004), 34–62, 58.

17 Aimé Césaire, *Cahier d'un retour au pays natal* (Paris: Présence Africaine, 1956), 62.

18 Fatou Diome, *Le Ventre de l'Atlantique* (Paris: Le Livre de Poche, 2005).

Relaying Stories of Imprisonment and Neglect: On States of Non-Arrival

Subsequent descriptions of the shipwreck include signs of immediacy and unexpectedness that precipitate the decision to welcome, or exclude, troubling Other bodies. With a brisk writing, or rather telling, style, Brigitte recalls, 'un déploiement de voitures dans une valse d'intermittentes lumières rouges et vertes, des crissements de pneus, un peuple d'uniformes, des claquements de bottes' (119) [a spread of cars with wavering red and green lights flashing on and off, screeching tires, a flock of uniforms and a pounding of boots] on the beach in Florida (148). Each respective metonymic element not only allows the reconstitution of the scene in its entirety, but also symbolizes a range of inhospitable responses to the presence of Haitian migrants, therefore establishing the basis for a testimony to states of non-arrival. With their entryway into the US blocked by police forces, survivors of the *Caminante* shipwreck are not permitted to ever truly reach their destination. Instead, they are detained at the Krome detention centre to wait for a formal hearing on deportation or political asylum.[19]

Numerous accounts of US-operated immigration detention facilities often find consensus over Charles's description of refugee detention centres such as Krome Camp in Florida, Fort Allen in Porto Rico and Guantánamo in Cuba as 'concentration camps', citing profusely his work of reportage, *De si jolies petites plages*.[20] Those imprisonment structures extend a state of non-arrival for Haitian migrants. In fact, building on the notion of 'concentration camp', these structures are the culmination of both physical

19 For a detailed description of US policy on Haitian migrants, in particular the 1981 US-Haiti Interdiction Agreement signed between Jean-Claude Duvalier and President Reagan on 23 September 1981, see Greenhill, *Weapons of Mass Migration*, 186–90.

20 See Michael J. Dash, *Haiti and the United States*; Dominique, 'L'Écriture baroque d'Ollivier et la crise des idéologies', 179–208; Cooreman, '"La Mer, la plage, l'épouvante": l'imaginaire des "Boat People" haïtiens dans la littérature caribéenne anglophone et francophone', 34–46.

and figurative closure. The historical analogy between Nazi concentration camps during the Second World War and immigrant detention facilities especially helps articulate the physical hardship and traumatic memories of 'boat people'. With Haitian migrants being kept away from any form of interaction with the outside world, except for interviews with journalists and immigration services (and eventually the character of Normand when he goes to Krome to interview one of the Haitian detainees, in the capacity of a retired sociologist), the possibility of a direct encounter with those bodies that have unsettled border spaces is continually delayed. Critics of *Passages* are in this regard correct when they describe those detention centres with a range of synonymous terms, such as the liminal condition of being 'between and betwixt two states'; an 'in-between'; a 'neither-here-nor-there-space'; or 'absolute non-places'.[21] In short, all note that Ollivier expresses a rupture between the enclosed world of Haitian 'boat people' and the world they are unable to reach, thus conveying ethical concerns regarding the impossibility of openness and comprehension.

An exclusive attention to the telling of closure fails, however, to explore the possibility of pulling out from the text ethical propositions for resisting it and developing, alternatively, interaction and exchange. While it is clear that Ollivier's *Passages* establishes a detailed picture of the imprisonment of Haitian migrants, it seems that concluding, as Christiane Albert suggests, that the writer merely offers 'some sort of disenchanted and hopeless contemplation of the fracturing of the world', appears as a limiting takeaway.[22] Rather, I am interested in questioning the potential of Haitian migrants' stories and the multiple narrative threads around them to contribute to the development of ethical sensibilities.

It is not uncommon, in contemporary times, to find distressing narratives by and about refugees and migrants disseminated in the public sphere. In an information session regarding the role and work carried out by the

21 In respective order: Michel Laguerre, *Diasporic Citizenship: Haitian Americans in Transnational America* (New York: St Martin's Press, 1998), 76; Martin Munro, 'Theorizing the Haitian Fragment and Fragmenting Caribbeanist Theory in Émile Ollivier's *Passages*', 46; Christiane Albert, 'L'Écriture de "L'Entre Deux" dans *Passages* d'Émile Ollivier', *Intercâmbio* 1/1 (2008), 67–76, 74.

22 Albert, 'L'Écriture de "L'Entre Deux" dans *Passages* d'Émile Ollivier', 75.

UN High Commissioner for Refugees during a graduate study program in Geneva in 2016, Melissa Fleming, chief spokesperson of the agency, chose to document and illustrate the story of a Syrian refugee in an attempt to create an emotional connection with viewers, raise awareness and stimulate understanding. A similar incentive is expressed in Fleming's *A Hope More Powerful Than the Sea* (2017), an account of the so-called 'refugee crisis' in Europe as experienced by a Syrian woman, but ultimately, literary critic and author Natasha Walter notes, it 'tells the kind of tale that is too often unheard or forgotten' in the context of a growing media spectacle.[23]

In this light, it seems that accounts of refugee experiences often fail to motivate the expected empathy as they are sometimes simply lost amidst the myriad stories that regularly find their way into mainstream media and turned into a mere banality. In the case of *Passages*, ways to resist the sense of closure experienced and conveyed by characters in the novel might constitute an ethical intervention for facilitating interaction and openness to others. In other words, once the issue of hospitality, in the sense of a welcoming gesture and/or attitude to unexpected and unsettling others, is raised, how can we incorporate and sustain an ethical outreach beyond closure?

Creating a Testimonial Dynamic: On Acts of Storytelling and Story-Listening to Effectively Resist Closure

The testimonial dimension around which the novel is structured is key to interrogating, if not resisting, the forms of closure I have outlined above. This dimension is initially reflected through the interplay between multiple narrative voices. Normand appears as the first and core voice for spreading Othered voices and bodies in the novel. After the *Caminante* shipwreck, he goes to Krome to meet the survivors. Normand's testimonial initiative is presented from the very beginning as rather different

23 Natasha Walter, '*A Hope More Powerful Than the Sea* by Melissa Fleming – Review', *The Guardian* (22 January 2017).

from the journalists' reporting activity at the detention centre. In particular, there is a clear disconnect between a group of journalists and the protagonist's attitude: on the day of his first visit to Krome, '[Normand] enfourne rageusement magnétophone, calepin et stylo dans son porte-documents. Il veut arriver tôt au camp de Krome et devancer ainsi la meute de journalistes qui ne manqueront pas de répondre à l'invitation du service de l'immigration' (121) [[Normand] shoved furiously a tape recorder, notepad and pen into his briefcase. He wants to arrive early at the camp at Krome and precede the horde of journalists who would not fail to accept the immigration people's invitation] (153). Unlike the self-serving curiosity of journalists invited 'pour mettre fin aux rumeurs qui circulaient sur les conditions d'internement des réfugiés haïtiens' (121) [to put an end to rumours concerning the conditions of internment that Haitian refugees were forced to live in] (150), Normand wishes to record Brigitte's testimony on an impulse without really knowing what he will do with it, but initiating exchange nonetheless.

Normand's initiative to encourage exchange moreover stands in contrast with testimony received in the context of asylum cases with American immigration services. Accounts of asylum interviews at Krome, and more generally asylum testimonies, often occur in a mechanized process of writing or telling, signalling, April Shemak notes, a possible 'institutionalization and commodification of testimony'.[24] Claiming, in addition, that the denying or silencing of Haitian testimonies is not rare, she continues to point that those 'are scrutinized for credibility, [...] become sites of surveillance and policing of national borders, as evidenced by the systematic denial of Haitian refugees' asylum applications'.[25] Alternatively, Brigitte's testimony to Normand breaks down the legal and normative framework on asylum status that diverts the expression of individual sensibility to fit a mechanical fact-checking storytelling process. After she has been released from Krome with a few others on humanitarian grounds, Brigitte announces

24 April Shemak, 'Introduction: The Poetics of Hospitality: Refugee, Migrant, Testimony' in *Asylum Speakers. Caribbean Refugees and Testimonial Discourse* (New York: Fordham, 2010), 1–44, 27.

25 Shemak, 'Introduction', 24.

her return to Port-à-l'Écu (197; 159), relieving further her testimony from a codified legal framework.

Brigitte's original testimony to Normand gives the first impulse to what I call a testimonial dynamic. That is to suggest that there is an incentive to make the critical importance of telling, sharing and being attentive to one another's stories apparent to readers. Just as places like Port-au-Prince and Miami are described as cultural hubs connecting people from diverse cultures and backgrounds in the novel, Normand represents a crossroads for the exchange of stories. Sustained circulation of the *Caminante* survivor's testimony is, in this respect, evidence that the testimonial dimension is constantly reactivated from one narrator to the next, giving shape to a continuous process of listening and telling.

In Ollivier's novel, connections and interactions among multiple addressees involved in turn in storytelling or story-listening, or both, are staged in the narrative. Acts of storytelling and/or story-listening necessitate encounters with others that are direct or indirect – such as the conversation between Normand and Brigitte recorded on cassettes – more or less intimate, or more or less distant. More specifically, such practices test the capacity to bear testimony, that is, to effectively listen to others whom one may not like and with whom one may disagree.

A striking example is found after Normand's death when his friend Régis, whose identity is only known to readers in the third part of the novel, explains that, 'Normand mort, [il] ressen[t] l'extrême urgence de relater à sa place l'odyssée de Brigitte Kadmon' (129) [Now Normand is dead, [he] feel[s] an urgent impulse to relate in his place Brigitte Kadmon's odyssey] (161). Régis's voluntary decision to recount Brigitte's story sustains the testimonial dynamic, as he was the one who encouraged Normand to go to the Krome detention centre, meet the *Caminante* survivors, and record their stories in the first place. In other words, Normand's urge to bear testimony to Haitian 'boat people's experiences, is carried on through Régis's narrative impulse. In this respect, Normand is the one unifying all the pieces together: the character never speaks in the first person and is the product of successive testimonial voices relating his life events. What all testimonial voices have in common is their knowledge of Normand eventually leading to unexpected and sometimes unwanted encounters among each other. These exchanges extend the scope of testimony beyond the refugee narrative, which served as a starting point, to cultivate habits of attentiveness and openness that could sustain an ethical sensibility.

Putting a Testimonial Dynamic to the Test: On Habits of Attentiveness and Openness to Others

For Gabrielle Napoli, the notion of bearing testimony, when not restricted to the legal dimension, 'comes down to presenting oneself as the bearer of a past of which we have become responsible for, and whose responsibility we must hand over to the addressee'.[26] Building on the idea of a 'bearer' and sharer of a given past, Normand's ability to pass on testimonial responsibility is achieved through Régis's impulse to undertake story-listening and storytelling after the death of his friend. Such a narrative configuration seems, however, to be dependent on displays of attentive interaction with originally distant others. Both Normand and Régis demonstrate commitment to mediate Othered perspectives, in the sense of experiences so far unknown or unacknowledged. In other words, while it is clear that the testimonial dimension is preceded by acts of careful and thoughtful openness to others, for it to become a testimonial dynamic requires finding ways to maintain exchange.

While Normand and Régis's testimonial initiative leads to productive interactions in the form of willing exchanges, the immediacy of unintended encounters with migrant bodies is met with closure and prevents effective interaction. A similar refusal to engage with a disturbing and unannounced Other is found when Leyda, Normand's wife, and Amparo, his lover, meet in Montreal a year after his death. The second chapter of the novel's first part opens with the narrator's (Régis) mention of Amparo's upcoming visit to Montreal and how Leyda received the news:

26 Gabrielle Napoli, 'Poétiques du témoignage: le retour spectral de l'Histoire comme condition éthique du récit', *Roman 20–50* 52 (2011), 141–54, 142.

> Elle [Leyda] attendait à déjeuner une jeune femme qu'elle ne connaissait pas [...]. Leyda avait répondu *avec beaucoup de réticence à cette intruse* [...]. À cette jeune femme qui lui téléphonait, elle avait donc répondu *un tantinet agacée*[27] qu'elle ne pouvait la rencontrer [...]. Amparo insista. Leyda accepta finalement de la rencontrer le vendredi de la semaine suivante (25).
>
> [She was waiting to serve lunch to a young woman she didn't really know [...]. Leyda had answered *this intruder rather coolly* [...]. To this young woman who telephoned her, she had replied *with slight irritation*, that she couldn't meet her [...]. Amparo insisted. Leyda finally received her the following Friday] (32).

The situation described above as it was probably told to Régis gives privileged access to Leyda's early appraisal of her meeting with Amparo. These early signs of discontent anticipate Leyda's disengagement from the prospect of a conversation with her late husband's lover. When the two women eventually meet, making clear allusion to her desire to end the conversation, Leyda reportedly asks herself after some time spent listening to a chatty Amparo: 'Comment mettre un terme à cette conversation? Comment se débarrasser de la jeune femme?' (142) [How could she bring this conversation to an end? How could she get rid of this woman?] (176). As Leyda grows increasingly weary of a presence she perceives as invasive, Amparo's flow of words is repeatedly interrupted by mentions of the host's inconclusive attempts to cut the conversation short, or simply by access to Leyda's inner thoughts.

The narrator identified as Normand's friend Régis notes, for example, that '[La] tentative de diversion [de Leyda] en proposant de se déplacer n'avait pas réussi et Amparo, les yeux hallucinés, avait recommencé à parler' (132) [[Leyda']s attempt at diversion by suggesting to change rooms did not succeed, and Amparo started speaking again with distraught eyes] (164). After a while, moreover, Leyda's thoughts simply start drifting away as she gets caught in her own memories of Normand and moments they spent together. This happens without Amparo's realizing that Leyda was no longer paying much attention, as the narrator observes that 'dans l'application obstinée qu'elle mettait à définir Normand, Amparo semblait avoir oublié la présence de Leyda. Elle ne parlait plus que pour elle-même' (143) [because of

27 Emphasis mine.

her obstinate efforts to define Normand, Amparo seemed to have forgotten Leyda's presence. It was as though she was only talking to herself] (178).

Conclusion: On the Ethical Exercise of Bearing Testimony

Described as such, the conversation between the two women fails to show signs of mindful listening to one another. Kwame Anthony Appiah highlights the benefits of making conversation regardless, suggesting it might be useful for people 'to develop habits of coexistence', since whether it is 'delightful' or 'vexing', it supports interaction and engagement with experiences and perceptions of others.[28] And yet the parting of the two women after what seems to have been an inconclusive exchange – Amparo tells Leyda she was 'hoping to leave this place feeling relieved' (167) – seems to obscure the prospect of a productive interaction. It is then that the possibility of teasing a testimonial dynamic out of Leyda and Amparo's conversation allows us to underline how bearing testimony, once conceived as an ethical exercise, can cultivate habits (uncoincidentally from the Greek *ethos*) of attentiveness and openness to others.

Leyda actually identifies herself as a potential bearer of Amparo's experiences with Normand, but this realization is immediately followed by her dismissal of the burden of having to endorse a testimonial voice (165; 205). Though dismissed by Leyda, the testimonial dynamic in *Passages* includes several layers, and is in turn recuperated by Régis's narrative voice. The character is not only bearing testimony to Amparo and Leyda's meeting by recounting details of their encounter but he also manages to reconnect their respective experiences by highlighting the complementarity that the two stories have with one another. The idea of complementarity allows us to propose a reassessment of Leyda and Amparo's differences and points of disagreement. While a first level of analysis dwells on Leyda's disengagement from conversation with an emphasis on her thoughts drifting away or

28 Kwame Anthony Appiah, 'Introduction', *Cosmopolitanism: Ethics in a World of Strangers* (New York: W. W. Norton, 2007), xi–xxi, xix.

points of disagreement between the two women, it is eventually at a second level that a set of contrasting stories about and memories with Normand come together, to bear testimony to the late multifaceted Haitian exile at different moments of his life.

A striking illustration of these two levels of analysis is found when Leyda and Amparo each give one word to describe Normand: while 'désenchantement' [disenchantment]; 'désaffection' [disaffection]; or 'désengagement' [disengagement] are the first words that come to Leyda's mind (142; 176), Amparo firmly disagrees as for her, the narrator notes, 'le terme désenchantement ne pouvait s'appliquer à Normand [...]. Elle, Amparo traduisait cela par un autre mot: la nonchalance' (143) [disenchantment could never be attributed to Normand [...]. She, Amparo saw him as a reflection of another concept: nonchalance] (177). Régis's narrative intervention, in this respect, consists not so much in appeasing or resolving the two women's disagreement – this being an integral part of the texture of their conversation – but rather in composing with their contrasting views. Commenting on the difficult exercise of bearing testimony to one another's complex and sometimes divergent experiences, Régis compares his steadfast patience to that of a spider as he carefully attends to the harsh words Leyda and Amparo had exchanged (134; 167). The incentive to sustain the testimonial dynamic initiated by Normand at the time of his first encounter with Brigitte is precisely what necessitates that Régis continuously cultivates habits of openness and attentiveness to others, revealed for instance when he pieces together the two women's histories and timelines. Despite a seeming distance between the two female characters, their testimonial voices are crucial for the completion of Régis's nuanced testimony to his late friend's life.

While Ollivier's novel raises several questions about how to generate audiences for and engagement with migrant and refugee narratives, or how to raise public awareness to the plight of migrants and refugees, the focus is also placed concomitantly on creating, sustaining and testing a testimonial dynamic among seemingly distant others. In endorsing a testimonial function following Normand's first impulse to bear testimony to Haitian migrants and also on behalf of his late friend, Régis's narrative voice attends to the development of habits of attentiveness and openness to others' stories, sensibilities and values. In light of the multiple forms of closure observed during numerous encounters with Othered bodies throughout the novel, bearing testimony to the presence of others is far from being inherently mutual; just as making conversation is on its own, I have argued, not enough to get used to each other's presence. Though Appiah makes clear that conversation does not need to involve consensus or harmonious interactions with others, making conversation nonetheless calls for a willingness to exchange and be attentive to experiences and/or views different from one's own, at least for it to meet his prospective results, that is, 'to develop habits of coexistence'.[29]

It is not my intention to suggest that bearing testimony is the magic panacea to sustain social interactions, but instead that it is a possible avenue to promote habits of attentiveness and openness. Similarly, the prospect of bearing testimony does not cancel marginalization or dismissal of unsettling others, but seems an effective way to actively resist it. In *Passages*, Régis makes use of his testimonial voice, and grapples with Amparo and Leyda's disengagement from each other as he carefully collects and interconnects contrasting narratives. Recognition of the testimonial function we can endorse for each other suggests for Régis (and others) to engage in activities that can expose a mutual responsibility as bearer and trader of many different stories and experiences.

The unexpected and sudden arrival of migrants off the coast of Southeast Florida triggers a testimonial dynamic on which recounting of all the entangled narratives relies. Successive attempts to bear testimony to others attest to the possibility of developing mutual participation and responsibility in accounting for one another's experiences and sensibilities. In *Passages*, the exercise of bearing testimony not only includes a reminder of the sometimes tenuous and difficult act of storytelling and/or story-listening, but also and more importantly, dwells on the process of producing testimony and learning to compose with socially and culturally diverse experiences. Therefore, concerns over engagement with migrant and refugee narratives may be tied back to the need to attend to habits of attentiveness and openness to others more generally. The focus is thus not

29 Appiah, 'Introduction', xix.

so much on engagement with and through testimonies already produced, but rather on the possibility to endorse a testimonial responsibility, especially challenging to cultivate in the immediacy and unexpectedness of the encounter with seemingly distant others.

Bibliography

Albert, Christiane, 'L'Écriture de 'L'Entre Deux' dans *Passages* d'Émile Ollivier', *Intercâmbio* 1/1 (2008), 67–76.

Appiah, Kwame Anthony, 'Introduction', *Cosmopolitanism: Ethics in a World of Strangers* (New York: W. W. Norton, 2007), xi–xxi.

Augé, Marc, *Non-Lieux. Introduction à une anthropologie de la surmodernité* (Paris: Seuil, 1992).

Bauman, Zygmunt, *Wasted Lives: Modernity and Its Outcasts* (Cambridge: Polity, 2003).

Césaire, Aimé, *Cahier d'un retour au pays natal* (Paris: Présence Africaine, 1956).

Charles, Jean-Claude, *De si jolies petites plages* (Paris: Stock, 1982).

Cooreman, Gaëlle, '"La Mer, la plage, l'épouvante": l'imaginaire des "boat people" haïtiens dans la littérature caribéenne anglophone et francophone,' *L'Esprit Créateur* 51/2 (2011), 34–46.

Danticat, Edwidge, *Krik? Krak!* (New York: Soho Press, 1995).

Dash, J. Michael, *Haiti and the United States: National Stereotypes and the Literary Imagination* (Basingstoke: Palgrave, 1997).

Diome, Fatou, *Le Ventre de l'Atlantique* (Paris: Le Livre de Poche, 2005).

Dominique, Max, 'L'Écriture baroque d'Ollivier et la crise des idéologies' in *Esquisses Critiques* (Port-au-Prince: Mémoires, 1999), 179–208.

Fleming, Melissa, *A Hope More Powerful than the Sea* (New York: Flatiron Books, 2017).

Greenhill, Kelly, 'An Invasion to Stop the Invasion: The United States and the Haitian Boatpeople Crises' in Kelly Greenhill, ed., *Weapons of Mass Migration: Forced Displacement, Coercion, and Foreign Policy* (Ithaca, NY: Cornell University Press, 2010), 180–226.

Laguerre, Michel, *Diasporic Citizenship: Haitian Americans in Transnational America* (New York: St Martin's Press, 1998).

Lambert, Fernando, 'Émile Ollivier, écrivain d'Haïti du Québec', *Notre Librairie*, 133 (1998), 154–59.

Munro, Martin, 'Theorizing the Haitian Fragment and Fragmenting Caribbeanist Theory in Émile Ollivier's *Passages*', *The Romantic Review* 97/2 (2006), 213–29.

Napoli, Gabrielle, 'Poétiques du témoignage. le retour spectral de l'Histoire comme condition éthique du récit', *Roman 20–50* 52 (2011), 141–54.

Ollivier, Emile, 'L'Enracinement et le déplacement à l'Epreuve de l'avenir', *Études Littéraires* 34/3 (2002), 87–97.

—— *Passages* (Montreal: Typo, 2005 [1991]); *Passages*, Leonard Sugden, trans. (Victoria, BC: Ekstasis, 2003).

Pierron, Jean-Philippe, 'De la fondation à l'attestation en morale. Paul Ricœur et l'éthique du témoignage', *Recherches de Science Religieuse* 91 (2003), 435–59.

Shemak, April, 'Introduction: The Poetics of Hospitality: Refugee, Migrant, Testimony', In *Asylum Speakers. Caribbean Refugees and Testimonial Discourse* (New York: Fordham, 2010), 1–44.

KATHRYN CHAFFEE

12 Dance as Encounter in the Films of Claire Denis

What do bodies *do* in cinema? What do we do with moving bodies? What happens when one body meets another? The aim of this chapter is to look at the dancing body as a site of encounter throughout the cinematic *œuvre* of Claire Denis: a drunk Englishman waltzes with a colonial housewife in *Chocolat* [*Chocolate*] (1988),[1] four long-time friends slow dance to the Commodores in a shuttered African restaurant in *35 Rhums* [*35 Shots of Rum*] (2008),[2] and a Parisian divorcée dances alone to Etta James before she is suddenly joined by a potential love interest in *Un beau soleil intérieur* [*Let the Sunshine In*] (2017).[3] In each scene, previously invisible aspects of intersubjectivity (and in some cases, subjectivity) take centre stage on the dance floor. From her first film to her most recent, Denis' films present a queer(y)ing of bodies, probing how bodies change and react to their environments in a way that challenges normative expectations. In turn, movement and dance act as a tacit response to the questions raised by Denis in her films, structuring experience and revealing latent aspects of the ways in which characters relate to themselves and to others.

Central to my conception of dance in this chapter is Deleuze's work on movement presented in *Cinema I*. More specifically, I argue that Deleuze's reading of Bergson's *Creative Evolution* and *Matter and Memory* is a type of phenomenology particularly well suited for analysing the queering/questioning of bodies presented in Denis' *œuvre*. Early on in *Cinema I: The Movement-Image* and following Bergson's first thesis, Deleuze argues that

1 Claire Denis, dir. *Chocolat*. Orion Classics, 1988. All translations are my own unless otherwise noted.

2 Claire Denis, dir. *35 Rhums*. Wild Bunch Distribution, 2008.

3 Claire Denis, dir. *Un beau soleil intérieur*. Curiosa Films, 2017.

movement is a way of dividing and experiencing space that also reveals the essential; movement uncovers fundamental qualities of bodies and relationships. Deleuze's following conception of movement is exceptionally relevant to this chapter and worth quoting at length:

> movement merely expresses a 'dialectic' of forms, an ideal synthesis which gives it order and measure. Movement, conceived in this way, will thus be the regulated transition from one form to another, that is, an order of *poses* or privileged instants, as in a dance. The forms or ideas … characterize the quintessence, the culminating point, the essential movement.[4]

Deleuze's assertion that movement is a type of dialectics is intensely related to the idea of dancing with another person. Movement becomes a conversation, a negotiation of desires and a distillation of what the relationship has been, or has the potential to become: 'The fall of a body presupposes another one which attracts it, and expresses a change in the whole which encompasses them both.'[5] Deleuze places the focus of his argument not on the body itself, but rather on the moments in which bodies interrelate.

I suggest that the dialectics of movement described by Deleuze also presents a 'queer(y)ing' of the expected and normalized corporeal boundaries as one body in motion is drawn towards another. In the context of Denis' films, dance specifically highlights bodily encounters in ways that problematize normative relationships between characters. In *Chocolat*, a waltz becomes an expression of attraction, a moment that crystalizes underlying sexual and racial tensions and violates the coded spaces of the colonial mansion. In *Beau travail* [*Beautiful Work*], the deftly executed, choreographed movements of the French *légion d'honneur* become a series of 'privileged instants' that reveal underlying homoerotic desires.[6]

Furthermore, Deleuze's conception of movement presented in *Cinema I* places an emphasis on specific temporal moments that represent essential elements of various interpersonal dynamics. He writes: 'Things and people

4 Gilles Deleuze, *Cinema I: The Movement-Image* (Minneapolis: University of Minnesota Press, 2013), 4.

5 Deleuze, *Cinema 1: The Movement-Image*, 8.

6 Claire Denis, dir. *Beau Travail*. Pyramide Distribution, 1999.

are always forced to conceal themselves, to have to conceal themselves when they begin … The essence of a thing never appears at the outset, but in the middle, in the course of its development, when its strength is assured.'[7] Following Deleuze, the 'essence' of a relationship is found not at its beginning, but rather at moments of particular intensity after the relationship has developed. The way in which Deleuze describes 'intensities' in his earlier work also elucidates his conception of movement and provides a generative way of reading moments of contact in Denis' films. In *Logic of Sense* (1969), intensities represent a movement outside of the self, a series of 'risings and falls' that happen between individuals, in between separate bodies[8] In a later characterization, Deleuze writes: 'Intensity aims at itself in aiming at the other, modifies itself in modifying the other, and returns finally onto its own trace. The dissolved self opens up to a series of roles … across and with multiple bodies.'[9] Similarly, in Denis' films, necessary moments of character development are revealed through the way in which bodies interrelate, movement between bodies becoming a reflection of the individual. Her dance scenes in particular highlight the type of social intensities that underscore the 'singular points which belong to movement'.[10]

Early Encounters: *Chocolat*

Critically acclaimed director Denis is remarkable not only for the sheer number of films in her *œuvre* – fourteen feature-length films, as well as several documentaries and short films – but also for the formal unity of her work, characterized by long takes and a sparsity of dialogue.[11] Born in Paris and raised in different locations throughout francophone Africa

7 Deleuze, *Cinema 1: The Movement-Image*, 3.

8 Gilles Deleuze, *The Logic of Sense* (New York: Columbia University Press), 289.

9 Deleuze, *The Logic of Sense*, 298.

10 Deleuze, *Cinema I: The Movement-Image*, 5–6.

11 See specifically Marjorie Vecchio's edited volume, *The Films of Claire Denis: Intimacy on the Border* (London: I.B. Tauris, 2014).

including Cameroon, Djibouti, and Burkina Faso, her films, as well as her biography, reflect a tension between France as destabilized centre and its former colonies.[12] Denis returned to France for her education, where she enrolled at the prestigious *Institut des hautes études cinématographiques* (or IDHEC), a formative experience not only for her training in cinema, but also for the connections she made during her studies. Perhaps most importantly, IDHEC is where she met Agnès Godard, with whom she has had a close working relationship since the beginning of her film career and who acted as director of photography for all of the films analysed in this chapter.

Denis' first feature-length film, *Chocolat*, is loosely based on her childhood and is set in the final days of French colonialism in Cameroon.[13] The film, nominated for the Palme d'or at the 1988 Cannes Film Festival and for a César for best first film in 1989, follows an adult France, a white woman living in France but raised in Cameroon, as she returns to her childhood home. *Chocolat* unfolds as a series of flashbacks primarily documenting France's relationship to Protée, the family's black servant who acts as France's primary caretaker and head of household during her father's absence. Throughout the film, underlying sexual tension between Aimée, France's mother, and Protée is revealed through the exchange of glances along with moments of brief and limited physical contact. In the sequence analysed below, a brief encounter between Protée and Aimée immediately precedes a waltz between Aimée and her drunken houseguest. While Aimée and Protée neither act on, nor verbalize, their basic physical desires at this point in the film, I suggest that the dance shared between Aimée and the English military official becomes a substitute for a forbidden physical contact with Protée. The sequence brings into question the 'fixed' racialized boundaries of the colonial mansion and presents a transgressive representation of sexuality within societal context of film. This moment in *Chocolat* also queries normative ideas about the boundaries of the body,

12 Judith Mayne, *Claire Denis* (Urbana: University of Illinois Press, 2005), xi–xii.

13 The film's title, taken from the phrase *être chocolat*, or 'to be cheated', is an implicit reference to the permanent state of disadvantage in which West Africans found themselves during colonial rule. The title should also be read as a nod to Cameroon's role a major producer of cacao beginning in the 1800s.

about contact between bodies, through touch, gaze, and through the way in which some bodies stand in for others.

In the scene leading up to the waltz, Denis establishes the relationship between Aimée and Protée through the way in which Aimée invites her 'boy', whose impressive stature and sculpted figure are typically masculine, into the private, socially coded space of her bedroom. Preparing for her formal dinner with the commander, Aimée, unable to close the back of her ball gown herself, calls to Protée for assistance. At first, Protée waits outside, asking if he should serve the drinks through the closed bedroom door. Aimée, aware that her request constitutes a social transgression and an abuse of her power within the home, begins a series of gently delivered, informal commands: 'attends, entre. Approche-toi' [wait, come here]. Protée, dressed for the special occasion, cautiously opens the door to Aimée's bedroom. 'Aide-moi, Protée, veux-tu?' [help me, Protée, would you?] She insists, and Protée steps hesitantly into her room. In the next shot, the spectator looks at Aimée as if from the inside of her full-length mirror, and we watch Protée approach from behind. He looks down, tightening the bodice of her dress before his eyes travel silently up her back and meet her gaze in the mirror. I suggest that this moment in the film functions as a Deleuzian intensity, a movement in between bodies that reveals an essential element of the relationship between the two, and a clear manifestation of unspoken sexual desire. The subtlety with which the transgressions in this scene take place challenges normative ideas about contact between bodies – gaze and movement into a private space reveal layers of complexity and attachment.

I read the second half of the sequence as an acting out of the desired physical contact between Aimée and Protée. The scene begins in the equally socially coded space of the formal dining room, and record music begins to play. Young France, barefoot in her pyjamas, watches from outside the house; her outfit marks the exceptional nature of her presence in the servants' quarters at that hour of the evening and reinforces the way in which the scene redraws boundaries between characters and spaces in and around the home. The following shot recreates France's point of view for the spectator as she watches her mother slow dance with the English officer. Protée remains visible in the frame, stationed just behind the dancing couple with his hands folded carefully behind his back. The camera slowly dollies in as the officer vocalizes his obvious enjoyment: 'you're a fine dancer, très bon, je ne le savais pas!' [you're a fine dancer, very good, I had no idea!] The subtext of his compliment suggests that Aimée would be just as talented on the dance floor as in the bedroom, and she laughs with a bemused disinterest: 'si vous voulez' [if you think so.] Her lack of enthusiasm is directly contrasted with the sexually charged exchange of glances shared with Protée at the beginning of the sequence. Finally, as evening comes to a close, another servant leads the Commander out of the room. He takes his arm, as if escorted by another dance partner – drunk, the Englishman moves awkwardly, his white, middle-aged body appears at once frail and overweight, his physique juxtaposed with the muscular, capable black men around him. While the officer takes his exit, Aimée once again exchanges glances with Protée before heading out of the room.

The sequence takes place with little dialogue, placing a greater emphasis on bodies and contact while racial differences and power dynamics separating characters are simultaneously reinforced and brought into question: Aimée gives orders to Protée with a subtext of sexual desire during the absence of her husband, the English Commander is at once 'socially superior' and physically inferior to the black men who run and organize the mansion. Although the waltz in *Chocolat* is the only example of dance in the film, Denis' presentation of movement and contact throughout the sequence prefigures the unique choreography of bodies and the Deleuzian 'culminating points' of various interpersonal relationships that guide her later works. The scene also introduces some of the overarching themes that reappear through dance across Denis' extensive *œuvre*: gazes that reveal unspoken connections, bodies that move in unison or act as replacements for others. Finally, this moment in *Chocolat* reveals the complexity of the ways in which Denis thinks through spaces of postcolonial encounter – Denis queries the boundaries that divide racial and social hierarches within the space of the colonial home, presenting dynamics of power and sexuality that are messier, more porous and multidirectional than the official French narrative would suggest.[14] Instead of a narrative in which whiteness

14 I refer specifically to the French colonial narrative outlined by Jules Ferry. In 'Les fondements de la politique coloniale' (28 July 1885), Ferry justifies French colonization as a unidirectional expansion of 'civilized' and 'humanitarian' ideas from the

'masters' interpersonal relationships, characters move through coded spaces in transgressive ways, illustrating the exact moments when seemingly fixed interactions between black and white bodies change.

The way in which Denis presents postcolonial encounter in *Chocolat* and throughout her other films resonates with Laura U. Marks's work in *The Skin of the Film: Intercultural Cinema, Embodiment, and the Senses* (2000). For Marks, cinema has a 'tactile and contagious quality'; it is something we 'brush up against like another body'.[15] As Denis' filmmaking brings into question the permeable boundaries between social class and race, Marks argues that intercultural cinematic works 'challenge the separateness of cultures and make visible the colonial and racist power relations that seek to maintain this separation'.[16] Marks goes on to highlight the '*social* character of embodied experience: the body is a source not just of individual but of cultural memory'.[17] Similarly, Zsuzsa Baross' work on encounter specifically within the context of Denis' films is deeply centred around tactile images and forms of exchange. Baross focuses on the ways in which bodies are 'caressed' by Denis' camera, and her description of encounter is presented in terms that evoke a transgression of the physical boundaries between bodies. Encounter is 'intrusion, penetration, touch; appropriation, theft, abduction; intercourse, […] modalities for entering, imposing, or being exposed to a relation by *contact*'.[18] Marks's vocabulary of 'haptic visuality' and 'multisensory images' and Baross's embodied account of contact give us the language to think through dance scenes in Denis' *œuvre*, moments when radically different types of bodies and different cultures 'brush up against' each other, queering and bringing into question relationships between individuals and socially constructed spaces.

French colonizer to the 'barbaric', 'inferior race'. In contrast, in the sequence from *Chocolat*, it is Aimée who is unable to follow the prescribed social conduct.

15 Laura U. Marks, *The Skin of the Film: Intercultural Cinema, Embodiment, and the Senses* (Durham, NC: Duke University Press, 2000), xii.

16 Marks, *The Skin of the Film: Intercultural Cinema, Embodiment, and the Senses*, xii.

17 Marks, *The Skin of the Film: Intercultural Cinema, Embodiment, and the Senses*, xiii.

18 Zsuza Baross, *Encounters: Gérard Titus-Carmel, Jean-Luc Nancy, Claire Denis* (Brighton: Sussex Academic Press, 2015), 2–4.

Queer Encounters: *Beau travail*

Denis returns to West Africa in her 1999 film, *Beau travail*. The film, which unfolds as a series of flashbacks, follows Galoup, a disgraced former member of the *legion d'honneur*, and Sentain, a handsome new recruit who arrives at the legion's military base in Djbouti. As in *Chocolat*, Denis privileges synchronized bodily movements through coded spaces over dialogue in order to tell her story. The opening sequence of *Beau travail* begins with the operatic score of *Billy Bud*, the opera adaptation of the Herman Melville play on which Denis' film is based, heard along with the sounds of wind and surf crashing against rocks.[19] The screen cuts from the opening credits to a lateral tracking shot, and the camera moves across a mural depicting soldiers ready for combat. Arms in hand, their bodies are dark silhouettes against rocky cliffs. Marching footsteps are added to the sounds of waves as soldiers begin to sing: 'après nos attentats … On veut des soldats valeureux' [after our battles … we want brave soldiers]. The song, along with the voyeurism of Denis' camera, seems to valorize the men for their sculpted physiques instead of their military prowess. The male voices are suddenly interrupted by the sound of a kiss, confirming the underlying homoeroticism embedded in the opening sequence and transporting both the viewer and the soldiers themselves to a busy nightclub. The jarring visual and auditory contrast between two radically different locations repositions boundaries between the urban centre and desert periphery and juxtaposes seemingly unrelated forms of movement and experiences of space. Instead of the thundering male chorus heard during the military training, young women of colour dance with the uniformed French *légion d'honneur* to high intensity nightclub beats. The young men and women's faces, shoulders and hair are highlighted by the warm glow of flickering lights as Denis' camera circles around the dancers' torsos.

19 Caroline Godart, *The Dimensions of Difference: Space, Time and Bodies in Women's Cinema and Continental Philosophy* (London: Rowman & Littlefield International Ltd, 2016), 32.

Denis' opening sequence of *Beau travail* suggests that the young male bodies are just as prepared for dancing as they are for military training. The opening images and sound prepare the spectator to read the practised movements of the legion as a type of choreography, presenting an aesthetics of movement just as central to the film's narrative as elements of plot and dialogue. The beginning sequence also 'sets the stage' for two later scenes in the film. The next time we hear the opera score, images of light and shadow are juxtaposed in the late afternoon light. Dark shadows trail behind rocks and brush; the chorus of male voices in harmony becomes increasingly louder. The camera pans across the sand, following elongated horizontal shadows until we finally see the legs of the soldiers from which the shadows originate. In one long take, the camera pans vertically up the body of one of the soldiers, revealing his bare chest, then panning laterally over the chests of the other men, their eyes closed, and their arms raised to the sky. Agnès Godard's camerawork under Denis' direction is transgressive, implicating the spectator in the sexualized gaze of the soldiers and drawing attention to textures and colours that would otherwise go unnoticed. Instead of the deep focus shots that would emphasize the hostile desert environment, Denis gives us close-ups of individual plants or abstract shadows elongated by the late afternoon light.

Furthermore, while more traditional filmic techniques would 'introduce' characters through camera angles held at torso height, Denis' camera begins with shadows of the soldiers' bodies transformed into surreal shapes stretched along the desert floor and altered by patterns in the sand. Next, each individual body is fragmented and cut in half by the movement of the camera, emphasizing the uniformity of the young male figures. Their skin appears smooth and luminous, highlighted by the afternoon sun and contrasted with the background of volcanic rock and blue sky around them. Throughout the scene, Denis queers boundaries between the human bodies and the surrounding landscape as well as between the young men, who appear interchangeable, their arms held to the sky, awaiting the inspection of the camera. The sculpted, uniformed men seem to exist solely for the viewing pleasure of the spectator, while the cinematography highlights specific elements of the *mise-en-scène*, emphasizing contrasting colours, surfaces and shapes. The scene evokes the type of 'haptic visuality' described by Marks, blurring the separation between viewer and diegesis. Heat seems to radiate off the sand and bodies and through the screen, the emphasis on skin and texture drawing the spectator into the world of the film.

The sexualized images of the soldiers also foreshadow the desirous gaze of Galoup, who, in the next scene, writes in his diary, narrating the arrival of Sentain: 'j'ai remarqué un type qui sortait de l'eau, un type mince, un jeune type distant qui n'avait rien à faire parmi nous .... C'est ce que je me suis dit. Quelque chose de vague et menacent a serré le cœur' [I noticed a guy coming out of the water, thin, distant, a guy who had nothing to do with us ... That's what I said to myself. Something vague and menacing gripped my heart]. In contrast with the lithe and almost feminine beauty of Sentain, Galoup describes his own physical decline: 'mes muscles sont rouillés, je me sens rouillé,' [my muscles are rusty, I feel rusty,] his body destroyed from years of military training as if 'attaqué par un acide' [attacked by acid]. His voiceover is immediately followed with a training sequence in the desert staged by the choreographer Bruno Montet. Young, limber, muscular male bodies crawl beneath wire obstacles positioned only a few inches above the ground. Next, the soldiers elegantly lift their bodies up and over a series of wooden beams, swinging over their legs and landing in one swift motion. In each shot, the camera follows the trained movements of the young soldiers as if to verify the precision of their routine and to confirm their physical and sexual prowess.

In contrast with the heteronormative space of the nightclub in the film's opening scene, the choreographed training sequence is deeply homoerotic, challenging normative expectations about sexuality and masculinity within the tightly controlled and socially coded space of the *légion d'honneur*. Furthermore, images of physically superior male bodies performing their choreographed 'dance' recreate Galoup's queer gaze for the spectator, and bring into question notions of encounter more generally. While explicit representations of homosexuality are absent from *Beau travail*, the film explores the ways in which haptic images present notions of contact that query sexual boundaries. Denis' film suggests that the tactile qualities of bodies in motion can provoke a queer encounter between characters within the film's narrative and between the spectator and the bodies on screen. Through movement and textures, bodies on screen are brought into contrast with heat, sand and water – qualities that we can almost feel. We brush up against the diegetic world of the film, implicated through gaze and Godard's voyeuristic, embodied cinematography in Galoup's homoerotic contemplation of the men around him.

Finally, in contrast with the nightclub scenes in which women dance alongside the men of the *légion d'honneur*, or the scenes in the desert where the young male bodies move together under the watchful eye of Galoup, *Beau travail* concludes with a frenetic modern dance solo to Corona's 'Rhythm of the Night'. In the scene, Galoup jumps and spins, the smoke from his cigarette shadowing his movements like a ghostly dance partner. The scene, which Denis has referred to as a 'dance of death', acts as a sort of narrative closure after Galoup's suicide in the film's penultimate sequence.[20] As Caroline Godart notes, the scene is at once 'a metaphor for Galoup's death' and 'a last, frenzied grip on life' – a final show of agency over his own body after a career tightly controlled by military protocol. The improvised dance, performed in an empty nightclub, also functions as an unspoken confirmation of Galoup's queer sexuality, alluded to up until this moment in the film through a series of gazes. The majority of the film's homoerotic elements are presented through eyeline match – shots that recreate the ways in which Galoup inspects the bodies of the young men around him for the spectator. However, in counter to the many scenes in which we see Galoup observe muscular, half-naked male bodies from afar, in the film's final scene, Galoup inspects his own fragmented reflection in the many diamond shaped mirrors of the empty nightclub. I suggest that Galoup's bodily movements are also queer. Dance and motion up until this point in the film are either represented through the heteronormative gyrating that happens between the soldiers and the women in the discotheque or through the tightly controlled and carefully practised training sequences in the desert. In contrast, Galoup's final solo is performed with reckless abandon that seems to question the limits of how bodies can jump, spin and gesture. His solo reveals the essential, the essence of his sexuality, the Deleuzian singularities that belong to movement.

20 Godart, *The Dimensions of Difference*, 33.

Family Encounters: *35 Rhums*

In Denis' 2008 film *35 Rhums*, motion and dance once again reveal implicit dynamics between characters. As in *Chocolat* and *Beau travail*, the film interrogates notions of contact through moments that reveal the underpinnings of subjectivity and intersubjectivity. The film, which takes place in the outskirts of Paris, follows the shifting interpersonal dynamics between long-time friends. Lionel, an aging railroad conductor, accepts the newly found independence of his adult daughter, Joséphine. Meanwhile, Joséphine's long-time friendship with her neighbour Noé becomes romantic, and Gabrielle reconnects with Lionel. The first time we meet each of the four protagonists, they are in motion: Lionel at the helm of his train, Joséphine on the metro on the way to her university, and Gabrielle in her taxi. Their moving bodies suggest the transient nature of their lives in the Paris *banlieue* as well as a certain ease and stability that the protagonists find in movement.

In contrast to the way in which each of the characters moves independently through the outskirts of the city, one scene in particular reveals the complexities of the ways in which the characters relate to each other. The scene underscores the tension between dialogue and the more essential pieces of information that are revealed through gaze, movement and contact. As the sequence begins, a potential suitor arrives to invite Josephine to a concert, delivering flowers. His unexpected arrival solicits curious glances from Gabrielle, and a simple question from Lionel: 'comment il s'appelle?' [what's his name?] The simplicity of Lionel's question runs parallel to the more important information revealed in this moment. Joséphine, dressed for the concert, appears even more adult – a woman with romantic interests and a social life independent of her father. The next shot of the sequence takes place in Gabrielle's taxi, where the music on the radio fills the silence in the car and provides a verbal confirmation of the unspoken romantic tension between Joséphine and Noé. While the radio sings: 'Can't live without you baby, can't live without you, no,' Gabrielle verbalizes both her attachment to and shared history with the group of friends in the car: 'ça fait tellement longtemps qu'on n'est pas sorti en famille' [it's been a long time since we've gone out as a family]. Gabrielle's comment reveals the complexity of her relationship to Lionel and Joséphine and also the way in which the scene provides a re-enactment of the type of outing they would have shared in the past.

Next, as Gabrielle's taxi breaks down en route to the concert, Lionel, Joséphine, Gabrielle, and Noé take shelter from the pouring rain in a closed African restaurant. The restaurant owner and her daughter bring out towels, the music turns on, and shots of rum appear on the bar counter. As soon as the dancing starts, the dialogue stops, and previously latent aspects of relationships between characters – old and new attractions, tensions around Joséphine's entry into adulthood – are brought out on to the dance floor. Furthermore, in contrast to the beginning of the sequence which alludes to past relationships between the film's protagonists, dance characterizes the 'presence of movement' described by Deleuze in his reading of Bergson and the 'privileged instants', the 'peaks and shouts' that push 'scenes to their climax and brings them into collision'.[21] Through dance, bodies are brought into contact, physical proximity and movement generating essential, embodied moments of connection. Lionel observes the open back of Gabrielle's dress before pulling her tightly into his arms. The camera circles around the pair as they slow dance, their faces and shoulders, pressed tightly together, fill the entirety of the frame. Gabrielle's laugh and her physical proximity to Lionel suggest a continued romantic attraction, and in the next shot, Joséphine watches the dance partners with a knowing smile. The music changes to the Commodores' 'Nightshift' as Lionel invites his daughter to dance. Resting her head against his shoulder, she appears momentarily younger than she is, evoking the past and a simpler period in their relationship.

Lionel passes Joséphine's hand to Noé, and, although the camera remains fixed in place, centred on the new pair, Lionel remains in focus as he

21 Deleuze, *Cinema I: The Movement-Image*, 1–5. In addition to a discussion of Bergson's *Creative Evolution*, Deleuze also refers specifically to the work of Soviet filmmaker Sergueï Mikhaïlovitch Eisenstein.

walks out of the frame. While his gestures constitute a silent permission, Lionel, now seated at the bar, continues to watch the couple carefully. He simultaneously acknowledges Joséphine's transition into adulthood while also keeping a close eye on the development of her new relationship. As Noé and Joséphine dance, intimacy builds. He turns her around, drawing her close to his body, before carefully undoing her hair clip and kissing her for the first time. Meanwhile, Lionel's gaze shifts to the body of a much younger waitress. Gabrielle watches as he takes her hand and pulls her to the centre of the floor; the movement is an unspoken confirmation of his unwillingness to commit to romantic attachment. Throughout the scene, dance allows the characters to question and to renegotiate interpersonal boundaries – bodies move to incite even closer physical contact, relationship dynamics are queried and impulses are acted upon in ways that would be impossible without a dance floor. As bodies shift towards and away from each other, proximity reveals unspoken connections. Dance becomes an acting out of unspoken desires, producing moments that embody how characters interrelate.

Furthermore, because the entirety of the dance takes place without dialogue, the scene also brings into question the ways in which information is revealed through movement and touch. Motion becomes the primary marker of the relationships between characters, suggesting the limitations of words in particular environments and circumstances – movement takes over when words fail. In contrast to the beginning of the sequence, where the sparse dialogue does little to illustrate the relationships between characters, the dance scene is the dramatic climax of the film – movement and physical proximity, a firm grab of a wrist or a head on a shoulder, reveal the complexity of the ways in which each of the four protagonists relate to each other. The scene also highlights important narrative and thematic elements: relationships and characters evolve, and as the pairs of dancers change and move their bodies together, Denis works through the ways in which certain characters trade places with others: Joséphine's love interests as an adult and newly found independence will alter her relationship with her father, Gabrielle's romantic attachment to Lionel does not preclude his desire for younger women.

Perhaps the most interesting aspect of Denis' use of dance is not the tacit acknowledgement of various relationship dynamics between characters, but rather the way in which these scenes draw the spectator into the diegesis. Her works present Deleuzian intensities, dialectics negotiated between bodies within the diegesis and presented as haptic, multisensory images accompanied by songs we sing along to, our bodies compelled to movement. In one of Denis' most recent films, *Un beau soleil intérieur*, Isabelle, a divorced Parisian artist played by Juliette Binoche, dances alone to the familiar opening lines of Etta James singing 'At Last'. Isabelle moves slowly from side to side, her eyes closed, her head back. Unlike Denis' other dance sequences, which feature groups of almost identical bodies, couples, or individual dancers lost in their own movement, Isabelle is centred in the camera's frame, her body towards the spectator. The scene suggests a more restrained interpretation of dance to come in Denis' *œuvre*, characterized by small movements that suggest a familiarity within one's body and a more explicit openness to the camera's gaze – an invitation to dance.

Throughout her films, Denis' bodies move, change and interact, revealing the essence of their experience, the 'privileged instants' that queer boundaries between separate bodies, between bodies and environments. Finally, dance reveals an evolution in how Denis thinks through movement. *Chocolat* presents Denis' first experiment with dancing bodies moving together, a simple waltz that prefigures the symbolically loaded dance scenes that reappear throughout her other works. Already, dance queries established social and physical boundaries between characters, movement revealing the unspoken. Later, *Beau travail* gives us both literal and figurative representations of dance; sculpted bodies move through the heat of the desert, evoking homoerotic gaze, while Galoup's exuberant modern dance solo queers the heteronormative space of a downtown nightclub. In *35 Rhums*, a slow dance in a closed restaurant uncovers both change and continuity through the ways in which characters relate to each other, presenting new elements of old relationships. Ultimately, dance poses the questions that guide Denis' filmmaking – movement incites characters to renegotiate their relationships to themselves and to others, and draws us into the world of her films.

Bibliography

Baross, Zsuzsa, *Encounters: Gérard Titus-Carmel, Jean-Luc Nancy, Claire Denis* (Brighton: Sussex Academic Press, 2015).

Deleuze, Gilles, trans. Barbara Habberjam, *Cinema I: The Movement-Image* (Minneapolis: University of Minnesota Press, 2013).

Deleuze, Gilles, trans. Mark Lester and Charles Stivale, ed. by Constantin V. Boundas, *The Logic of Sense* (New York: Columbia University Press, 1990).

Denis, Claire, dir. *Beau travail*. Pyramide Distribution, 1999.

—— *Chocolat*. Orion Classics, 1988.

—— *35 Rhums*. Wild Bunch Distribution, 2008.

—— *Un beau soleil intérieur*. Curiosa Films, 2017.

Godart, Caroline, *The Dimensions of Difference: Space, Time, and Bodies in Women's Cinema and Continental Philosophy* (London: Rowman & Littlefield International, 2016).

Marks, Laura U, *The Skin of the Film: Intercultural Cinema, Embodiment, and the Senses* (Durham, NC: Duke University Press, 2007).

Mayne, Judith, *Claire Denis* (Urbana: University of Illinois Press, 2005).

Vecchio, Marjorie, *The Films of Claire Denis: Intimacy on the Border* (London: I.B. Tauris, 2014).

POLLY GALIS, MARIA TOMLINSON AND ANTONIA WIMBUSH

Conclusion

The chapters of this volume have collectively defied rigid definitions of bodily identity and behaviour, and shed light on the divisive systems underlying such norms, such as: gender, class and racial inequality; homophobic attitudes; migration policy; colonial legacy; globalization and consumerism; and cultural prejudice. The act of queering or querying bodily norms in this book has therefore been framed as an intersectional form of social critique and, ultimately, as a means of contesting hegemonic power structures within francophone culture and society, from the 1900s to today.

The studies in this volume also threw into question what we mean by the body in the first place. The weaponization and mutilation of limbs at war, the digitalization of dating via apps, and the cloning of humans or the evolution of IVF make us reassess the point when the body begins and stops being a body. This queer(y)ing of bodily origins, form and purpose calls into question how far our sense of self is defined by our biological body. On the one hand, this volume's contributors showed that, according to the cultural works examined, flesh and blood are still the defining features of human existence, sexuality and desire. On the other, they stressed the benefits of transcending traditional conceptualizations of corporeal identity, as showcased by the depiction of queer bodies, transgender bodies, obese bodies, migrant bodies, disabled bodies, cloned bodies and robotic bodies, to name a few. In this way, the studied works were shown to expand the parameters of what we consider to be 'normal' bodies and to depict bodily identity as something which is open to continual review and reconstruction. Reflective and regenerative representations of this kind, we conclude, are what can allow for restrictive gazes, spaces and associated power networks to be problematized.

The authors were especially interested in how queer identity involves spatial as well as gendered and sexual (re)orientations. Queer identity is something which involves complex negotiations and renegotiations between the local places we inhabit, as well as re-evaluations of our relationships with the people within them. To queer a bodily norm often involves a 'turn' towards an alternative one, one which is not considered the 'appropriate' norm for us, such as identifying with masculine traits when one has been assigned female at birth, or vice versa. Queering bodily norms involves forms of resistance to the status quo of a given place and people, such as resisting the bourgeois domestic ideals of family members, or the societal expectations of friends in terms of how we should look and behave. Some spaces in this volume were seen to lend themselves to more liberating bodily action and interactions, such as gay bars and nightclubs. Querying normative spaces therefore reflects the extent to which our bodily apperception (how we perceive our own bodies) is intimately informed by the views of other people, and reminds us that low self-esteem, body dysmorphia and denial of one's sexual orientation are frequently the product of judgemental gazes and views. Queer(y)ing bodily norms therefore constitutes a reorientation of public opinion as a way of producing more accepting and illuminating spaces of representation and living.

In line with this perspective, contributors focused on bodily movements through space, including travel, dance, migration, erotic encounters and violent body-to-body combat. They explored what such movements could teach us about the shape and potentiality of bodies themselves, about their connections to other bodies, and about the social institutions and regulations proper to those spaces. Once again, then, queer(y)ing bodily norms took on a critical dimension. This fluid portrayal of bodily identity was substantiated by an emphasis on fictional characters' childhood and teenage years, given the emphasis on gender and sexual development in this volume. The various studies reminded us that bodily identity is not something which remains the same throughout our lives, but on the contrary, evolves with every passing day.

Many of the authors complemented these political, ontological and existential considerations with a reassessment of language itself, playing with etymological roots to draw on the unexplored potential of words, turning over well-trodden expressions to explore them anew. This volume has also drawn on a range of disciplines and genres, examining examples of queer or querying bodily norms in literature, film, plays and online dating apps, thereby querying lexical, formal and disciplinary 'norms' too.

Such an expansive approach to viewing the body is critical, this volume showed, to highlighting and celebrating a multiplicity of bodily experiences and desires, and to providing subsequently more inclusive representational spaces in the contemporary francophone world, counter to oppressive social regimes. This volume explored bodies of varying nationalities, races, genders, classes, gender orientations and identification, and abilities, as well as digitalized and posthuman bodies, and we recommend that future studies take this initiative further by examining the body (human and animal more broadly) in relation to the ecological crisis, in terms of illness and chronic pain, and as a tool for political activism. We also hope that this queer(y)ing approach will be applied to scholarly studies beyond as well as within the francophone world, to begin a comparative conversation about different ways to celebrate and protect bodily diversity and individual freedoms.

Notes on Contributors

RAY BALSTAD is a PhD student and Graduate Instructor in the Department of French and Italian at the University of Minnesota – Twin Cities. They are presently the recipient of a Summer 2020 Interdisciplinary Dissertation Proposal Development Fellowship. Their dissertation research explores visual and filmic representations of weight and the resonances in its representation across its myriad literal and figurative forms. Considering all weight – emotional, physical, mental, etc. – as embodied, this research interrogates the perceived corporeal, epistemological and often antagonistic split between the Self and the 'true', 'correct' or 'ideal' confines of the body and mind.

SARA BÉDARD-GOULET is ASTRA Professor of Romance Studies at the College of Foreign Languages and Cultures of the University of Tartu. Her main research interests in the field of contemporary French-language literature include ecocriticism and geopoetics, reader-response theories, literature and psychoanalysis. She has worked extensively on the novels of French author Jean Echenoz and the novels, plays and autobiographical narratives by Quebec author Michel Tremblay.

KATHRYN CHAFFEE is the author of 'Young Love and Everyday Politics: Abdellatif Kechiche's *La Faute à Voltaire* and *La Vie d'Adèle*' in *Screening Youth: Contemporary French and Francophone Cinema* (Spring 2019) and 'Adèle as Subject in Pursuit and Object Pursued: Narrative Structure in Abdellatif Kechiche's *Blue is the Warmest Color*' in *Revue CELAAN: Regards sur les films d'Abdellatif Kechiche*, Vol. 12, No. 2 (Spring 2016). She is a PhD candidate at the University of California, Los Angeles, where she is writing her dissertation on dance and movement in the films of Claire Denis, Abdellatif Kechiche and Céline Sciamma.

SETH COMPAORÉ was born in Abidjan, Ivory Coast and grew up in Ouagadougou, Burkina Faso. He completed his undergraduate work in French Literature at the University of Ouagadougou, then became a French-language teacher in Yako. In November 2009, he relocated to the United States. After a brief stay in New York City, he moved to Louisville, Kentucky where he eventually enrolled in a graduate program at the University of Louisville. In 2015, he received his Master of Arts in French Literature. He completed his Doctorate in Francophone Cinema and Film Studies in July 2020 at the University of Missouri-Columbia.

KATE FOSTER is an early-career researcher specializing in text-image relations. Her research focuses on mannequins, androids and cyborgs in modern visual art and literature. Kate's thesis suggests that the idea of the machine-man took on renewed significance in late modernity. Her work examines the inherent ambiguity of such artificial copies of the human body, whose unstable categorization (and fictional status) make them an ideal locus for questions of gender, human-made perfection and identity.

POLLY GALIS is a Senior Research Associate at the University of Bristol, conducting research into post-1950s literature by francophone sex workers, funded by the SFS Postdoctoral Prize Fellowship. She completed a PhD in French at the University of Leeds, and is revising her thesis for publication with Peter Lang (*Frank French Feminisms: Sex, Sexuality and the Body in the Work of Ernaux, Huston and Arcan*) as a winner of the Young Scholars Competition.

VANESSA LEE is an academic and playwright whose research interests include postcolonial theatre and film, gender studies, and European, Asian and Caribbean theatres. She holds a DPhil from the University of Oxford, where she taught French and postcolonial literature. Her articles have appeared in the *Global Media Journal*; *Journal of Romance Studies*; *Transtext(e)s Transcultures*; *Bulletin of Francophone Postcolonial Studies* and the University of Edinburgh's *Dangerous Women Project*. As a playwright and theatre practitioner she has written and translated plays, and directed and performed in several productions in the UK, France, Ireland and Sweden.

JENNIFER BOUM MAKE is Assistant Professor in the Department of French & Francophone Studies at Georgetown University. Her teaching and research include a focus on migration, (post)colonial memories and hospitality in contemporary Francophone contexts. Her broad areas of interest include: Francophone postcolonial theory; Caribbean and Mediterranean Studies; ethics; as well as questions of mobility and circulation of people and cultures. She has published or has forthcoming publications in *Crossings: Journal of Migration and Culture*, *Convergences Francophones*, *Nouvelles Études Francophones*, and the *Lincoln Humanities Journal*. She is also currently co-editing a special issue on the representations and discourses of food in contemporary Francophone literatures for Modern and Contemporary France (forthcoming in 2021).

CRISTINA ONESTA obtained a PhD in French Studies at Boston University in May 2020. She is currently a Lecturer in French at Kore University in Italy. Her research interests focus on the representation of women's sexuality and body, immigration and memory in Contemporary Francophone Literature and Cinema. She is the author of an essay on Ananda Devi's work titled 'Pluralité du corps et corporalité de l'espace: *Les jours vivants* d'Ananda Devi', *Mosaïque*. Cameroon: Université de Maroua, Vol.3, 2018.

KATHLEEN RIZY completed a PhD in Romance Languages at the University of Georgia. She is currently a Lecturer in the Department of French Literature, Thought & Culture at New York University, where she teaches all levels of undergraduate courses. As a specialist of twentieth- and twenty-first-century French literature, Kathleen's work explores the intersections between the environment and literature in modern and contemporary France. Her research interests also include women's and gender studies, women's writing and animal studies.

ADINA STROIA is an early-career researcher in the field of women's life-writing and visual culture. A former Visiting Fellow at the Centre for the Study of Contemporary Women's Writing, IMLR, Adina's research focuses on psychoanalysis, thanatography, ageing, ethics of care and visual studies. Her most recent publications include 'Camille Laurens: L'écriture depuis soi' in *Dalhousie French Studies* and 'The Traumatic Structure of the *récit de mort*: Camille Laurens's *Philippe*' in *French and Francophone Studies*. Her current project investigates the ways in which Agnès Varda mobilizes the tension between photography and moving image to represent her own aging process in her late documentaries.

MARIA TOMLINSON is a Leverhulme Early Career Fellow in the department of journalism at the University of Sheffield. Her project is entitled 'Menstruation and the Media: Reducing Stigma and Tackling Period Poverty'. Her PhD examined the representation of menstruation, childbirth and the menopause in women's writing from Algeria, Mauritius and France. Her resulting monograph, *From Menstruation to the Menopause: The Female Fertility Cycle in Contemporary Women's Writing in French*, is soon to be published with Liverpool University Press. She has published articles and chapters in her specialist areas which include the body, feminism, gender and postcolonial studies.

BRIAN TROTH is an HIV/AIDS and French gay culture specialist who earned his PhD from The Ohio State University in 2019. His work confronts filmic and literary interpretations of the HIV epidemic to show the ways in which sexual health and risk has evolved both medically and in how they are perceived by gay men. Dr Troth's recent work has examined the various ways in which gay men interact via social media and social networking apps, the creation of digital personae, the effects of preventative medicine on sexual practices/perceptions, and gay identity in France.

ANTONIA WIMBUSH is a Leverhulme Early Career Researcher at the University of Liverpool, where she is working on a project which explores cultural responses to French Caribbean migration in the post-war era. She completed a PhD at the University of Birmingham, funded by the AHRC Midlands3Cities, and her first monograph, *Autofiction: A Female Francophone Aesthetic of Exile*, is forthcoming with Liverpool University Press. She has taught French language, literature, history and politics at the University of Birmingham and the University of Bath.

LOREN K. WOLFE received her doctorate in Romance Languages and Literatures from Harvard University in 2013, specializing in twentieth and twenty-first century literature. She served for three years as a faculty member in Barnard College's Department of French, teaching French and Comparative Literature before moving to Paris, where she has taught in the Columbia Masters program in History and Literature. Her research explores the intersections between medical and literary discourse. She is working on a book project entitled *Immunity, Modernity, Masculinity* that cuts across the disciplines of literature, biology, philosophy and sociology.

Index

abject, the 21, 157–9, 161, 219–20
ableism 4–5, 12
abortion 9, 34, 47, 96, 218
'Abus de la société' 128
activism 5, 17, 169, 265
Adorno, Theodor 82
advertising 2
affect 13, 15, 49, 71, 81–4, 135
Africa 7–8, 25, 112, 125, 132, 159, 211, 217–22, 233, 247, 249, 254–61
 Cameroon 16, 250, 269
 Mauritania 16
 Senegal 16
 Tunisia 16
ageing 120–3
agency 17, 21–2, 91, 109, 114, 121, 153–9, 169–84, 257
Ahmed, Sara 20, 22, 67–84, 210–24
androcentrism 21, 91
Apocalypse bébé 48
Archetypes of Literature, The 134–5
autofiction 55–6, 180, 270

Bachelard, Gaston 70, 80
Baise-moi 52
Bakhtin, Mikhail 155–7
BAME 14
Barthes, Roland 127, 138
Basic Writings 91
Baudrillard, Jean 31, 38, 40, 153
Beau travail 248, 254–8, 261
beauty 18–9, 159, 161, 192, 199, 256
Beauvoir, Simone de 8–10, 73
Belgium 16
Berlant, Lauren 37–9
Berliner, Alain 20, 71
Bessette, Jean 1–2
Best, Victoria 56
binaries
 gender 91–2
 mind-body dualism 168, 197–204
Black Lives Matter 9, 14
body, the
 blood 21, 29, 60, 116, 138, 155, 159–60, 175, 182, 212, 217, 221, 263
 flesh 21, 58, 166, 151, 157–60, 179, 203, 263
 touch 192, 201–2, 210–25, 251–3, 160, 260
Boisclair, Isabelle 11
Boni-Claverie, Isabelle 21, 149–65
Bourdieu, Pierre 181, 184
bourgeoisie 103
Boyle, Claire 7
Bruno, Giuliana 82–3
Butler, Judith 6–8, 47, 178, 214

Cahn, Arthur 20, 29, 31, 44
Cairns, Lucille 49
Canada 16, 230–2
 Quebec 11, 231, 244, 267
camp
 concentration 234–5
 detention 227–39
Capitalisme et schizophrénie 1: l'anti-œdipe 31, 34
Carbajal, Alberto Fernández 3
Cardinal, Marie 9
Caribbean, The 21, 107–24, 229, 231
 Guadeloupe 115
 Martinique 115–23, 211, 216–17

Césaire, Ina 21, 109–24
Chargois, Marianne 17
Chauvin, Sébastien 37
Chamoiseau, Patrick 115, 117, 122–3
Chocolat 247–61
Cinema I 248–9
ciscentrism 4–5, 71
class 2, 9, 12, 17, 72, 101, 111–9, 253, 263, 265
cloning 18, 21, 89–103, 263
colonization 117, 219
Collard, Cyril 37
comics 2
consumerism 160, 162, 263
contraception 9, 96
corporality 144, 156, 218
coronavirus *see* COVID-19
COVID-19 x, 12, 14, 89
Creed, Barbara 51
Crowley, Martin 56, 59
cyborgs 7, 22, 89–103, 167, 187–204
  automaton 187, 189, 197
  doll 197, 203
  machine 7, 22, 31, 91, 95, 187–90, 195, 197–203
cryogenics 21, 90, 101, 103

Darrieussecq, Marie 21, 89–103
Davis, Oliver 6–7
Davis, Shardé 9
Deleuze, Gilles 12–3, 15, 20, 22, 29, 31, 34–5, 131, 247–9, 259
Delphy, Christine 9
Denis, Claire 22–3, 247–61
desire 4, 18, 20, 21, 29, 31, 32–3, 35, 44, 47, 49, 51–65, 67–8, 71, 75, 84, 111, 130–2, 137, 140, 142–3, 151–4, 157–62, 180, 201, 203, 210, 212, 215, 240, 248–52, 260, 263–5
Deuxième sexe, Le 8, 73
Derrida, Jacques 33
Despair 50
Despentes, Virginie 47–8, 52
deterritorialization 131
Devi, Ananda 21, 149–65
disability 1, 4–5, 21, 150, 157, 159, 162
disembodiment 187, 203
Discours sur l'origine et les fondements de l'inégalité parmi les hommes 102
domesticity 76
Domino 54–5
Dracius, Suzanne 21, 109, 114–20, 124
Duvalier, Jean-Claude 227–8, 231, 234

Eaubonne, Françoise d' 94
Echenoz, Jean 21, 167–84
ecocriticism 150
embodiment 4, 21, 91, 102, 108, 116, 124, 131, 180, 187, 193, 200–3, 253
energy 19, 61, 118, 143, 188–9, 193–4, 197–8, 200, 203
Engels, Frederick 95
Epistemology of the Closet 6
ethics 16, 164, 230
ethnicity 2, 9, 12, 14
Eurocentrism 12
Evans, Elliot 17
exile 22, 227–31, 242

family 11–3, 20, 31, 60, 72–7, 90, 95, 110, 122, 128, 131–4, 190–2, 224, 250, 258–61, 264
Fanon, Frantz 7
feminism 3, 5, 11, 56, 94–5
  ecofeminism 94–5
  intersectional 5, 10, 16, 263
  postfeminism 56
  second-wave 9
  third-wave 12
fertility 89–103

fetishism 43, 72, 83
food 150, 156–8, 233, 269
Foucault, Michel 7, 20, 68–71, 75, 81–2
France 5–17, 20, 29–30, 54, 89–90, 96, 101, 109, 112–3, 116, 128–9, 133, 155, 168, 175, 181, 190, 250
Frankenstein 33, 191, 193, 196
Fischer, Lucy 51
fluidity 38, 54, 62, 229
Freud, Sigmund 10, 97–8, 137, 142, 210
Front homosexuel d'action révolutionnaire 5
Frye, Northrop 134–5
Fuss, Diana 7
Future Sex 32

Garréta, Anne 48–9
gaze 21, 50, 70, 78, 79, 83, 138, 139–41, 149, 162–3, 251, 252, 255–7, 261, 263, 264
  touristic 82–3
Gender Trouble 6, 8, 73
Génie d'Abou, Le 21, 149, 151, 159–62, 164
girlhood 72, 78
Glissant, Édouard 115
Gouines rouges, Les 5
Guattari, Félix 12, 13, 15, 20, 29, 31, 34, 35, 131
Guibert, Hervé 209–10, 211, 215, 216, 217, 219, 221, 222–5
gynocentrism 99

habitus 181
Haiti 227, 228, 230, 231–2, 234, 235, 237, 238
Halberstam, Jack 82
Haraway, Donna 7, 22, 93, 94, 169, 187, 188, 200
healthcare 30
hegemony 37, 67, 71
Heidegger, Martin 91
Heine, Henrich 50
heteronormativity 4, 11, 20, 29, 37, 44, 47, 59, 68, 77, 145, 204, 210–11, 224, 256, 261
heterosexuality 3, 11–2, 22, 23, 38, 47, 52, 57, 63, 68, 71–2, 74, 76–7, 80, 82, 191
  compulsory 219
  contingent 210, 214–5, 224, 225
HIV-AIDS 16–7, 30, 38, 43, 209, 210–11, 217, 219, 220, 223–4
Hoffman, E.T.A. 50
homophobia 1, 16
homosexuality 20, 22, 38–40, 49, 57, 72, 128–9, 132, 137, 144
Hooker, Evelyn 38, 39, 40, 43
Horkheimer, Max 82
humanism 197, 202, 204
  posthumanism 95, 188, 203
  transhumanism 203
Humphrey, Laud 37
hybridity 149, 187, 200–1

imaginary, the 70, 80, 233
In a Queer Time and Place: Transgender Bodies Subcultural Lives 82–3
Inceste 52
inequalities 14, 15, 162, 233
  gender 12
Insurrection of Southern Martinique, The 21, 115–19
Interpretation of Dreams, The 97–8, 137
intersex 4, 16
Irigaray, Luce 7, 10
IVF 16, 21, 89, 90, 92–4, 263

Jordan, Shirley 52, 64
Juste, Mylène 17

Kapital, Das 95
Kollias, Hector 6–7

Koplin, Julian 40–1
Kristeva, Julia 9, 157–8, 219

Lacan, Jacques 7, 10, 141–2
Lagerfeld, Karl 52–3, 61
Larquier, Jeanne Sarah de 53
Lauretis, Teresa de 50
Leclec, Annie 9
Lerch, Arnaud 37
Leroux, Gaston 22, 187, 188–9, 193, 195, 201, 202, 203, 204
LGBTQ+ 1, 4–5, 15, 41
  homosexuality *see* homosexuality
  Lesbianism 8–9, 10–11, 16, 20, 47–52, 210
  transgender identity 4, 16, 30, 77, 82–3, 263
Lorde, Audre 9
love 31, 39, 43, 50–1, 56, 57–8, 143–4, 156–7, 159, 189, 190–2, 197, 212, 213, 218, 219, 225
Lumina Sophie dite Surprise 109, 115–20

Ma Vie en rose 68, 71–3, 74, 76–8, 79–81, 83–4
Macron, Emmanuel 13
Manger l'autre 21, 149, 150–9, 160, 161, 162–4
Manifesto of the Communist Party 95
marginalization 2, 14, 16–7, 21, 113–5, 117, 120, 124, 152–4, 243
Marks, Laura 253
marriage 39
  same-sex 16
  ceremony 79–81
Marx, Karl 95
Mausolée des amants, Le
Mbembe, Achille 161–2
McCaffrey, Enda 33
Medeiros, Ana de 63
Mémoires d'île 109, 120–3
menstruation 3–4
Mercier, Louis Sébastien 128, 143, 144
Merleau-Ponty, Maurice 216–7
migration 227–8, 231, 233–4, 263, 264
  'boat people' 227–8, 231, 235
  immigration 234, 237
  refugees 22, 228, 229, 233, 234, 235–7, 239, 242–3
military 176, 179, 180, 250, 254–7
mirror stage, the 141–2
modernity 31, 38, 40, 153, 193
Moi, Toril 62–3
'Mon mari le clone' 89–103
Morello, Nathalie 55
Morocco 16
movement 22, 31, 67–8, 69, 75, 76–7, 79, 84, 109, 113–4, 119, 121, 135, 193, 217–8, 221, 225, 247–9, 251, 255–6, 258–61, 264
  dance 22–3, 117, 119, 121–3, 160–1, 247–9, 250–61
  travel 112–3, 211, 222–3, 264
  displacement 233
motherhood 20, 74, 90–1, 94, 95–101, 103, 110–11
Mouvement de libération des femmes 9
Mulvey, Laura 139–41
Mythologies 127, 138

Nabokov, Vladimir 50
Navarro-Ayala, Luis 7–8
neocolonialism 5
neoliberalism 68
New Wave cinema 130–1
Nimier, Marie 20, 52–56, 61–4
non-binary identity 4, 11, 22, 170
nonhuman 22, 167, 168–73, 175, 176–8, 182, 183, 184, 202
Nouvelle pornographie, La 52–3, 55–7, 61, 64

obesity 21, 154, 158–61, 163, 164, 165, 263
Ollivier, Emile 22, 227–9, 230–1, 235

On Female Body Experience: 'Throwing Like a Girl' and Other Essays 3–4
Orbach, Susie 19
Other, the 22, 50–1, 53, 55–7, 59–60, 63–4, 157, 163, 203, 214, 229–30, 232–4, 239, 243
space 70–1

Pas un jour 48
Paradis, Le 211, 216–7, 219, 222
Passages 22, 227–31, 233, 235–6, 241, 243
patriarchy 96, 102, 112
patriotism 13
perception 21, 43, 53–4, 91, 93, 101, 108, 142, 149, 157, 199, 241, 270
apperception 264
Peirce, Kimberley 83
penis 32, 36
performativity 82, 112, 176, 178, 212
Perreau, Bruno 7
pétroleuses 116–19
phallus 155
Photo-photo 52, 55, 61, 64
Poetics of Space, The 70
pornography 44, 51–2, 55, 57, 153–4
postcolonial studies 2–3, 21, 107–8, 114–5, 117, 124, 150, 161–2, 165, 252–3
postmodernism 18, 20, 53, 55–6, 64, 153, 179
Poupée ashanti, La 109–12, 114
Poupée sanglante, La 22, 187, 192, 199
power 3, 20, 39, 51, 63, 69–71, 75–6, 84, 91, 95, 99, 110, 112, 121, 149, 151, 155–7, 159–65, 200, 214–5, 251–3, 263
Preciado, Paul B. 17, 47
pregnancy 81, 91, 96–7, 99, 101–3, 116, 136
pride 1, 4–5, 42
Protocole compassionnel, Le 211–2, 219, 223–4
Proust, Marcel 7
psychonalysis 10, 55

Quand on a 17 ans 21, 127–33, 135–6, 138–9, 142, 144
QTIPOC 16
Queer Phenomenology: Orientations, Objects, Others 22, 71, 210
Queering Transcultural Encounters 7
queer 20, 22, 29, 51, 53–4, 57, 59–60, 64–5, 67, 71, 73–4, 77, 82–4, 107, 127, 145, 167–9, 178, 184, 191, 193, 204, 210, 215, 224, 247–8, 254, 256–7, 263–5
activism 15–8
approaches 1–15, 19, 23
community 2
culture 39
organizations 16, 69
spaces 41, 68–9, 71, 79, 253, 255, 261, 264
theory 1–12, 17–8, 71

race 2, 9, 12, 17, 101, 151, 154, 161, 219, 253, 265
Rank, Otto 51
religion 9
Christianity 72, 79
Rémès, Erik 42–3
reproduction 18, 21, 68, 81–2, 89–92, 95, 97–100, 103, 181, 191, 193, 210–11, 218, 224
Rich, Adrienne 8
Rincon, Giovanna Murillo 16–7
Rodgers, Catherine 55
Room of One's Own, A 156
Rousseau, Jean-Jacques 102
Rye, Stellen 51

Saint-Martin, Lori 11
Sciamma, Céline 20, 73, 133

science 73, 90, 97–8, 101, 187–9, 193–7, 202, 223
Sedgwick, Eve 2, 6–7, 15
sexism 11, 110
sex work 3, 16–17
Sibalis, Michael 5–6
Simians, Cyborgs, and Women: The Reinvention of Nature 188
Sirène 54
Skin of the Film: Intercultural Cinema, Embodiment, and the Senses, The 253
slavery 107, 110, 115, 117, 119, 233
Smith, Zadie 3
Sphinx 48
sport 16, 35, 40–1
  football 76, 78–9
social media 9, 18, 30, 42, 270
  Facebook 30
  Grindr 31–7, 39–44
  OKCupid 34, 27
  Pinterest 30
  Tinder 34, 37
space 1, 4–5, 13–4, 17, 20–1, 29–30, 37–40, 42, 51, 54–5, 67–71, 73–7, 79–82, 84, 97, 109, 112–4, 117–8, 121, 124
sterility 31, 91–4, 98
stigma 4, 16–7, 270
STDs 218
storytelling 83, 117–8, 172, 183, 229, 236–9, 243
  testimony 22, 131, 182, 229–31, 234, 237–9, 241–3
surrogacy 101, 187
Surveiller et punir: la naissance de la prison 75
Suzanne et Louise 223

taboo 9
Tearoom Trade 37
Téchiné, André 21, 127–37, 139–40, 142, 144
technology 18, 21, 30–1, 90–3, 95, 97–100, 102–3, 187–8
Tendencies 2
Tomboy 20, 68, 71, 73
transgender identity 4, 16, 30, 77, 82–3, 263
transgression 18–9, 21, 47, 57, 60, 63, 72, 121, 122, 155, 191, 194, 250–1, 253, 255
trauma 47, 77, 107, 119, 152, 170, 235
Truismes 89–90, 97

United Kingdom, The 14–15
United States, The 7, 15, 30, 109, 227, 268

vagina, the 60
Vacances du petit Renard, Les 20, 29, 31, 35, 42
Vernon Subutex 48
violence 14, 17, 21, 29, 75, 77, 119, 127–8, 132–4, 136–8, 140, 143–4, 152–3, 160, 162, 170, 218, 264
vulva 218

Waelti-Walters, Jennifer 49
Warner, Michael 37–9
water 13, 141–2, 256–7
  beach 211, 218–9, 228, 232–4
  ocean, the 219
  sea, the 218, 233, 236
  shipwreck 23–4, 236
  shore 15, 216, 233
war 117, 132, 170, 175, 177, 180–3, 263
  Algerian War 132
  First World War 22, 96, 169, 171–3, 181, 183
  Second World War 235
Widdows, Heather 19
Witt, Emily 32, 36
Wittig, Monique 10–11, 17
Woolf, Virginia 156
womxn 11

writing 17, 20, 22, 48, 52–5, 57, 62, 91, 103, 109, 117–8, 130, 167, 169, 172, 176, 211, 220–2, 225, 229–30, 234, 237

Young, Iris Marion 3–4

14 21–2, 167, 169, 170–1, 177, 180, 183
35 Rhums 247, 258, 261–2

Modern French Identities

Edited by Jean Khalfa

This series aims to publish monographs, editions or collections of papers based on recent research into modern French Literature. It welcomes contributions from academics, researchers and writers worldwide and in British and Irish universities in particular.

Modern French Identities focuses on the French and Francophone writing of the twentieth and twenty-first centuries, whose formal experiments and revisions of genre have combined to create an entirely new set of literary forms, from the the- matic autobiographies of Michel Leiris and Bernard Noël to the magic realism of French Caribbean writers.

The idea that identities are constructed rather than found, and that the self is an area to explore rather than a given pretext, runs through much of modern French literature, from Proust, Gide, Apollinaire and Césaire to Barthes, Duras, Kristeva, Glissant, Germain and Roubaud.

This series explores the turmoil in ideas and values expressed in the works of theorists like Lacan, Irigaray, Foucault, Fanon, Deleuze and Bourdieu and traces the impact of current theoretical approaches – such as gender and sexuality studies, de/coloniality, intersectionality, and ecocriticism – on the literary and cultural interpretation of the self.

The series publishes studies of individual authors and artists, comparative studies, and interdisciplinary projects and welcomes research on autobiography, cinema, fiction, poetry and performance art and/or the intersections between them.

Volume 1	Victoria Best & Peter Collier (eds): Powerful Bodies. Performance in French Cultural Studies.
220 pages. 1999. ISBN 3–906762-56-4 / US-ISBN 0–8204-4239-9

Volume 2	Julia Waters: Intersexual Rivalry. A 'Reading in Pairs' of Marguerite Duras and Alain Robbe-Grillet.
228 pages. 2000. ISBN 3–906763-74-9 / US-ISBN 0–8204-4626-2

Volume 3	Sarah Cooper: Relating to Queer Theory. Rereading Sexual Self-Definition with Irigaray, Kristeva, Wittig and Cixous.
231 pages. 2000. ISBN 3–906764-46-X / US-ISBN 0–8204-4636-X

Volume 4	Julia Prest & Hannah Thompson (eds): Corporeal Practices. (Re) figuring the Body in French Studies.
166 pages. 2000. ISBN 3–906764-53-2 / US-ISBN 0–8204-4639-4

Volume 5	Victoria Best: Critical Subjectivities. Identity and Narrative in the Work of Colette and Marguerite Duras.
243 pages. 2000. ISBN 3–906763-89-7 / US-ISBN 0–8204-4631-9

Volume 6	David Houston Jones: The Body Abject: Self and Text in Jean Genet and Samuel Beckett.
213 pages. 2000. ISBN 3–906765-07-5 / US-ISBN 0–8204-5058-8

Volume 7	Robin MacKenzie: The Unconscious in Proust's A la recherche du temps perdu.
270 pages. 2000. ISBN 3–906758-38-9 / US-ISBN 0–8204-5070-7

Volume 8	Rosemary Chapman: Siting the Quebec Novel. The Representation of Space in Francophone Writing in Quebec.
282 pages. 2000. ISBN 3–906758-85-0 / US-ISBN 0–8204-5090-1

Volume 9	Gill Rye: Reading for Change. Interactions between Text Identity in Contemporary French Women's Writing (Baroche, Cixous, Constant).
223 pages. 2001. ISBN 3–906765-97-0 / US-ISBN 0–8204-5315-3

Volume 10	Jonathan Paul Murphy: Proust's Art. Painting, Sculpture and Writing in A la recherche du temps perdu.
248 pages. 2001. ISBN 3–906766-17-9 / US-ISBN 0–8204-5319-6

Volume 11	Julia Dobson: Hélène Cixous and the Theatre. The Scene of Writing.
166 pages. 2002. ISBN 3–906766-20-9 / US-ISBN 0–8204-5322-6

Volume 12 Emily Butterworth & Kathryn Robson (eds): Shifting Borders. Theory and Identity in French Literature.
226 pages. 2001. ISBN 3–906766-86-1 / US-ISBN 0–8204-5602-0

Volume 13 Victoria Korzeniowska: The Heroine as Social Redeemer in the Plays of Jean Giraudoux.
144 pages. 2001. ISBN 3–906766-92-6 / US-ISBN 0–8204-5608-X

Volume 14 Kay Chadwick: Alphonse de Châteaubriant: Catholic Collaborator.
327 pages. 2002. ISBN 3–906766-94-2 / US-ISBN 0–8204-5610-1

Volume 15 Nina Bastin: Queneau's Fictional Worlds.
291 pages. 2002. ISBN 3–906768-32-5 / US-ISBN 0–8204-5620-9

Volume 16 Sarah Fishwick: The Body in the Work of Simone de Beauvoir.
284 pages. 2002. ISBN 3–906768-33-3 / US-ISBN 0–8204-5621-7

Volume 17 Simon Kemp & Libby Saxton (eds): Seeing Things. Vision, Perception and Interpretation in French Studies.
287 pages. 2002. ISBN 3–906768-46-5 / US-ISBN 0–8204-5858-9

Volume 18 Kamal Salhi (ed.): French in and out of France. Language Policies, Intercultural Antagonisms and Dialogue.
487 pages. 2002. ISBN 3–906768-47-3 / US-ISBN 0–8204-5859-7

Volume 19 Genevieve Shepherd: Simone de Beauvoir's Fiction. A Psychoanalytic Rereading.
262 pages. 2003. ISBN 3–906768-55-4 / US-ISBN 0–8204-5867-8

Volume 20 Lucille Cairns (ed.): Gay and Lesbian Cultures in France.
290 pages. 2002. ISBN 3–906769-66-6 / US-ISBN 0–8204-5903-8

Volume 21 Wendy Goolcharan-Kumeta: My Mother, My Country. Reconstructing the Female Self in Guadeloupean Women's Writing.
236 pages. 2003. ISBN 3–906769-76-3 / US-ISBN 0–8204-5913-5

Volume 22 Patricia O'Flaherty: Henry de Montherlant (1895–1972). A Philosophy of Failure.
256 pages. 2003. ISBN 3–03910-013-0 / US-ISBN 0–8204-6282-9

Volume 23 Katherine Ashley (ed.): Prix Goncourt, 1903–2003: essais critiques.
205 pages. 2004. ISBN 3–03910-018-1 / US-ISBN 0–8204-6287-X

Volume 24 Julia Horn & Lynsey Russell-Watts (eds): Possessions. Essays in French Literature, Cinema and Theory.
223 pages. 2003. ISBN 3–03910-005-X / US-ISBN 0–8204-5924-0

Volume 25 Steve Wharton: Screening Reality.
French Documentary Film during the German Occupation.
252 pages. 2006. ISBN 3-03910-066-1 / US-ISBN 0-8204-6882-7

Volume 26 Frédéric Royall (ed.): Contemporary French Cultures and Societies.
421 pages. 2004. ISBN 3-03910-074-2 / US-ISBN 0-8204-6890-8

Volume 27 Tom Genrich: Authentic Fictions.
Cosmopolitan Writing of the Troisième République, 1908–1940.
288 pages. 2004. ISBN 3-03910-285-0 / US-ISBN 0-8204-7212-3

Volume 28 Maeve Conrick & Vera Regan: French in Canada.
Language Issues.
186 pages. 2007. ISBN 978-3-03-910142-9

Volume 29 Kathryn Banks & Joseph Harris (eds): Exposure.
Revealing Bodies, Unveiling Representations.
194 pages. 2004. ISBN 3-03910-163-3 / US-ISBN 0-8204-6973-4

Volume 30 Emma Gilby & Katja Haustein (eds): Space.
New Dimensions in French Studies.
169 pages. 2005. ISBN 3-03910-178-1 / US-ISBN 0-8204-6988-2

Volume 31 Rachel Killick (ed.): Uncertain Relations.
Some Configurations of the 'Third Space' in Francophone Writings of the Americas and of Europe.
258 pages. 2005. ISBN 3-03910-189-7 / US-ISBN 0-8204-6999-8

Volume 32 Sarah F. Donachie & Kim Harrison (eds): Love and Sexuality.
New Approaches in French Studies.
194 pages. 2005. ISBN 3-03910-249-4 / US-ISBN 0-8204-7178-X

Volume 33 Michaël Abecassis: The Representation of Parisian Speech in the Cinema of the 1930s.
409 pages. 2005. ISBN 3-03910-260-5 / US-ISBN 0-8204-7189-5

Volume 34 Benedict O'Donohoe: Sartre's Theatre: Acts for Life.
301 pages. 2005. ISBN 3-03910-250-X / US-ISBN 0-8204-7207-7

Volume 35 Moya Longstaffe: The Fiction of Albert Camus. A Complex Simplicity.
300 pages. 2007. ISBN 3-03910-304-0 / US-ISBN 0-8204-7229-8

Volume 36 Arnaud Beaujeu: Matière et lumière dans le théâtre de Samuel Beckett: Autour des notions de trivialité, de spiritualité et d'« autre-là ».
377 pages. 2010. ISBN 978-3-0343-0206-8

Volume 37 Shirley Ann Jordan: Contemporary French Women's Writing: Women's Visions, Women's Voices, Women's Lives.
308 pages. 2005. ISBN 3-03910-315-6 / US-ISBN 0-8204-7240-9

Volume 38 Neil Foxlee: Albert Camus's 'The New Mediterranean Culture': A Text and its Contexts.
349 pages. 2010. ISBN 978-3-0343-0207-4

Volume 39 Michael O'Dwyer & Michèle Raclot: Le Journal de Julien Green: Miroir d'une âme, miroir d'un siècle.
289 pages. 2005. ISBN 3-03910-319-9

Volume 40 Thomas Baldwin: The Material Object in the Work of Marcel Proust.
188 pages. 2005. ISBN 3-03910-323-7 / US-ISBN 0-8204-7247-6

Volume 41 Charles Forsdick & Andrew Stafford (eds): The Modern Essay in French: Genre, Sociology, Performance.
296 pages. 2005. ISBN 3-03910-514-0 / US-ISBN 0-8204-7520-3

Volume 42 Peter Dunwoodie: Francophone Writing in Transition. Algeria 1900–1945.
339 pages. 2005. ISBN 3-03910-294-X / US-ISBN 0-8204-7220-4

Volume 43 Emma Webb (ed.): Marie Cardinal: New Perspectives.
260 pages. 2006. ISBN 3-03910-544-2 / US-ISBN 0-8204-7547-5

Volume 44 Jérôme Game (ed.): Porous Boundaries: Texts and Images in Twentieth-Century French Culture.
164 pages. 2007. ISBN 978-3-03910-568-7

Volume 45 David Gascoigne: The Games of Fiction: Georges Perec and Modern French Ludic Narrative.
327 pages. 2006. ISBN 3-03910-697-X / US-ISBN 0-8204-7962-4

Volume 46 Derek O'Regan: Postcolonial Echoes and Evocations: The Intertextual Appeal of Maryse Condé.
329 pages. 2006. ISBN 3-03910-578-7

Volume 47 Jennifer Hatte: La langue secrète de Jean Cocteau: la mythologie personnelle du poète et l'histoire cachée des Enfants terribles.
332 pages. 2007. ISBN 978-3-03910-707-0

Volume 48 Loraine Day: Writing Shame and Desire: The Work of Annie Ernaux.
315 pages. 2007. ISBN 978-3-03910-275-4

Volume 49 John Flower (éd.): François Mauriac, journaliste: les vingt premières années, 1905–1925.
352 pages. 2011. ISBN 978–3-0343-0265-4

Volume 50 Miriam Heywood: Modernist Visions: Marcel Proust's A la recherche du temps perdu and Jean-Luc Godard's Histoire(s) du cinéma.
277 pages. 2012. ISBN 978–3-0343-0296-8

Volume 51 Isabelle McNeill & Bradley Stephens (eds): Transmissions: Essays in French Literature, Thought and Cinema.
221 pages. 2007. ISBN 978–3-03910-734-6

Volume 52 Marie-Christine Lala: Georges Bataille, Poète du réel.
178 pages. 2010. ISBN 978–3-03910-738-4

Volume 53 Patrick Crowley: Pierre Michon: The Afterlife of Names.
242 pages. 2007. ISBN 978–3-03910-744-5

Volume 54 Nicole Thatcher & Ethel Tolansky (eds): Six Authors in Captivity. Literary Responses to the Occupation of France during World War II.
205 pages. 2006. ISBN 3–03910-520-5 / US-ISBN 0–8204-7526-2

Volume 55 Catherine Dousteyssier-Khoze & Floriane Place-Verghnes (eds): Poétiques de la parodie et du pastiche de 1850 à nos jours.
361 pages. 2006. ISBN 3–03910-743-7

Volume 56 Thanh-Vân Ton-That: Proust avant la Recherche: jeunesse et genèse d'une écriture au tournant du siècle.
285 pages. 2012. ISBN 978–3-0343-0277-7

Volume 57 Helen Vassallo: Jeanne Hyvrard, Wounded Witness: The Body Politic and the Illness Narrative.
243 pages. 2007. ISBN 978–3-03911-017-9

Volume 58 Marie-Claire Barnet, Eric Robertson and Nigel Saint (eds): Robert Desnos. Surrealism in the Twenty-First Century.
390 pages. 2006. ISBN 3–03911-019-5

Volume 59 Michael O'Dwyer (ed.): Julien Green, Diariste et Essayiste.
259 pages. 2007. ISBN 978–3-03911-016-2

Volume 60 Kate Marsh: Fictions of 1947: Representations of Indian Decolonization 1919–1962.
238 pages. 2007. ISBN 978–3-03911-033-9

Volume 61 Lucy Bolton, Gerri Kimber, Ann Lewis and Michael Seabrook (eds): Framed!: Essays in French Studies.
235 pages. 2007. ISBN 978-3-03911-043-8

Volume 62 Lorna Milne and Mary Orr (eds): Narratives of French Modernity: Themes, Forms and Metamorphoses. Essays in Honour of David Gascoigne.
365 pages. 2011. ISBN 978-3-03911-051-3

Volume 63 Ann Kennedy Smith: Painted Poetry: Colour in Baudelaire's Art Criticism.
253 pages. 2011. ISBN 978-3-03911-094-0

Volume 64 Sam Coombes: The Early Sartre and Marxism.
330 pages. 2008. ISBN 978-3-03911-115-2

Volume 65 Claire Lozier: De l'abject et du sublime: Georges Bataille, Jean Genet, Samuel Beckett.
327 pages. 2012. ISBN 978-3-0343-0724-6

Volume 66 Charles Forsdick and Andy Stafford (eds): La Revue: The Twentieth- Century Periodical in French.
379 pages. 2013. ISBN 978-3-03910-947-0

Volume 67 Alison S. Fell (ed.): French and francophone women facing war / Les femmes face à la guerre.
301 pages. 2009. ISBN 978-3-03911-332-3

Volume 68 Elizabeth Lindley and Laura McMahon (eds): Rhythms: Essays in French Literature, Thought and Culture.
238 pages. 2008. ISBN 978-3-03911-349-1

Volume 69 Georgina Evans and Adam Kay (eds): Threat: Essays in French Literature, Thought and Visual Culture.
248 pages. 2010. ISBN 978-3-03911-357-6

Volume 70 John McCann: Michel Houellebecq: Author of our Times.
229 pages. 2010. ISBN 978-3-03911-373-6

Volume 71 Jenny Murray: Remembering the (Post)Colonial Self: Memory and Identity in the Novels of Assia Djebar.
258 pages. 2008. ISBN 978-3-03911-367-5

Volume 72 Susan Bainbrigge: Culture and Identity in Belgian Francophone Writing: Dialogue, Diversity and Displacement.
230 pages. 2009. ISBN 978-3-03911-382-8

Volume 73 Maggie Allison and Angela Kershaw (eds): Parcours de femmes: Twenty Years of Women in French.
313 pages. 2011. ISBN 978-3-0343-0208-1

Volume 74 Jérôme Game: Poetic Becomings: Studies in Contemporary French Literature.
263 pages. 2011. ISBN 978-3-03911-401-6

Volume 75 Elodie Laügt: L'Orient du signe: Rêves et dérives chez Victor Segalen, Henri Michaux et Emile Cioran.
242 pages. 2008. ISBN 978-3-03911-402-3

Volume 76 Suzanne Dow: Madness in Twentieth-Century French Women's Writing: Leduc, Duras, Beauvoir, Cardinal, Hyvrard.
217 pages. 2009. ISBN 978-3-03911-540-2

Volume 77 Myriem El Maïzi: Marguerite Duras ou l'écriture du devenir.
228 pages. 2009. ISBN 978-3-03911-561-7

Volume 78 Claire Launchbury: Music, Poetry, Propaganda: Constructing French Cultural Soundscapes at the BBC during the Second World War.
223 pages. 2012. ISBN 978-3-0343-0239-5

Volume 79 Jenny Chamarette and Jennifer Higgins (eds): Guilt and Shame: Essays in French Literature, Thought and Visual Culture.
231 pages. 2010. ISBN 978-3-03911-563-1

Volume 80 Vera Regan and Caitríona Ní Chasaide (eds): Language Practices and Identity Construction by Multilingual Speakers of French L2: The Acquisition of Sociostylistic Variation.
189 pages. 2010. ISBN 978-3-03911-569-3

Volume 81 Margaret-Anne Hutton (ed.): Redefining the Real: The Fantastic in Contemporary French and Francophone Women's Writing.
294 pages. 2009. ISBN 978-3-03911-567-9

Volume 82 Elise Hugueny-Léger: Annie Ernaux, une poétique de la transgression.
269 pages. 2009. ISBN 978-3-03911-833-5

Volume 83 Peter Collier, Anna Magdalena Elsner and Olga Smith (eds): Anamnesia: Private and Public Memory in Modern French Culture. 359 pages. 2009. ISBN 978-3-03911-846-5

Volume 84 Adam Watt (ed./éd.): Le Temps retrouvé Eighty Years After/80 ans après: Critical Essays/Essais critiques.
349 pages. 2009. ISBN 978-3-03911-843-4

Volume 85 Louise Hardwick (ed.): New Approaches to Crime in French Literature, Culture and Film.
237 pages. 2009. ISBN 978–3-03911-850-2

Volume 86 Emmanuel Godin and Natalya Vince (eds): France and the Mediterranean: International Relations, Culture and Politics.
372 pages. 2012. ISBN 978–3-0343-0228-9

Volume 87 Amaleena Damlé and Aurélie L'Hostis (eds): The Beautiful and the Monstrous: Essays in French Literature, Thought and Culture.
237 pages. 2010. ISBN 978–3-03911-900-4

Volume 88 Alistair Rolls (ed.): Mostly French: French (in) Detective Fiction.
212 pages. 2009. ISBN 978–3-03911-957-8

Volume 89 Bérénice Bonhomme: Claude Simon: une écriture en cinéma.
359 pages. 2010. ISBN 978–3-03911-983-7

Volume 90 Barbara Lebrun and Jill Lovecy (eds): Une et divisible? Plural Identities in Modern France.
258 pages. 2010. ISBN 978–3-0343-0123-7

Volume 91 Pierre-Alexis Mével & Helen Tattam (eds): Language and its Contexts/ Le Langage et ses contextes: Transposition and Transformation of Meaning?/ Transposition et transformation du sens?
272 pages. 2010. ISBN 978–3-0343-0128-2

Volume 92 Alistair Rolls and Marie-Laure Vuaille-Barcan (eds): Masking Strategies: Unwrapping the French Paratext.
202 pages. 2011. ISBN 978–3-0343-0746-8

Volume 93 Michaël Abecassis et Gudrun Ledegen (éds): Les Voix des Français Volume 1: à travers l'histoire, l'école et la presse.
372 pages. 2010. ISBN 978–3-0343-0170-1

Volume 94 Michaël Abecassis et Gudrun Ledegen (éds): Les Voix des Français Volume 2: en parlant, en écrivant.
481 pages. 2010. ISBN 978–3-0343-0171-8

Volume 95 Manon Mathias, Maria O'Sullivan and Ruth Vorstman (eds): Display and Disguise.
237 pages. 2011. ISBN 978–3-0343-0177-0

Volume 96 Charlotte Baker: Enduring Negativity: Representations of Albinism in the Novels of Didier Destremau, Patrick Grainville and Williams Sassine.
226 pages. 2011. ISBN 978–3-0343-0179-4

Volume 97 Florian Grandena and Cristina Johnston (eds): New Queer Images: Representations of Homosexualities in Contemporary Francophone Visual Cultures.
246 pages. 2011. ISBN 978-3-0343-0182-4

Volume 98 Florian Grandena and Cristina Johnston (eds): Cinematic Queerness: Gay and Lesbian Hypervisibility in Contemporary Francophone Feature Films.
354 pages. 2011. ISBN 978-3-0343-0183-1

Volume 99 Neil Archer and Andreea Weisl-Shaw (eds): Adaptation: Studies in French and Francophone Culture.
234 pages. 2012. ISBN 978-3-0343-0222-7

Volume 100 Peter Collier et Ilda Tomas (éds): Béatrice Bonhomme: le mot, la mort, l'amour.
437 pages. 2013. ISBN 978-3-0343-0780-2

Volume 101 Helena Chadderton: Marie Darrieussecq's Textual Worlds: Self, Society, Language.
170 pages. 2012. ISBN 978-3-0343-0766-6

Volume 102 Manuel Bragança: La crise allemande du roman français, 1945–1949: la représentation des Allemands dans les best-sellers de l'immédiat après-guerre.
220 pages. 2012. ISBN 978-3-0343-0835-9

Volume 103 Bronwen Martin: The Fiction of J. M. G. Le Clézio: A Postcolonial Reading.
199 pages. 2012. ISBN 978-3-0343-0162-6

Volume 104 Hugues Azérad, Michael G. Kelly, Nina Parish et Emma Wagstaff (éds): Chantiers du poème: prémisses et pratiques de la création poétique moderne et contemporaine.
374 pages. 2013. ISBN 978-3-0343-0800-7

Volume 105 Franck Dalmas: Lectures phénoménologiques en littérature française: de Gustave Flaubert à Malika Mokeddem.
253 pages. 2012. ISBN 978-3-0343-0727-7

Volume 106 Béatrice Bonhomme, Aude Préta-de Beaufort et Jacques Moulin (éds): Dans le feuilletage de la terre: sur l'œuvre poétique de Marie- Claire Bancquart.
533 pages. 2013. ISBN 978-3-0343-0721-5

Volume 107 Claire Bisdorff et Marie-Christine Clemente (éds): Le Cœur dans tous ses états: essais sur la littérature et l'art français.
230 pages. 2013. ISBN 978-3-0343-0711-6

Volume 108 Michaël Abecassis et Gudrun Ledegen (éds): Écarts et apports des médias francophones: lexique et grammaire.
300 pages. 2013. ISBN 978-3-0343-0882-3

Volume 109 Allison and Imogen Long (eds): Women Matter / Femmes Matière: French and Francophone Women and the Material World. 273 pages. 2013. ISBN 978-3-0343-0788-8

Volume 110 Fabien Arribert-Narce et Alain Ausoni (éds): L'Autobiographie entre autres: écrire la vie aujourd'hui.
221 pages. 2013. ISBN 978-3-0343-0858-8

Volume 111 Leona Archer and Alex Stuart (eds): Visions of Apocalypse: Representations of the End in French Literature and Culture.
266 pages. 2013. ISBN 978-3-0343-0921-9

Volume 112 Simona Cutcan: Subversion ou conformisme ? La différence des sexes dans l'œuvre d'Agota Kristof.
264 pages. 2014. ISBN 978-3-0343-1713-9

Volume 113 Owen Heathcote: From Bad Boys to New Men ? Masculinity, Sexuality and Violence in the Work of Éric Jourdan.
279 pages. 2014. ISBN 978-3-0343-0736-9

Volume 114 Ilda Tomas: Arc-en-ciel: études sur divers poètes.
234 pages. 2014. ISBN 978-3-0343-0975-2

Volume 115 Lisa Jeschke and Adrian May (eds): Matters of Time: Material Temporalities in Twentieth-Century French Culture.
314 pages. 2014. ISBN 978-3-0343-1796-2

Volume 116 Crispin T. Lee: Haptic Experience in the Writings of Georges Bataille, Maurice Blanchot and Michel Serres.
316 pages. 2014. ISBN 978-3-0343-1791-7

Volume 117 Ashwiny O. Kistnareddy: Locating Hybridity: Creole, Identities and Body Politics in the Novels of Ananda Devi.
208 pages. 2015. ISBN 978-3-0343-1814-3

Volume 118 Michaël Abecassis et Gudrun Ledegen (éds): De la genèse de la langue à Internet: variations dans les formes, les modalités et les langues en contact.
278 pages. 2015. ISBN 978-3-0343-1798-6

Volume 119 Peter D. Tame: Isotopias: Places and Spaces in French War Fiction of the Twentieth and Twenty-First Centuries.
592 pages. 2015. ISBN 978-3-0343-0837-3

Volume 120 Daniel A. Finch-Race et Jeff Barda (éds): Textures: Processus et événements dans la création poétique moderne et contemporaine. 242 pages. 2015. ISBN 978-3-0343-1898-3

Volume 121 Hélène Sicard-Cowan: Vivre ensemble: éthique de l'imitation dans la littérature et le cinéma de l'immigration en France (1986–2005). 149 pages. 2016. ISBN 978-3-0343-1944-7

Volume 122 Mercedes Montoro Araque et Carmen Alberdi Urquizu (éds): L'entre- deux imaginaire: corps et création interculturels. 216 pages. 2016. ISBN 978-3-0343-1926-3

Volume 123 Maureen A. Ramsden: Crossing Borders: The Interrelation of Fact and Fiction in Historical Works, Travel Tales, Autobiography and Reportage.
191 pages. 2016. ISBN 978-3-0343-1995-9

Volume 124 Jean Khalfa: Poetics of the Antilles: Poetry, History and Philosophy in the Writings of Perse, Césaire, Fanon and Glissant.
388 pages. 2017. ISBN 978-3-0343-0895-3

Volume 125 Mathilde Poizat-Amar: L'Eclat du voyage: Blaise Cendrars, Victor Segalen, Albert Londres.
252 pages. 2017. ISBN 978-1-78707-296-1

Volume 126 Philippe Willemart: L'Univers de la création littéraire: Dans la chambre noire de l'écriture: Hérodias de Flaubert.
160 pages. 2017. ISBN 978-1-78707-458-3

Volume 127 Margaret Atack, Alison S. Fell, Diana Holmes and Imogen Long (eds): French Feminisms 1975 and After: New Readings, New Texts. 276 pages. 2018. ISBN 978-3-0343-2209-6

Volume 128 Matt Phillips and Tomas Weber (eds): Parasites: Exploitation and Interference in French Thought and Culture.
284 pages. 2018. ISBN 978-3-0343-2266-9

Volume 129 Zoe Angelis and Blake Gutt (eds): Stains / Les taches: Communication and Contamination in French and Francophone Literature and Culture.
274 pages. 2019. ISBN 978-1-78707-443-9

Volume 130 Michaël Abecassis avec Marcelline Block, Gudrun Ledegen et Maribel Peñalver Vicea (éds): Le Grain de la voix dans le monde anglophone et francophone.
332 pages. 2019. ISBN 978-1-78874-107-1

Volume 131 Philippe Willemart: L'écriture à l'ère de l'indétermination: Études sur la critique génétique, la psychanalyse et la littérature.
232 pages. 2019. ISBN 978–1-78874-631-1

Volume 132 Augustin Voegele: De l'unanimisme au fantastique: Jules Romains devant l'extraordinaire.
382 pages. 2019. ISBN 978-1-78874-513-0

Volume 133 Maggie Allison, Elliot Evans and Carrie Tarr (eds): Plaisirs de femmes: Women, Pleasure and Transgression in French Literature and Culture.
278 pages. 2019. ISBN 978-1-78874-383-9

Volume 134 Aaron Prevots: Bernard Vargaftig: Gestures toward the Sacred.
144 pages. 2019. ISBN 978-1-78997-357-0

Volume 135 Susie Cronin, Sofia Ropek Hewson and Cillian Ó Fathaigh (eds): #Noussommes: Collectivity and the Digital in French Thought and Culture. 184 pages. 2020. ISBN 978-1-78874-767-7

Volume 136 Anaïs Stampfli: La coprésence de langues dans le roman antillais contemporain. 456 pages. 2020. ISBN 978-1-78874-578-9

Volume 137 Philippe Willemart: Les mécanismes de la création littéraire: Lecture, écriture, génétique et psychanalyse. 214 pages. 2020. ISBN 978-1-78997-737-0

Volume 138 Maureen A. Ramsden: The Evolution of Proust's 'Combray': A Genetic Study.
152 pages. 2020. ISBN 978-1-78997-785-1

Volume 139 Charlène Clonts: Gherasim Luca: Texte, image, son.
454 pages. 2021. ISBN 978-1-78997-916-9

Volume 140 Polly Galis, Maria Tomlinson and Antonia Wimbush (eds): Queer(y)ing Bodily Norms in Francophone Culture. 304 pages. 2021. ISBN 978-1-78997-514-7

www.ingramcontent.com/pod-product-compliance
Lightning Source LLC
Chambersburg PA
CBHW071538110726
47908CB00007B/1930

* 9 7 8 1 7 8 9 9 7 5 1 4 7 *